The Mystery of Mysteries

The Mystery of Mysteries:
Cultural Differences and Designs

Samuel Coale

Bowling Green State University Popular Press
Bowling Green, OH 43403

Copyright 2000 © Bowling Green State University Popular Press

Library of Congress Cataloging-in-Publication Data
Coale, Samuel.
    The mystery of mysteries : cultural differences and designs / Samuel
Coale.
        p.   cm.
    Includes bibliographic references.
    ISBN 0-87972-813-2 -- ISBN 0-87972-814-0 (pbk.)
    1. Detective and mystery stories, American--History and criticism.
2. Hillerman, Tony--Criticism and interpretation. 3. Heilbrun, Carolyn
G., 1926--Criticism and interpretation. 4. Burke, James Lee, 1936--
Criticism and interpretation. 5. Mosley, Walter--Criticism and interpre-
tation. 6. Detective and mystery stories--Authorship. 7. Novelists,
American--20th century--Interviews. 8. American fiction--20th century
--History and criticism. I. Title.
PS374.D4 C55 1999
813'.087209-dc21
                                                                99-055806

Cover design by Dumm Art

DEDICATION

To Gray and Sam and Ariel
Mysteries are never enough

CONTENTS

PREFACE AND ACKNOWLEDGMENTS

Read mysteries? Bite your tongue! When I was in graduate school at Brown and long after, I never deigned to read a mystery. It was obviously beneath me. My eye was on deconstruction, Hawthorne, Toni Morrison, post-structuralism, and the postmodern tremors of the American psyche.

But then . . .

On my honeymoon, marooned on an island off the coast of Greece with literally nothing to read, fearing I would go mad without the printed word at my finger tips, I borrowed an Agatha Christie mystery from Gray, my wife.

And that was it.

When we returned to the States, I read every Christie mystery. And then turned haphazardly to others, everyone from Robert Barnard to Sue Grafton, Sara Paretsky to Peter Dickinson, Japanese mysteries on golf courses to Indian mysteries in the crowded streets of Calcutta. It became a mania, an obsession, a sheer delight.

"Can you recommend a good mystery writer?" I would ask friends.

I began reviewing mysteries, six or seven at a clutch for the *Providence Journal*. And still do. That, and my aberrant taste for gothics by the likes of John Saul and Stephen King and James Herbert, keep me immersed in "formula fiction."

Someone recommended Tony Hillerman. I was hooked.

Another suggested Amanda Cross. That was it.

I myself stumbled upon James Lee Burke at the bookstore with a paperback copy of his earlier novel, *The Lost Get-Back Boogie,* enclosed with a new Robicheaux mystery.

And Walter Mosley's *Devil in a Blue Dress* mesmerized me.

I was asked to give a paper on popular fiction at an MLA Convention in Toronto in 1993 and turned out a long complicated and convoluted piece on Stephen King, Hillerman, Cross and Dean Koontz, "King, Koontz, Cross and Hillerman: Popular Fiction as Exorcism, Subversive Moralism, and Mythic (Re)Models." Egad! The angle? How certain writers "subverted" old formulas; how King loved to side with his demonic characters or creatures who always got defeated in the end but who were fascinating before their final demise; how Hillerman's interest in the Navajo raised issues that the "enlightened" and rational mystery formula essentially had to marginalize; how Cross' feminism upended the patriarchal plots and trajectories of most mysteries.

Deep into a second book on Hawthorne, on mesmerism as a structuralist principle in his creation of the dark American romance, I took "time off" to write articles on mysteries, three of which were published by *Clues: A Journal of Detection*. These included "Hillerman and Cross: The Re-Invention and Mythic (Re)-Modeling of the Popular Mystery" (1995), "The Dark Domain of James Lee Burke: Mysteries within Mystery" (1997), and "Carnage and Conversion: The Art of P. D. James" (1999). Without *Clues'* support, this book would not have been possible.

I wholeheartedly want to thank Pat Browne, Karen Wiechman, and the staff at Popular Press for being so helpful, thoughtful, and encouraging. You always write in isolation and are more than grateful when someone "out there" endorses your project, complete with all the attendant risks.

Much of this book would also not have happened without the willingness of Tony Hillerman, Amanda Cross (Carolyn Heilbrun), James Lee Burke, and Walter Mosley to bear with my questions, ramblings, asides, and often muddled transcripts. Hillerman sent me into the desert in New Mexico with much goodwill where I tried to inhabit, however briefly, his favorite landscapes. Cross' wit and good humor in her New York apartment and Burke's relaxed, supportive manner on the phone and at his New York hotel helped me strengthen my interviews by allowing me to talk with them a second time. And Walter Mosley, also on the phone, was forthright and precise, an approach which all these writers share. So, thank you, publicly now, for your time and your patience.

My old black lab Mavro saw me through the Hawthorne years. And Ariel, the basset, appropriately born on Halloween, sat beneath my desk this go-round, always making it possible for me to leap up and insist upon a walk when things weren't going well.

Son Sam, college-bound, sports his own sense of mystery, laced with the eerie and the atmospheric—and the films of Steven Spielberg. He was always around to talk with and cajole me out of darker moods.

But if Gray hadn't leant me that Christie mystery on the isle of Spetsai—the same island where John Fowles conjured up *The Magus,* a metaphysical mystery of seductive sweep and skill (and I was fortunate to talk with him in 1996)—none of this would have come about. She made it literally possible, and her presence and support over the years have sustained me utterly. Without her, nothing is possible.

1

THE MYSTERY OF MYSTERIES:
RITES, REASONS, AND RESOLUTIONS

It is the nature of mystery novels to perform their own demise. They must also serve a pre-conceived formula as they simultaneously self-destruct. The solution that usually concludes this process necessarily undermines it, since once it is discovered, the fiction is concluded. Such a structure presents a distinct chain of events in a horizontal sequence that purports to reflect and constitute the social and historical external world we inhabit (Bonnycastle). In doing so, however, any other "mysteries"—the nature of human choice, of evil, of circumstance and accident—must be intentionally marginalized and evaded, repressed and hidden for the self-eviscerating process to take place.

Popular mysteries rely on formula. The re-enactment of that formula and, therefore, the process of the narrative itself must include the initial set-up of the cast, the characters, and the context in which they operate; the crime that disrupts all of these; the discourse of investigation and inquiry, usually built upon a series of interviews and interrogations; and the final solution or recognition of the underlying truth of the crime and the culprit who performed it.

The appeal of the mystery formula is understandable—and profitable.[1] It creates a rational world amid an irrational or at the very least a non-rational world. It substitutes rational discourse for metaphysical speculation, which nevertheless relies on the metaphysical certainty that the truth is out there. It underscores faith in a systematic series of revelations in place of ultimate unknowns, and in doing so must marginalize that unknown territory as best it can so as not to sink the ship. The formula clearly supports and upholds the western belief and faith in objective discourse and careful analysis, or as Anne Williams has suggested, in the Patriarchal Symbolic order of language, logic, chronology, and genealogy, the organization of a male-oriented culture which provides "a relatively stable arrangement of chains of association . . . a basic structure of interpersonal relationships" (263).

All such literary formulae play to our sense of expectation within severe limitations at the same time that they reinforce our desire to believe that the world works in such a recognizable and reasonable manner. They re-play our sense that this is the way the world always works, and that in our reading of these generic texts, we re-enact the similar situations and expectations of each of these formulaic stories. As Joyce Carol Oates suggests, "Readers of genre fiction, unlike readers of what we presume to call 'literary fiction,' assume a tacit contract between themselves and the writer: they understand that they will be manipulated, but the question is how? and when? and with what skill? and to what purpose? However plot-ridden, fantastical, or absurd, populated by whatever pseudo-characters, genre fiction is always resolved" (*New York Times* Book Review 31 Oct. 1996: 50). We experience not the shock but the comfort of recognition, knowing full well that genre fiction supports the status-quo of contemporary conventional opinion and does so by avoiding the ambiguity and the uncertainty of the more complex world in which we live. In submitting ourselves to the re-enactment of the formula, therefore, we preserve the present order of things.[2]

Such formulas play directly into the distinctions that Jacques Barzun has made between the tale and the novel in "The Novel Turns Tale" (131). While the novel "professes to illuminate life by pretending to be history," the tale "is a narrative too, but [it] appeals to curiosity, wonder and the love of ingenuity. If it 'studies' anything, it is the calculating mind rather than the spontaneous emotions, physical predicaments rather than spiritual." As John Fowles comments directly after this, writers like Conan Doyle belong "to the tale-tellers, in the long modern line from Poe to Ross Macdonald." As Barzun continues, "One goes to a tale because it is a marvellous invention, because it is ingenious, full of suspense and concentrated wisdom . . . and [because it] appeases the heart by its love of reason" (131). The mystery formula, then, springs more directly from the tale than from the more "literary" novel.

There are literally too many excellent mystery writers to choose from, but I have selected my own personal favorites to discuss, who by now have created a significant and diverse body of work and in doing so can stand as examples of many others: Tony Hillerman, Amanda Cross (Carolyn Heilbrun), James Lee Burke, and Walter Mosley. They pursue social and cultural differences in their mysteries, which lie outside the usual landscape of the genre's formula—Hillerman's Navajos, Cross' feminist academics, Burke's Cajun-Southern Louisianans, and Mosley's urban blacks. Often the confrontation between formula and content results in some very interesting twists and fictional situations. As Michiko Kakutani has suggested, "By manipulating the conventions of the detective story, writers are able to comment both on its formal limitations and on the limitations of its philosophical outlook" (37).

Nevertheless all four writers have chosen to write within the time-honored framework of the mystery formula. Thus, as Martin E. Marty might define them, they situate their tribal subjects and values within a popular totalizing perspective.[3] That choice necessarily demands various strategies, as they attempt to remain true to both cultural differences (which, in many cases, actually contradict the basic premises of the mystery) and the structure of popular fiction. It is this on-going process in their fiction that has led to this study.

These four authors and several previous and contemporary ones—such as Dashiell Hammett (who is one of the several members of the hard-boiled "school" of earlier American mystery writers), P. D. James (who probably spearheads the modern revival of the British Golden Age of such mystery writers as Dorothy Sayers and Agatha Christie), John Fowles, Tim O'Brien, and Joan Didion, among others—both subvert and maintain the mystery formula. The form has become so widespread that such very different writers as Gabriel Garcia Marquez and Paul Auster have also used it in their fiction in a calculated attempt to undermine its rational and linear construction of experience.

The linear structure of the mystery formula stems in part from the philosophy of Rene Descartes, certainly one of the best exemplars and founding patriarchs of the belief in rationalism. "Ever since Descartes and the Rationalists elevated humans above nature by emphasizing our ability to *think* rather than merely to act and *feel*, Western ideology has valued almost exclusively the ability to solve problems through rational, linear, conscious thought," suggests David L. Calof (13). Descartes' method, which preceded but proved to be a great influence upon the Enlightenment in the eighteenth and nineteenth centuries, initiates an empirical procedure in which he re-created a series of steps followed in a logical order based on his own immediate experience and observation often without due regard for system and theory. Such observations, he thought, could be verified or disproved by further observation or experiment. In this process he, like the mystery formula, had to repress certain "ultimate" or metaphysical mysteries, or at least try to finesse them, and at the same time to produce a methodology which relied upon cause and effect, the underlying faith of what came to be the belief in western progress heralded and upheld by the Enlightenment. In re-tracing Descartes' steps, we can see both what the analytical mystery formula can accomplish and what it must marginalize.

Descartes at first accepted what his senses revealed to him and then doubted them. His senses could obscure and confuse him in terms, for example, of how he actually saw the sun and what he knew about its real size and dimensions. He assumed that he had to be a thinking thing, that his own consciousness and his awareness of his very existence proved to be one and the same thing. Therefore his mind had to be separate from his senses. It must dominate the body, since it "is distinct from and superior to matter" (Descartes 19). In effect he recognized in his conscious self "the will to dominate, to control events, [and] to eliminate chance and the irrational" (21). By examining what his senses revealed to him, by using those senses, and by combining them with his memory and understanding, he could therefore "link and join present knowledge to past" and thereby unearth the causes of whatever errors he had made (168).

From this methodology Descartes arrived at the idea that the facts of consciousness and of the world, of subject and object, mind and matter, can be misinterpreted but once known are based solely on a strict causality and physical laws which lead inevitably to predictability (22). Every effect or consequence must have its agent or motive, every result its antecedent, every outcome its determinant, exactly in the same manner of his own conscious methodology. Thus, the cosmos reproduced his methodological approach: "The laws which govern the physical world and which will continue to govern it to the end of all time may be discovered and used by man for his own ends," and the facts of existence, based mathematically as they must be on extension and motion, must reflect "the notion of the unity of mathematics" (16). If outward signs suggest appearances only, these can be re-interpreted in the light of experience and understanding and the underlying, predictable prior cause known.

When it comes to the existence of God, however, and other metaphysical speculations, Descartes must fudge things a bit. First of all he makes it clear to himself that he can distinguish dream from reality, sleep from waking. When one is awake and only when one is awake, memory connects all things. Only when one is awake can one know the place from which memory comes, the present place in which one exists, and the time in which these appear and thus link all these perceptions to the rest of one's conscious life. Proof appears to reside in the belief that one can distinguish consciousness from the unconscious because of all of the above. Of course this is precisely what occurs in the mystery formula. Signs may reveal themselves as clues and not merely as mysteriously elusive icons in dreams, because the formula excludes the latter and focuses on the former.

In proving the existence of God, Descartes asserts that things outside the mind can project and imprint themselves upon it, producing ideas within it. There also exist very real differences between actual objects and the ideas generated or inaugurated by those objects in the form of ideas. God is obviously infinite in a way that the human mind and the physically visible world cannot possibly be. Therefore an infinite God, a first cause, must produce the objects which imprint themselves on the human mind, as the infinite can and must produce the finite. And the pictures, images, and ideas that the mind produces must themselves lead back to that first cause, as the finite must lead back by its very limitations to the infinite, which alone can contain all things. If one, therefore, has the idea of God, God must exist, for the idea must have been put there. That idea of infinite perfection can only come from an infinite being, since human imperfection itself could never conjure up such a thing: "I would not, nevertheless, have the idea of an infinite substance, since I am a finite being, unless the idea had been put into me by some substance which was truly infinite. . . . The idea, I say, of this supremely perfect and infinite being is entirely true" (Descartes 125). So Descartes' will to power must itself come from somewhere else, and he must submit to that infinite will that must exist to create his own. Therefore God as a first cause must exist. Such assumptions would crumble under Nietzschean scrutinies and contemporary skeptical strategies and would never make it into the mystery formula. While Descartes in his time felt the need to prove the existence of an infinite God, the mystery formula obviously does not. And Descartes' own methodology reveals its shortcomings in producing a logical but "bizarre" series of assumptions that belie his own formulaic procedures.

The nature of Descartes' God partakes of the nature of geometry: extension, cause, and effect have helped to produce him. But the assumptions Descartes must rely upon to make what we would call a leap of faith cannot stand up under the scrutiny of his own methodology and thus of course must be discarded from most Enlightenment thought. "It is very obvious that there must be at least as much reality in the cause as in its effect. . . . the cause must equally be a thinking thing, and possess within it the idea of all the perfections that I attribute to the divine cause" (Descartes 128, 131, 134). Obvious to whom? Attributions by whom? Descartes continues: "Everything I perceive clearly and distinctly cannot fail to be true. . . . I know already that I cannot be deceived in judgments the reasons of which I know clearly. . . . But even if I were asleep, everything which is presented to my mind clearly, is absolutely true" (149).

In accepting Descartes' analytical approach as one of the most influential within western scientific and Enlightenment thought, one must necessarily lop off those other parts of it which today strike us at best as clever and at worst absurd. But if one part can be doubted, the whole must be doubted as well. Decartes admits that his proof for the existence of God "is apprehended by the intuition rather than by deductive reasoning" (20) and yet at the same time confesses, "I notice further that this power of imagination which is in me, in so far as it differs from the power of conceiving, is in no way necessary to my nature or essence . . . that is to say, to the essence of my mind; for, even if I did not have it, without doubt I should still remain the same as I am now, whence it seems that one can conclude that it depends on something different from my mind" (151). Thus, Descartes must marginalize and exclude those very speculations and uncertainties that the mystery formula must. In doing so he re-enacts the built-in marginalization and provides us with the limitations of his own analytical reasoning upon which the believer in western progressive thought and the reader of mysteries must depend. At the philosophical core of the modern method, then, rests the contradictions and assumptions that must be transcended or buried for that method to function as we popularly know it.

The Cartesian discourse at the heart of the western enlightened tradition of philosophical and analytical thought was, of course, preceded by certain religious and/or mythic patterns in western culture. W. H. Auden, for instance, in "The Guilty Vicarage," "saw detective fiction as the Christian morality play restated in modern dress" (95). C. Day Lewis described the pattern of the detective novel as formalized as a religious ritual, comparing the crime or murder to sin, the criminal to the high priest of this rite, and the detective to a yet higher power who appears on behalf of the victim of such rites (400). And of course in the very ritual of discovering, exorcizing, and expelling the scapegoat, the criminal, in the midst of normal society, the mystery formula performs an act of exorcizing all guilt and criminality, guilt being that universal psychological condition that underlies everything from Oedipus' crimes to Cain's. "In the beginning there was guilt: the basic motive for reading crime fiction," Julian Symons insists, "is the religious one of exorcizing the guilt of the individual or the group through ritual and symbolic sacrifice" (9). After all "victim, murder, investigation, all have a hieratic and ritual quality" (12).

As Peter Brooks makes clear, a certain psychological pattern, what he calls Freud's master plot, also underlies and supports the rites and patterns of the narrative in general, the mystery in particular, and the Cartesian discourse which parallels it (287-99). For Freud life ultimately desires death; the need for an ending is contained within the organism itself; ends are implicit in beginnings. Thus, the beginning of any narrative initiates desire and anticipation for what is to come. And the end results in a recognition or revelation which completes that initial desire and arousal: "What operates in the text through repetition is the death instinct, the drive toward the end. . . . the narrative must tend toward its end, seek illumination in its own death. Yet this must be the right death, the correct end" (Brooks 293-94). That end in the mystery, of course, involves the adding up of specific clues which, if done correctly, produces the final revelation and resolution. And the pursuit of those clues occupies the detective's consciousness with a vengeance. He or she is obsessed in terms of finding out exactly what has happened. The web of the text re-enacts this sense of demonic possession, this pursuit of the answer, just as clearly as does the detective himself or herself. Text and character, therefore, perform similar actions.

Unlike other more "open" or literary narratives, however, the mystery with its clues, its demonic drive within the text, and its detective to reveal, discover, master, and exhume what has already happened are themselves carefully enclosed within the mystery formula. The formula itself is a repetition of previous mystery formulas, welcoming the reader into its already known and recognized patterns. All the psychic drives toward repetition and death, including the narrative's own, are carefully embodied in the structure of the formula, thus encapsulating and making comfortable those very psychic drives that it so regularly unleashes and reins in. In a mystery the text and the reader return to the origins of the plot that the author has known from the beginning. We are reassured that things can be unearthed and spelled out. The return to origins usually does not involve a return of the repressed but sets us on our formulaic way to clear identities, verifiable explanations, and certain truths. Thus, mysteries are, at least, doubly repetitive, and they seal their own comforting fates.

Quasi-religious rites and psychological explanations, however, only parallel the formula that the mystery embodies. They allegorize the process and in a way substitute themselves for it, not finally explaining how the formula actually functions. As Barbara Johnson has said, psychological analysis is "capable of finding only itself wherever it looks. . . . [It is an] act . . . of mere *recognition* of the expected" (34). While it is true that "the theoretical frame of reference which governs recognition is a constitutive element in the blindness of any interpretive insight" (342), it is also true that narratives are more dynamic than static, more "operational" than "timeless," and it is to Brooks' credit that he points out the dynamics of narrative as well, viewing it as essentially sequential and successive, a re-enactment of a plot and story.

Every mystery also suggests a novel of manners, a creature of its own time and social milieu, both the author's and the reader's. We view the characters, as the author has created them, as visible products of their society, dominated by the manners of that society which "exert control [and are] a determinant upon [their] actions" (Tuttleton 10). Thus, these characters seem to be realistically drawn and representative of certain social classes, ethnic groups, economic backgrounds, and the like. And this sociological determinant encourages us to view the murder, say, as a "dramatic violation of commonly held ethical values" (Tuttleton 12), a disruption of conventional manners and taboos. No wonder so many mystery writers from Robert Barnard to Amanda Cross write satirically and ironically, since in effect they are criticizing certain social myths by reason of their mysteries and characters. Cross, for instance, attacks and undermines the American myth of homogeneity and political egalitarianism by revealing the clear stratification of social groups, the complexities of their customs, and the gender biases of their myths and outlooks. Barnard works similarly in satirizing the profound class consciousness of his English characters.

Much of this, of course, has contributed to the popularity of mysteries in the last one hundred and fifty years. The formula itself comforts and clarifies. As David S. Reynolds tells us about Poe and the invention of the detective story, the mystery re-enacts the "ultimate imaginary victory over the irrational. . . . [Poe's] invention of the modern detective story stems directly from . . . [his superimposition of] ideas from contemporary science or pseudoscience upon sensational situations. . . . In creating the brainy detective, Poe gained victory over the popular Subversive imagination" (247, 238, 248). Marcus Klein proves that the private eye was indeed the product of the Gilded Age and rapid urbanization in America, what he refers to as the "ghettoization of urban America" (5), and the growth of finance capitalism, the industrial revolution, and mass immigration. Klein's detective is obviously very different from the kind Julian Symons describes. Symons scrutinizes only British writers from the Golden Age, whose detectives are products "of a class in society that felt it had everything to lose by social change" (11). One thinks immediately of Dupin, Holmes, Lord Peter Wimsey, and Hercule Poirot. These white, upper-class, brainy fellows from the 1830s onwards reassured the reading public, members of a more privileged class which had the time to read such things, that "those who tried to disturb the established order were always discovered and punished" (Symons 11).

And yet part of the fascination with the mystery formula resides in what it both tries to exclude and marginalize and what it cannot. First of all, the formula must severely restrict its scope in order to function, and that restriction previously exists within the limitations of the Cartesian analytical point of view, itself restricted by what the mystery formula tends to ignore, i.e., Descartes' more metaphysical speculations, despite his attempts to embody them in his methodology. But it must also exclude other dimensions of the wider vision of mystery. The formula must marginalize inscrutable enigmas and problems, puzzles which perpetually baffle and perplex and remain inexplicable, existing beyond one's powers to discover, understand, or explain. It must exclude religious mysteries that can be known only by revelation and cannot fully be comprehended. It must also skirt religious sacraments and the secret religious rites of certain mystery cults. The philosophical riddles involved with the (possible) freedom of human choice—why, for instance, does the murderer choose to murder? What entices one to cross the line?—the existence of all kinds and degrees of evil in the world, and (possible) pre-determined acts of hubris, fate, and even accident must be, in some way, ignored. Anything that may suggest the unknowable and the unfathomable, whether religious or otherwise, must be virtually and carefully excluded from the text for it to operate successfully within the boundaries of its formula. The mystery writer, as David I. Grossvogel suggests, "establishes surrogates for the beyond on this side of the divide . . . inviting a mock penetration of the unknown" and by inventing such incarnations hopes to short-circuit the larger issues he may stumble upon (13).

Traditional Mysteries: Hammett and James

The story of the invention and development of the detective and crime narrative has been told successfully in many other places. The line from Poe's Dupin to Doyle's Holmes, Sayers' Wimsey, and Christie's Poirot, among others, is clear and clean, and such diverse writers as the American Dashiell Hammett and the British P. D. James build on this tradition, the former by rejecting the "British country house" atmosphere and plots, the latter by extending and deepening them.

Hammett at one time worked as a Pinkerton detective. In the United States the first police force in New York was organized in the 1840s, and it led to Allan Pinkerton's founding the first detective agency in 1873. Interestingly enough the Pinkerton operative's main job was union-busting, infiltrating the labor unions as a spy to report on the radical agitators and their plans: "Labor spying was the main source of revenue for the agency" (Klein 176). Pinkerton agents were still actively involved in strike breaking during and after World War One. In the Ludlow Coal Strike in Colorado, they were deputized by the local sheriff and involved in the massacre of miners. Hammett fictionalizes the situation with his Continental Op in *Red Harvest*. History thus underscores the essentially conservative if not reactionary basis of what would become the mystery formula.

The real American breakthrough in the history of the mystery came in the 1920s and the 1930s in the rise of *Black Mask*, the most famous of the crime pulp magazines, which were themselves an outgrowth of the sensationalistic Dime Novels of the late nineteenth century. *Black Mask* and others created the stylistic frame for the hard-boiled short story and in doing so insisted on simplicity, realism, a terse and minimalist language, and "the classless, restless man of American democracy, who spoke the language of the street" (Klein 182), in the words of Ross Macdonald, the American mystery writer. Real detectives had been described as rogues, thieves, and deceivers, as lowlifes as much affected by the criminal world as trying to correct it. Wrote early critics of the trade, "the life of a detective is a living lie. . . . [he is] the outgrowth of a diseased and corrupted state of things, and is, consequently, morally diseased himself. His very existence is a satire upon society" (Klein 156, 158). Such creatures or operatives embodied no moral values themselves; they were close to the genuine secrets of how American society functioned in all its criminality and deception and were professionals in the fundamental sense of the word. The image of the tough, half-criminal detective preceded Hammett's apotheosis of him, but the manner of presentation of the *Black Mask* writers in general and Hammett in particular—he began by reviewing detective fiction in the magazine—created a "fundamentally American" type (Klein 193).

"We were trying to get murder away from the upper classes, the week-end house party and the vicar's rose-garden," wrote Raymond Chandler in 1944 in his famous essay, "The Gentle Art of Murder," "and back to the people who are really good at it" (Klein 180). Consequently the new breed of private eyes or policemen exuded a deliberate cynicism, proud of, as Marcus Klein has put it, the "integrity of their disenchantment," wearing their "civic despair as style" (179, 194). These characters opposed the dandified Holmeses and Poirots as hardened products of a tough urban milieu that surpassed the idealized country house and village in mystery fiction. Frederick Karl relates detective and western fiction to the combat novel in American fiction and suggests that these popular offshoots brought "back the sole frontier remaining to us and provide[d] an alternative to bourgeois society, which deals death to the instinctual life" (95). Such fiction reawakened these basic American themes, within which "violence establishes a purity with its own rules, its own field of force" (Karl 25).

The literary triumph of these tough-guy tales existed in the terse and minimalist style Hammett and others after him honed and perfected. For Claude-Edmonde Magny, Hammett employed "the aesthetics of the stenographic record," based on the aesthetics of American films. His sparse, objective prose relied upon the use of juxtaposition, ellipses, the change of camera angles, and the crosscuts that film relied upon to tell its story. Such a behaviorist approach in which "the psychological reality of a person . . . is limited to what can be perceived by a purely external observer [and is essentially] reduced to a succession of acts" (40), proved to be immensely successful in the rendering of a mystery, since the author worked "to conceal the essential fact from the reader in order to oblige him to reconstruct it, little by little, by conjectures and make it gradually emerge from the matrix of mystery in which it was hidden" (Magny 49). Such a manner also hid characters' motives the way Hemingway managed to do in his best fictions and added to the aura of mystery and deceit. This style continued in the mysteries of Chandler, Macdonald, Robert B. Parker, George V. Higgins, Elmore Leonard, and James Lee Burke.

Sam Spade in Hammett's *The Maltese Falcon* (1929), of his five novels arguably his masterpiece, is one of the first and most famous tough-guy detectives. Calm, self-possessed, poised, wary, he speaks tersely and observes quietly. Nothing gets in the way of his investigations, and his values are relatively simple: "When a man's partner is killed he's supposed to do something about it. It doesn't make any difference what you thought of him" (Hammett 226). When it comes to the possibility of love, even that won't interfere. As he tells Brigid O'Shaughnessy, "All we've got is the fact that maybe you love me and maybe I love you. . . . I've been through it before" (227). And despite his wheeling and dealing and innate cynicism, "Don't be too sure I'm as crooked as I'm supposed to be" (227).

Spade is very resourceful when it comes to money. He takes $200 from Brigid early on, even though he doesn't believe her story. He takes $200 from Joel Cairo to search for the falcon, even though Cairo's interests may be different from O'Shaughnessy's. He takes $50 as a downpayment from another client on the side. He keeps $1,000 of the $10,000 Caspar Gutman gives him for his trouble. And when Cairo offers him $5,000 for the bird, he tells Gutman it was $10,000, so that Gutman goes on to offer him $25,000 down, $25,000 later, and $500,000 when he gets and sells the falcon.

Gender roles are clearly drawn. The only other men who aspire to Spade's expertise are Sid Wise, Spade's sharp-eyed lawyer, and Casper Gutman who admires Spade's skills in the game as much as Spade admires his. The unskilled others include the homosexual Cairo, the young inexperienced thug named Wilmer Cook, and Spade's easy-going lout of a partner, Miles Archer. Both Wise and the clever but fat bulbous Gutman are aptly named.

Spade's attitude toward women is well known. They are either children, sisters, angels or babes. "God, you women" (107), Spade sputters to the whining jealous Iva Archer. To his sidekick, Effie Perrine, whose intuition proves to be false—she dislikes Iva and supports Brigid—he exclaims revealingly, "You're a damned good man, sister" (167). Brigid, of course, exudes sex appeal and cunning, both of which Spade finds impossible to resist despite or more likely because of her lies and deviousness. And Brigid even stoops to doping Gutman's seventeen-year-old daughter Rhea as part of his plan.

The social Darwinism of crude capitalism and the nightmarish accidents of life embody the world that Spade inhabits in the true tough-guy tradition. Falcon or no, everybody is a crook; everybody has an angle. The labyrinthine levels of double-cross and triple-cross boggle the mind. The history of the falcon itself is one long tale of greed and thievery, and despite the references to the Saracens, the Emperor Charles, and the Templars, Gutman insists, "We all know that the Holy Wars to them . . . were largely a matter of loot" (128). Spade would agree: "Most things in San Francisco can be bought, or taken" (56).

The story of Flitcraft, which Spade tells, points to the essential randomness of life, as well as the repetitious routines and habits that people rely upon to evade that darker vision. A beam falls and just misses Flitcraft, and he recognizes that "life could be ended for him at random. . . . [so] he would change his life at random by simply going away" (66). This he does, deserting his family and disappearing. But once away he re-establishes his old habits, now based on his developing vision of exactly what had happened to him: "He adjusted himself to beams falling, and then no more of them fell, and he adjusted himself to them not falling" (67). Within the intricate maze of Hammett's plot lies the irrational sudden event that can unhinge any attempt at constructing a life that appears to be clean, orderly, sane and responsible. That amoral eruption, a glimpse into the abyss, undercuts the binary morality of the mystery formula, which is still played out to the end, however battered and bruised, and calls attention to its very artifice. It's a fine balancing act on Hammett's part and lends Spade a certain philosophical perspective, in which he consistently expects the unexpected, trusts no one except his own instincts, and realizes the very gamesmanship of his career.

But it is Hammett's style that succeeds best of all and embodies his dark vision. The minimalist approach, swift and enigmatic, necessarily masks human motive and reflects Spade's self-possessed approach to things, as detail stands out to be observed and interpreted during the process of the investigation: "He talked in a steady matter-of-fact voice that was devoid of emphasis or pauses, though now and then he repeated a sentence slightly rearranged, as if it were important that each detail be related exactly as it had happened" (63). Hammett's emphasis on eyes reveals the nature of his method in which he focuses most often on characters gazing at one another, at cigarettes, at drinks, seeing and being seen:

> She *looked* at Spade again. He did not in any way respond to the appeal in her *eyes*. He leaned against the door-frame and *observed* the occupants of the room with the polite detached air of a disinterested *spectator*. The girl turned her *eyes* up to Dundy's. Her *eyes* were wide and dark and earnest. (77, italics mine)

Remarks Spade to Brigid: "You're good. You're very good. It's chiefly your eyes, I think" (36). "He stood beside the fireplace and looked at her with eyes that studied, weighed, judged her without pretense that they were not studying, weighing, judging her" (56).

Hammett conjures up his characters by using stark and telling physical details. Casper Gutman reveals "a great soft egg of a belly . . . with bulbous pink cheeks. . . . As he advanced to Spade all his bulbs rose and shook and fell separately with each step" (108). In contrast Spade is all sharp edges, "his chin a jutting v under the more flexible v of his mouth. . . . The v *motif* was picked up again by thickish brows rising outward" (3). Brigid reveals "cobalt-blue eyes that were both shy and probing. . . . She wore two shades of blue. . . . The hair curling from under her blue hat was darkly red, her full lips more brightly red" (3-4). Fight scenes are carefully detailed, gesture by gesture: "The elbow struck him beneath the cheek-bone. . . . Cairo let the pistol go the instant that Spade's fingers touched it. . . . The fist struck Cairo's face. . . . Cairo shut his eyes and was unconscious" (47, 48).

At the same time Hammett's terse dialogue suggests an almost Jamesian fascination with jockeying for position, keeping one's agenda hidden and masked, creating a pose that necessarily fits into the external situation, and playing a role crisply and succinctly. One thinks of Brigid's rhetorical plea to Spade in her use of repetitious phrases carefully cultivated: "I haven't lived a good life. . . . I've been bad. . . . You know I'm not all bad, don't you? . . . Help me, Mr. Spade. . . . You can help me. Help me" (36). Spade is quick to pick up on Brigid's set pieces: "You told me that this afternoon in the same words, same tone. It's a speech you've practiced" (57). And the dialogue between Spade and Gutman reveals two cunning men at the top of their craft.

To turn from the very American Hammett to the very British P. D. James is to leap from Spade's cynical one-liners to Adam Dalgleish's more brooding and refined reveries. In fact in the eyes of most literary and popular critics, P. D. James in her full-bodied, richly detailed, and psychologically probing mysteries has extended and enhanced the tradition of Agatha Christie and Dorothy Sayers, as in many ways have Elizabeth George and Martha Grimes, American authors writing in the British tradition. James has not only continued "the novel of straight detection" (Symons xiv); "she has pushed, as a modernist must, against the boundaries of the classical detective story" and been "called a natural successor to Sayers [with] the same care in plotting . . . the accuracy of minor points . . . and like Sayers gives us dialogue that is convincing rather than entertaining" (Tuttleton 212, 211). At the same time she "persistently raise[s] questions that reflect such evidence of ourselves as we have been able to gather, about honesty, duty, courage, and all those virtues" (Winks 97), thus deepening the psychological compulsions and moral issues her characters must face.

In James' case the tough-guy private eye in contemporary mystery fiction has been superseded by the more humane, more flawed detective. P. D. James' police detective, Adam Dalgleish, for example, occupies a position similar to other modern detectives, in that he is given an interesting and intriguing personality, complete with his own self-doubts and contradictions: "He is introspective, brooding, mournful" (Symons 61). He is "the poet who no longer writes poetry. The lover who substitutes technique for commitment. The policeman disillusioned with policing" (61). As James herself has said, "I made my detective a very private and detached man who uses his job to save himself from involvement with other human beings because of tragedies in his own life" (Cooper-Clark 21). He would fit Glenn W. Most's interpretation that "the true mystery in a mystery novel is . . . the nature of the detective who solves it" (342). And Richard Alewyn's assessment that detectives are essentially romantic artists, "the ones who know how to read the clues and to interpret the signs which remain invisible or incomprehensible to normal men, [revealing as romantics do] an everyday and peaceful deceptive surface, with abysses of mystery and danger underneath" (77, 76).

For the most part James' mysteries—which include *A Taste for Death* (1986), *Devices and Desires* (1990), and *Original Sin* (1995)—have also been described as essentially novels of manners focusing on the professional upper-middle classes. Although she displays "an almost obsessional zest in describing furniture and fittings" (Symons 211), most critics have praised her innovative subjects and sites, such as a home for incurables, a publishing house, and a forensic research laboratory. Such a view suggests that readers see and assess her characters, as she has created them, as visible products of a particular society, dominated by the manners of that society. Such significant conflict and confrontation, therefore, arise from the clash between professional manner and personal distress.

But there is an even greater dimension to the mystery formula that James has pursued. As we have seen, certain religious and mythic patterns in western culture extend and deepen the Cartesian discourse at the heart of the western enlightened tradition of empirical and analytical thought, which itself was built upon Judeo-Christian traditions. The mystery can resemble a Christian morality play, as well as a novel of manners—one does not necessarily exclude the other and might, in fact, reinforce one another—with all its formal and ritualistic characteristics, complete with exorcism, expulsion, guilt, and a final scapegoat.[4]

As Dennis Porter has pointed out, P. D. James "clings to one central concept of Christian faith, namely Pauline caritas," a religion of love and self-sacrifice, in a world which seems to have outlived both, mired in its own evils and self-obsessions, and offers us "models of right conduct" which suggest that "to read one of her novels is to risk a kind of conversion."[5] Her novels reveal what Elaine Pagels has described as "the struggle within Christian tradition between the profoundly human view that 'otherness' is evil and the words of Jesus that reconciliation is divine" (184). And in doing so James capitalizes on the modernist interest in myth and psychology, in ritual and possible redemption, within the boundaries of the rationalistic formula of the traditional mystery.

For the rite of exorcism to take place, James creates a world that is pervaded by sin, guilt, human culpability, and complicity, a dark world full of the darker ambiguities of human choice and motive that always outlast and transcend the single apprehension of the murderer. Guilt spreads and stains the whole of her domain. "It isn't as simple as that to solve the problem," James has said. "The problem may be solved but other problems are left unsolved, because these are problems of the human heart and problems about which perhaps nothing effective can be done" (Cooper-Clark 19). In effect, as she continues, "Detective fiction may be a substitute for the old morality plays [, but] because the detective is increasingly becoming a human being, that part of his personality which is evil has to be shown. So, to an extent, this destroys the old ideas that you have the good and evil, the dark and the light" (18).

James' sense of a world stained by sin and guilt, within which love and self-sacrifice may be possible, a descent of grace in a world of evil, parallels in many ways Paul Ricoeur's ideas on the subject in *The Symbolism of Evil*. "It is in confession," Larry D. Bouchard suggests about Ricoeur's thought, "that we most closely approach the inward experience of evil," and the primary symbols "in the language of confession [are] stain, sin, and guilt" (39). According to Bouchard, Ricoeur believes that "the development from one symbol to the next—the turning from exteriority (stain) to interiority (guilt) through the broken relation of humanity 'before God' (sin)—is dialectical, not chronological" (39). In other words each interacts with the other. Murder provides the exterior stain, James pursues the interior guilt of her characters, and both participate, in the characters' estrangement from one another and from themselves, in the religious act of sin. The pervasive vision conjures up "the terrifying fact of the irreducibility of evil. . . . to the extent that original sin makes guilt inevitable and objective, there is a penultimate possibility of the tragic, but to the extent that the ultimate answer to the demonic is not heroic defiance but saving grace, the tragic is transcended" (Bouchard 46, 92). The mystery formula and James' sense of caritas and love transcend the tragic in her novels, but the inevitable stain of guilt found there does not.

James' titles often suggest this religious and moral vision. *Devices and Desires* (1989) comes from the Anglican prayer of confession. *Original Sin* (1995) speaks for itself. And in discussing the final choice of the title, *Innocent Blood* (1980), James relates that choice directly to the Bible: "It immediately struck me as a very good title because it had this ambiguity about it as to whether the blood she had inherited [Philippa in the novel] was or was not innocent. And, of course, it ties up with the section in Ecclesiastes about it being an abomination to the Lord that one should shed innocent blood" (Cooper-Clark 32).

In short, in her mysteries James does not exclude or marginalize inscrutable enigmas and puzzles which perpetually baffle, perplex, and remain inexplicable. She often focuses on essential religious mysteries which involve a scapegoat and the exorcism of his/her crimes, some of which can be suggested only by revelation and cannot be fully comprehended. Essentially murder victimizes all of her characters, and that sense of victimhood pervades all of her novels. "It is, in short, no surprise," writes Dennis Porter, "if her plots recall both the bloody familial dramas of Greek myths and the tortured family romance of psychoanalytic theory" (16).

At first *The Children of Men* (1993), a dystopian novel in the tradition of Aldous Huxley's *Brave New World*, may seem an anomaly in James' fiction. It is not a mystery but a cautionary tale of the future in the year 2021. No baby has been born since 1995, and those that were born in that year, called Omegas, have become cruel, arrogant, and violent. England is run by the tyrant-warden, Xan Lyppiatt, who has organized private armies, a state security police, distant penal colonies, a system to import slaves known as Sojourners, and the Quietus ceremony which ritualizes the mass suicide of the old. The narrative is almost evenly divided between the diary entries of Theodore Faron, historian of the Victorian age, a self-declared, uncommitted, dispassionate observer (and cousin of the infamous, all-powerful Xan), and the third-person narrative which James writes to implicate him in the circumstances that come to surround and seduce him. The plot of this fable and Faron's decision to participate in it reveal that sense of self-sacrifice, love, and caritas—the jacket painting is a detail from Bartolomeo Schedone's "Christian Charity"—that James sees as the only possible way toward some kind of human if not traditionally religious redemption.

The text is saturated with religious imagery and yearnings. A revolutionary committee which opposes Xan's rule of terror and treachery calls itself the Five Fishes, an ancient Christian symbol, and at first pretends to be merely the Cranmer Club, interested in studying the old Book of Common Prayer.[6] The priest Luke performs a Eucharist later in the book. And at the very beginning Faron wonders if people will ever remember what deity St. Paul's Cathedral was built for: "Will they be curious about his nature, this deity who was worshipped with such pomp and splendour, intrigued by the mystery of his symbol, at once so simple, the two crossed sticks, ubiquitous in nature, yet laden with gold, gloriously jewelled and adorned?" (James, *Children* 4).

The fable itself, of course, reveals the answer. Theodore becomes involved with the Five Fishes and joins them when they attempt to flee Xan's spies and soldiers. His uncommitment turns to passionate conviction in the process. He abandons order for justice. James creates suspense with the flight of the revolutionaries, several of whom are grotesquely murdered along the way. Julian, one of the women in the group, has become pregnant by Luke, the priest, and Faron accompanies her deep into the forest to allow the birth to take place far from Xan's control. A boy is born, and Faron feels as if "he was both participant and spectator, isolated . . . in a limbo of time in which nothing mattered" (227). He describes the child as "the new Adam, begetter of the new race, the saviour of mankind" (66), Julian is described by Xan, who finds them in the forest, as "the most important woman in the world but she isn't the Virgin Mary" (238), and all have fled to prevent Xan's being able to announce the birth to the world as part of his regime: "There would be no simple shepherds at this cradle" (198). Theodore murders Xan, and he and Julian christen the baby at the novel's end.

It is helpful to trace this Christian vision briefly in several of James' other novels. In *Devices and Desires*, for instance, she conjures up the bleak Norfolk coast—she makes much of the fact that place often determines the tale she pursues[7]—because of its symbolic desolation which represents man's fallen state. Interestingly enough the victim and the murderer emerge from the long-standing mutual guilt shared by a brother and sister. This suggestively incestuous relationship between a brother and sister often appears in James' novels—one thinks of Alex and Alice Mair in this novel, Gabriel and Claudia Etienne in *Original Sin*, and Barbara Swayne Berowne and Dominic Swayne in *A Taste for Death*. Both Dominic Swayne and Alice Mair are murderers, and Gabriel Etienne is the primary victim of murder, a recognition perhaps of murder's earliest stirrings: "Crime stories certainly go back before the Bible. It is rather interesting, isn't it, that you get Cain and Abel in the first stories of the Bible and this is the story of a murder" (Cooper-Clark 20).

In any case in *Devices and Desires* the Mairs do not go for help when their father injures himself but wait until he dies. There are extenuating circumstances, but what survives longest is Alice's sense that "I've been made to feel guilty from childhood. And if at the heart of your being you feel that you've no right even to exist, then one more cause of guilt hardly matters" (413). She murders Alex's mistress to enhance his career, the guilty but devoted act of the single sister to prevent the mistress from continuing to blackmail him.

In *Innocent Blood,* in many ways more of a novel about the search for personal identity rather than a straightforward mystery, Philippa Rose Palfrey is mesmerized by the "whole mythology of identity" and sets out to discover who her real parents are in an effort to overcome or come to terms with once and for all "the loneliness of the self" (51, 95). In the course of the novel the self-absorbed and arrogant Philippa more or less encourages her real mother to commit suicide and exonerates the man, the father of the little girl her mother and father murdered years ago, who has come to kill her mother but instead stabs her when she is already dead. The tale of vengeance and revenge moves with the certainty of myth and ritual, even to the point where Philippa gives herself for one night to her adopted father.

James seems to praise High Anglicanism in *Innocent Blood* as "a satisfying compromise between reason and myth, justified by the beauty of its liturgy, a celebration of Englishness" (114). Her true vision comes at the end, where Philippa begins to realize that "it is only through learning to love that we find identity. . . . She hoped one day to find hers. She wished [the father of the murdered daughter] well. And perhaps to be able to wish him well with all that she could recognize of her unpracticed heart, to say a short, untutored prayer for him and his Violet [the blind woman he has decided to marry], was in itself a small accession of grace" (348-49).

In *Original Sin*, the river Thames underscores James' dark vision of the world as "a dark tide of horror," above which "a cluster of low cloud lay over London, stained pink like a lint bandage which had soaked up the city's blood" (71, 68). Peverell Press occupies Innocent House along its dark banks, and the murder victim is found with a toy snake wrapped around his neck. But the real horror and guilt of the book are embodied in a past murder at Innocent House and the Holocaust. Both permeate the entire atmosphere of the novel in a way that suggests all people are if not murderers capable of betrayal, treachery, and murder. Real snakes haunt a character's real nightmares.

Original Sin is very self-consciously a writer's book with its focus on the publishing world, on archives, diaries, letters, manuscripts, book-signings, even including Esme Carling, a failing mystery writer who ends up murdered. The titles of the five sections make this clear: "Foreword to Murder," "Death of a Publisher," "Work In Progress," "Evidence In Writing," and "Final Proof." James seems to connect the art of writing mysteries with the very pervasive guilt that stains every one of her pages. Authors themselves, of course, are creators of the crime and share the villain's plot and ingenious strategies. In many ways the writer elevates the very outlawed powers she is pretending to denounce, thus participating in the dark rites that initiate the need for love and possible human redemption. As readers we, too, participate in these dark rites.

James' masterpiece is *A Taste for Death,* in which religious revelation becomes the driving force of the narrative, embodied in the victim, Sir Paul Berowne, which leads him to submit to his own murder. His accumulated guilt, involving his first wife's death, the abortion, suicide, and drowning of women in his employ, his marrying his dead older brother's fiance to carry on the line, and his disaffection with his ministerial post in Parliament, leads him to spend the night at St. Matthew's Church. There his brother-in-law, eager to keep the Berowne status and money that his pregnant sister, Berowne's second wife, clings to, as he must cling to her, kills him. Exclaims the murderer, Dominic Swayne, "He wanted to die. . . . He practically asked for it. He could have tried to stop me, pleaded, argued, put up a fight. He could have begged for mercy. . . . That's all I wanted from him. . . . But he knew what I'd come for. . . . As if I had no choice. Just an instrument. . . . But I did have a choice. And so did he. Christ, he could have stopped me. Why didn't he stop me?" (444).

The mystery that haunts the center of the novel is Berowne's passion for revelation, a passion that cannot be explained but that occupies the heart of darkness of the murder mystery. Whatever drives him "had been something more profound, less explicable, than disillusionment, midlife restlessness, the fear of a threatened scandal. Whatever had happened to him on that first night in St. Matthew's vestry had led him, the next day, to change the whole direction of his life. Had it also led him to his death?" (53). "He told me that he had had an experience of God," proclaims another character (264). In a world of greed, social status, and envy such experiences may necessarily lead only to death. In any case the mystery of Berowne's sudden conversion infects Dalgleish, and his subordinates begin to see a likeness between the two. The revelation remains unrevealed, but it haunts all the pages of this novel and is not dissipated by the more rational mystery's solution. The novel concludes with a sermon: "If you find that you no longer believe, act as if you still do" (459). It seems to be James' ultimate advice.

At one point James takes us into Sarah Berowne's flat. She is a photographer and the left-leaning estranged daughter of Paul, and the reader is shown some of her work. One photograph in particular stands out at the end of the paragraph, that of "a buxom grandmother, noted for her detective stories, who gazed mournfully at the camera as if deploring either the bloodiness of her craft or the size of her advance" (216). One need not spend much time in guessing whose self-portrait this might be. Murder and the writing about murder fill the air with a certain madness: "To be part of a murder investigation [or to conjure one up?] was to be contaminated by a process which would leave few of their lives unchanged. Murder remained the unique crime. Peer and pauper stood equal before it" (260). This is the source and dark heart of P. D. James' art of fiction. And no amount of rational explanation can make it disappear.

Certainly this darker, more complex vision of things underscores James' strength as a writer of mysteries. The novel of bad manners, the atmosphere, and the furnishings serve only to anchor her wider and more moral, more human concerns and doubts. What James seeks is that essential man, a common humanity, however ambiguous and self-serving, in all its complexities and complicities: "Scrape away the carefully acquired patina of professional success, prestige, orthodox good manners, and the real man was there" (55). It is this pursuit which fuels her dark fictions. The manners and the essential human matter exist in an uncertain equilibrium in regard to one another. From the carnage of her vision, however, she pursues the conversion of her characters, readers, and probably herself, as she initiates the rites of mystery over and over again, playing out the ritual of exorcism and possible redemption, although she recognizes that blood is never innocent, that original sin contaminates our devices and desires, and that we all have a taste for death.

Clearly the mysteries of Dashiell Hammett and P. D. James are a world apart, not to mention the ocean between them, but they once again reveal the flexibility of the form. In renouncing the "British country house" plot, Hammett helped create the American hard-boiled mystery.

In continuing the "country house" tradition, James reinvigorated that specifically British sub-genre. Both attest to the popularity of the mystery structure and suggest very distinct ways in how it can be both deepened and extended.

Subverting the Formula: Faulkner, Fowles, and Others

There are also many ways in which the mystery formula may be not only broadened and enriched, as James has done, but subverted from within. The formula rests upon its own certified binary oppositions, the good guy and the bad guy, the detective and the murderer, the recognition of clues and the resolution of the plot. Such oppositions can appear to be monolithic and hierarchical, producing a kind of master-slave structure; at first the murderer is the master, but the tables are turned when he and his crime are discovered by the detective. As we know from Jacques Derrida's theory of deconstruction, however, this binary scheme, inherent in western thought, can become notoriously unstable, once the functional relationships between them are revealed and exposed. The process of narrative itself thwarts such a monolithic structure. "Literature exists in and through the act by which it questions what at the same time it proposes," Richard Poirier insists (147-48). "One obvious characteristic of a literary text is that its words tend to destabilize one another and to fall into conflicted or contradictory relationships. . . . such contradictions are inherent to the mystery of human existence in time and to the very words by which we have imagined it" (Poirier 147-48). In another sense mystery writers are playing with fire. They are themselves the creators of the crime, and the villain thus shares their own sense of plot and ingenious strategies. In many ways these writers elevate the very outlawed powers they are pretending to denounce (Reynolds 109) and violate those very taboos their tales are advising us not to.

The identification between writer and villain extends to include the reader as well, a process within which the good and the bad are less clearly defined. "The true [mystery] addict," Symons asserts, "is a sort of Manichee and his spirits of light and darkness, the detective and the criminal, are fighting each other for ever" (9). This constant confrontation leads to questions concerning the relationship between good and evil and the coexistence of both in the same person. As Gabriel Sarrazin has described such conundrums, "It has remained to our century and to America to erect evil and good upon equal pedestals and read in them an equal purpose" (Reynolds 112). If such subversive elements and perspectives can be smuggled into the mystery text or themselves are the result of the self-contradictory powers of language and literature, then as

Lehman acknowledges, "no solution, however convincing, can quite measure up to the riddle it unravels" (Symons 41). And we are left with Robin Winks, forced to recognize that "many mysterious elements relating to precise actions and precise motivations at precise times, as opposed to general explanations of motive, will almost certainly and properly be left unresolved" (Winks 105).

In many contemporary American mysteries, there is another element that destabilizes the traditional mystery formula. Several authors envision a world in which moral values no longer dictate the outcome of confrontations. Many re-enact their discovery of a violent chaotic society whose very exposure in their fiction undercuts any idea of a lasting ethical order. This recognition of a darker, wider, chaotic realm, akin as it is to the nightmarish domain of gothic novels, threatens all possible frameworks of law and order and plunges both reader and characters into an unendingly visceral and savage "new world order." Things may threaten to remain unresolvable because they cannot be adequately comprehended, and we have therefore entered newer, darker, and uncharted territories of both the individual psyche and society.

The mystery formula has become such a popular genre in the twentieth century that several writers, including many who are neither American nor British, have toyed with it in their own literary fiction and have consciously chosen to subvert and undercut it. Examples include everything from William Faulkner's *Sanctuary* (1931) and Paul Auster's *City of Glass* (1985), from his *New York Trilogy* (the only one we could consider here as a "genuine" mystery writer), to more recent fiction such as Tim O'Brien's *In The Lake of the Woods* (1994) and Joan Didion's *The Last Thing He Wanted* (1996), among others. And of course other writers have taken aim at the formula as well, including John Fowles in his short story, "The Enigma" (1974), and Gabriel Garcia Marquez in *Chronicle of a Death Foretold* (1982). In each the standard mystery approach has either been subverted from within, terminally disrupted and dispatched, reversed, or transcended.

Andre Malraux referred to *Sanctuary* as "the infusion of Greek tragedy into the detective story." Faulkner conjures up such a corrupt and evil world that its demonic workings-out inevitably overwhelm all attempts to try and solve the complex case of Popeye's murder of Tommy and his rape with a corncob of Temple Drake. The lawyer, Horace Benbow, attempts to convict Popeye of both the murder and the rape, but Temple refuses to cooperate and, because she is either in awe or terrified of Popeye, confesses on the witness stand that it was Lee Goodwin who actually killed the defenseless Tommy in the barn at the Old Frenchman's Place. Benbow is so stunned by Temple's testimony that he lets his case collapse, and Popeye goes free—to be convicted and executed later for a crime he didn't commit, a kind of Flitcraft's revenge. Faulkner builds his novel carefully, withholding the climactic scenes of rape and murder as in the most standard of mysteries. Readers, therefore, cannot discover what has actually happened until the conclusion. At the same time Faulkner creates a nightmarish realm of cryptic events, each gesture and action clearly recorded but lacking a discernible motive and explanation. Readers feel trapped in a kind of pure present in the first thirteen chapters, where people come and go, run in circles, and play a kind of hide-and-seek at the Old Frenchman's Place, where Gowan Stevens has stopped with Temple to pick up some bootleg liquor. Consequently the reader can see the actions but not understand exactly what is going on: "Motionless, facing one another like the first position of a dance, they stood in a mounting terrific muscular hiatus" (Faulkner 114). Hiatus gives way to cinematic blurr and sudden ellipses in the narrative, as the meaning of events remains uncertain and undiscovered, "like sitting before a series of printed pages turned in furious snatches, leaving a series of cryptic, headless and tailless evocations on the mind" (Faulkner 204).

Throughout the novel Faulkner creates a corrupt world in which no sanctuary exists or exists only as mere mask and facade, whether it be social status and respectability, money, traditional gender roles, the gangster code of "ethics," or a belief in good and evil, right and wrong. Horace's sister Narcissa will do anything to keep her social position intact. Temple Drake half-enjoys the rape and her incarceration at the whorehouse in Memphis. Gowan Stevens, who is dating Narcissa, escapes from the Old Frenchman's Place, leaving Temple there on her own. Clarence Snopes, a local politician, trades payoffs for information and will sell anything to anyone if the price is right. Each family group is in some way distorted and dysfunctional. And even Horace Benbow's belief in the law and justice crumbles in the face of so many betrayals and lies.

Horace discovers that "there's a corruption about even looking upon evil, even by accident; you cannot haggle, traffic, with putrefaction" (152). He recognizes that it involves his own sexuality and his own yearning for his step-daughter, that he is as guilty of a possible violation of social codes as is Temple, and that "the Snake was there before Adam, because he was the first one thrown out of heaven; he was there all the time" (181):

Perhaps it is upon the instant that we realise, admit, that there is a logical pattern to evil, that we die, he thought, thinking of the expression he had once seen in the eyes of a dead child, and of other dead: the cooling indignation, the shocked despair fading, leaving two empty globes in which the motionless world lurked profoundly in miniature. (266)

In such a world there can be no justice but only collapse, waste and ener-vation, in which the "monotonous pitch" of insects suggest "the chemi-cal agony of a world left stark and dying above the tide-edge of the fluid in which it lived and breathed" (267). Eliot's wasteland overwhelms the mystery formula, all justice is betrayed, and the would-be detective story concludes with its vision of a "sullen and discontented" Temple Drake in the Luxemborg Gardens with her father the judge, who has engineered in part her exoneration, staring at "the dead tranquil queens . . . and on into the sky lying prone and vanquished in the embrace of the season of rain and death" (380).

Building perhaps on Faulkner's displacement of the mystery for-mula, such diverse authors as Paul Auster, Tim O'Brien, and Joan Didion radically eviscerate it, as their texts set up mysteries to be solved and then collapse, remaining open-ended and curiously incomplete. Auster, for instance, suggests that "in the good mystery there is nothing wasted. . . . nothing must be overlooked. Everything becomes essence; the center of the book shifts with each event that propels it forward" (15). But as *City of Glass* unfolds, characters vanish, clues proliferate, and the would-be detective, Daniel Quinn, unable to decipher these clues, fades away. Quinn explains that "what interested him about the stories he wrote was not their relation to the world but their relation to other stories" (14). He also writes mysteries under the pseudonym of William Wilson, creates a detective named Max Work, assumes the iden-tity of "Paul Auster" when a would-be client calls the Auster Agency to seek advice, and pursues one of two look-alike men named Stillman he spies arriving at Grand Central Station.

For Edgar Allan Poe, to whom Auster refers several times in *City of Glass*, doubling always suggested dissolution, so much so that one nec-essarily includes the other. When a character meets his double in a final showdown, the result is inevitable death and destruction, as in "The Fall of the House of Usher." When Roderick Usher is confronted by his twin sister Madeline, whom he has buried alive, the two collapse one upon the other, and the entire house sinks into the dark tarn that reflects it. Similarly in "William Wilson" the narrator, William Wilson (which he admits is not his real name, so that the reader is never certain exactly who the narrator is), finally confronts his double (whether in reality or in his imagination Poe leaves provocatively ambiguous) and kills him. Thus William Wilson 1 kills William Wilson 2, but the actual event can be interpreted as either a suicide or a murder, and Poe leaves the final denouement problematic.

Likewise in *City of Glass*, Quinn discovers the "real" Paul Auster in New York, who of course is being invented by Paul Auster, the author. Quinn discovers that he and Auster's son are both named Daniel, that Quinn's dead son Peter has the same name as his client, Peter Stillman, and that his initials, DQ, are the same as *Don Quixote*, which Cervantes wrote as "an attack on the dangers of make-believe" and that "had to claim that it was real" (151). Quinn recalls that Poe's detective Dupin believed that it was necessary to identify "the reasoner's intellect with that of his opponent" (65), the detective's with the villain's. He also expresses his own pursuit of finding a place "where one could finally disappear" (167), "by flooding himself with externals, by drowning himself out of himself" (98) like Melville's Bartleby or Poe's A. Gordon Pym. The upshot results in the complete undermining of the mystery's faith in closely observed details which will inevitably lead to a solution: "The implication was that human behavior could be understood, that beneath the infinite facade of gestures, tics, and silences, there was finally a coherence, an order, a source of motivation" (105). *City of Glass* conducts the reader into a realm of reflective mirrors, which finally reflect only absence and the abandoned red notebook in a dark empty room where Quinn has been hiding out. "What will happen when there are no more pages in the red notebook?" (200). All will vanish. And the nameless narrator can only admit, "[Quinn] will be with me always. And wherever he may have disappeared to, I wish him luck" (203).

Auster, like O'Brien and Didion, is writing in a postmodern world in which the very nature of language has been questioned. Does it illuminate or imprison, reveal or re-veil, connect us to the world or isolate us in our own solipsistic imaginings? Auster focuses on the apparent collapse of language in contemporary times, that deconstructionist and poststructuralist vision that "names became detached from things; words devolved into a collection of arbitrary signs; language had been severed from God" (70). In such a world, as the character Stillman suggests, all has fallen into ambiguity and contradiction, which also involves "a knowledge of evil" (70). Evil in *Sanctuary* destroyed common morality and justice; in *City of Glass* it destroys or at least eviscerates language and the detective as well. The mystery beckons to Quinn and to us and then dissolves before our eyes, as if analogy (this tale is like one of Poe's) breeds causation. It also comments upon Poe's fiction, which leads to an ultimate identification, duplicating Poe's use of doubles that results in dissolution and death.

Tim O'Brien, who has written several stunning novels on his experiences in Vietnam, delights in confronting the mystery formula with ultimate metaphysical mysteries, a dialectic he reveals in his numerous footnotes to *In the Lake of the Woods*: "There are certain mysteries that weave through life itself, human motive and human desire. Even much of what might appear to be fact in this narrative—action, word, thought —must ultimately be viewed as a diligent but still imaginative reconstruction of events" (30). The impossibility of ultimately knowing anything about human motive and desire builds throughout the footnotes: "The man's soul remains for me an absolute and impenetrable unknown. . . . We are fascinated, all of us, by the implacable otherness of others. . . . they are all beyond us" (103). Perhaps his justification lies in the necessity "to bear witness to the mystery of evil" (203). Perhaps the book exists "to remind me. To give me back my vanished life" (301). Or perhaps he is mesmerized by "our love of enigma. . . . No answers, yet mystery itself carries me on" (269). Ultimately

there *is* no end. . . . Nothing is fixed, nothing is solved. . . . Mystery finally claims us. . . . One way or another, it seems, we all perform vanishing tricks, effacing history, locking up our lives and slipping day by day into the graying shadows. Our whereabouts are uncertain. All secrets lead to the dark, and beyond the dark there is only maybe. (304).

O'Brien has discovered that mysterious void at the center of all human experience, motive, and desire. Faulkner remarked that he wrote about "the human heart in conflict with itself," Hawthorne about the unfathomable mystery of the human heart. We can hear echoes of their words in O'Brien's: "Blame it on the human heart," the line which precedes the quotation above which begins, "One way or another, it seems, we all perform vanishing tricks" (304). And O'Brien has made very clear that the convoluted and inexplicable human heart has always been his first concern:

Writing fiction . . . display[s] in concrete terms the actions and reactions of human beings contesting problems of the heart. . . . The heart *is* dark. We gape into the tangle of this man's soul, which has the quality of a huge black hole, ever widening, ever mysterious, its gravity sucking us back into the book itself. . . . To reach into one's own heart, down into that place where the stories are, bringing up the mystery of oneself. ("Magic" 176, 182-83)

John Wade, the boy-magician turned politician in *In the Lake of the Woods,* has deleted his own dark deeds from the Army records of the My

Lai massacre in March 1968, in Vietnam and decides to run in a Democratic primary for the United States Senate. He thinks he can evade his past mistakes and dazzle his constituents with his charismatic personality and flair. The records, however, are discovered, and their publication in the press destroys his political career. He had believed that he could conjure up a self of his own choosing and devising and is one more representative in American fiction of those willfully self-made male American "heroes" like Ahab, Jay Gatsby, and Thomas Sutpen who spring from the Platonic conceptions of themselves. Wade's nickname is "Sorcerer," which is the perfect name for such a character—as is "Wade": the human condition can wade in darker waters but forever skirts the ultimate seas. He does it with smoke and mirrors. O'Brien himself admits to loving magic tricks as a child: "I liked the aloneness, as God and other miracle workers must also like it. . . . I liked shaping the universe around me. I liked the power" ("Magic" 175).

Of course what happens to such a self is that not only must it self-destruct, but its past exploits and history must inevitably catch up with it. When Wade loses the primary for the United States Senate, his political career is finished, as is the Sorcerer's ability to keep pulling rabbits out of the hat: "Wade felt an estrangement from the actuality of the world, its basic nowness, and in the end all he could conjure up was an image of illusion itself, a head full of mirrors" *(Lake* 281). No wonder O'Brien quotes Hawthorne's description of Wakefield near the very end of the novel: "He had happened to dissever himself from the world—to vanish—to give up his place and privilege with living men, without being admitted among the dead" *(Lake* 297).

History in *In the Lake of the Woods* does not just correct Wade's image of himself as Sorcerer and successful politician; it annihilates it. The wilderness swallows him whole, and he literally vanishes in the novel, as has his wife Kathy a few weeks before him. We never know what has happened to them. The mystery remains insoluble. But of course this is exactly what has attracted O'Brien: "Mystery everywhere—permeating mystery—even in the most ordinary objects of the world . . . infinite and inexplicable. Anything was possible" (2). Ultimate mystery has devoured the mystery formula, revealing its artifice and structure, and leaves us "in the deep unbroken solitude, age to age, [where] Lake of the Woods gazes back on itself like a great liquid eye. Nothing adds or subtracts. Everything is present, everything is missing. . . . [it is] where the vanished things go" (290, 243).[8]

In Joan Didion's latest novel, *The Last Thing He Wanted,* things such as facts do not vanish, but they remain virtually unexplained. We get them all but not within any final resolution. As in both Auster's and

O'Brien's novels, the text participates in its own demise and becomes a mystery in its own right, a gathering of facts and possibilities, a fluid pursuit of answers with none to give, so that the reader finds herself imprisoned in the process of revelation that is never satisfied. We eventually discover that Elena McMahon, daughter of an arms-dealer, has been assassinated on a Caribbean island in 1984, that she had become involved with a "crisis junkie," Treat Morrison, from the State Department or CIA, and that she was shot by the local police, who are connected to the Salvadoran and counterterrorist Colonel Alvaro Garcia Steiner. He may have also tried to kill Morrison and blame it on Elena, whose father had been selling arms to the Sandinistas in the Nicaraguan civil war. Didion clearly takes government bureacracy and secrecy to task and wants to expose the incestuous corruption that underscored the American support for the Contras in Nicaragua in the 1980s, but her narrative method, with her use of ellipses, flashbacks, sudden epiphanies and flashforwards—all of them fractured and splintered in terms of memory and monologue—just as clearly reveals the ultimate inability of understanding exactly what has gone on. She is aware finally of "a momentary phantasmagoria in which everyone focused on some different aspect and nobody at all saw the whole" (Didion 203).

Didion's famously obsessive fragmentary style—she circles, repeats, and juxtaposes tales and events with speculations, rumors, asides, and incomplete memoirs—destroys any possibility of continuity, of cause and effect, and thus sabotages the clear investigatory path of the mystery formula. Like O'Brien she senses a larger mystery, a yawning dread, in the world, a heart of darkness Joseph Conrad would have appreciated. And therefore in her pursuit of connecting "every moment . . . to every other moment, every act to have logical if obscure consequences, an unbroken narrative of vivid complexity" (56), she realizes that government policy in our information age creates "entire layers of bureaucracy dedicated to the principle that self-perpetuation depended on the ability not to elucidate but to obscure," that everything can be "obfuscated by acronym" (169, 91). Consequently these "glimpses of life on the far frontier of the Monroe Doctrine" (10) lack an ultimate coherence or solution. Mystery becomes a way of life, a mode of technical mastery, and Elena McMahon, one of its more prominent victims, "remained remote most of all to herself, a clandestine agent who had so successfully compartmentalized her operation as to have lost access to her own cutouts" (152).

The true price of such overwhelming obfuscation and loss of direction results in what Jerzy Kosinski, author of such novels as *The Painted Bird* and *Being There*, has called the theft of the self. The real mystery is that that self can never be retrieved and thus never "solved." Motives vanish in "Elena's apparently impenetrable performances in the various roles assigned her" (Didion 154), and the reader is left desperately trying to "correct or clarify whatever misunderstandings or erroneous impressions might or might not have been left" (170). We are left with Didion's own "half-mad gaze" (47) in which no mystery formula, at least in its more popular guise, can appease us or survive.

There are so many other writers, who are not American, who have played with and re-fashioned the mystery formula in contemporary fiction, and these include John Fowles and Gabriel Garcia Marquez. Fowles' *The Magus* offers solution after solution to the mysterious rites that Nicholas Urfe has gotten himself into, but in each and every instance, the solution at hand is seen to be a ploy, a fake, a staged theatrical display which leads to further mysteries. Eventually Urfe must face himself alone in Fowles' existential climax, freed from all preordained scripts, left with the ultimate mystery that life itself provides without explanation. Fowles is a superbly seductive writer, building his plot of Chinese boxes carefully and then, as in *The French Lieutenant's Woman*, offering multiple solutions or endings. The idea is to keep the process and the pursuit open, as it is in life, and leave the reader to face the tantalizing void of no answers or all possible ones.

In "The Enigma" 57-year-old John Marcus Fielding—family man, happily married, rich, a Conservative Member of Parliament, owner of a magnificent Elizabethan manor house in the country—vanishes. There are few clues to pursue, but Michael Jennings, the police sergeant who comes from a family of fine policemen and who essentially "saw life as a game, which one played principally for oneself and only incidentally out of some sense of duty" (Fowles, *Ebony* 213), is convinced that he can solve the case. In fact he makes two lists of possible solutions, the first he calls "*State of Play*," the second, which is more speculative, "*Wild Ones*." He finally interviews Isobel Dodgson, the former French girlfriend of Peter Fielding, the missing minister's son, and slowly falls in love with her. During the interview Isobel speculates about the nature of John Fielding and suggests but offers no proof whatsoever of what might have happened to him. In doing so Fowles eviscerates the mystery formula, claiming that it is truer to life to do so, since "the unreal literary rules" (239) of the mystery do not exist in the real world of mind and matter.

Isobel describes the entire Fielding household as more or less a decorous masquerade, in which each member of the family believes in or questions their facade of propriety and status but does nothing to change it. Some may be hypocritical; others may fit their appropriate roles easily; "someone alive" may be "playing dead" (224). According to Isobel, Fielding may have thought that "there was an author in his life. In a way. Not a man. A system, a view of things? Something that had written him. Had really made him just a character in a book" (240). And so on the spur of the moment he decides to opt out, to vanish. It is his way of achieving immortality, of performing "God's trick . . . Deus absconditus . . . Walking out" (242). In doing so he will remain forever an unsolved mystery which, as Isobel points out (certainly to Fowles' eternal delight), is "the one thing people never forget . . . the unsolved. Nothing lasts like a mystery" (242).

On this point Faulkner, O'Brien, Didion, and Fowles would all agree, and to assure that the mystery remains unsolved and therefore open-ended and seductive, they create their fictions accordingly. When Jennings and Dodgson discover their mutual attraction, they realize, as has Fowles before them, that "the tender pragmatisms of flesh have poetries no enigma, human or divine, can diminish or demean—indeed, it can only cause them, and then walk out" (247).

Gabriel Garcia Marquez pursues such pragmatisms of flesh by standing the mystery formula on its head. He reveals the crime, the killers, and the victim early on in *Chronicle of a Death Foretold* and in doing so pursues the human motives and complex cultural reasons that have participated in and initiated this murder. "There had never been a death more foretold" (57), explains the narrator, and he wants to reconstruct the events that led up to it not "from an urge to clear up mysteries but because none of us could go on living without an exact knowledge of the place and the mission assigned to us by fate" (113). The mystery of fate and why it seems to rule everyone in the Caribbean backwater village is exactly what Marquez and the narrator are pursuing twenty-seven years after the fact: "I returned to this forgotten village, trying to put the broken mirror of memory back together from so many scattered shards" (5).

What Marquez discovers is that racism, social codes no longer believed in but maintained at all costs, notions of traditional gender-based honor, and the community's submerged longing for a scapegoat help to account for the murder of the Arab, Santiago Nasar, by the twins, Pedro and Pablo Vicario, who have heard that Nasar deflowered their sister Angela, a desecration that is discovered on her wedding night by her husband, the mysterious Bayardo San Roman. Never in the novel do we find out that Nasar is indeed the culprit. Angela has said that he was, but there is no proof. Thus, at the center of the mystery lurks the unresolved issue of why she selected him as her lover in the first place. Why did she point the finger at him?

Marquez offers suggestive cultural clues. First of all, brothers must defend the virginal honor of their sisters. Explains Pablo's fiance, Prudencia Cotes, "I never would have married him if he hadn't done what a man should do" (72). Elaborates the narrator, "Most of those who could have done something to prevent the crime and did not consoled themselves with the pretext that affairs of honor are sacred monopolies, giving access only to those who are part of the drama" (114). In fact at one point the Vicario twins decide not to kill Nasar. It seems that only human inertia and a misguided belief in fate egg them on toward the final denouement. The machismo code of honor permeates the entire culture, as the narrator reveals by describing the several relationships between men and women, bachelors and whores, married men and mistresses, owners and servants, all of which reinforces it. The Vicarios are justified in killing Nasar, according to them, because the code demands it.

At the same time the narrator realizes how many people are "dominated then by so many linear habits" (113). They don't so much believe these habits as let them stand unassailed. The investigating magistrate in a marginal note on his report scrawls, "*Give me a prejudice and I will move the world*" (117). In another marginal note he writes, "*Fatality makes us invisible*" (133), thus suggesting that fate is the perfect smokescreen, excuse, and justification for people's actions or the lack of them. Fate embodies the cultural past, the religious need for an occasional scapegoat, the code of honor. It can be relied upon to act out its own premeditated drama with no personal need or desire to consider otherwise. If no one is responsible, then no one can prevent the crime. Each can only vaguely fathom "their part of the destiny that life had assigned them" (96). All view themselves as mere witnesses to a *fait accompli*, and the killers, as they cut and slaughter Santiago Nasar at the front door of his house, "didn't hear the shouts of the whole town, frightened by its own crime" (140). Marquez has upended the typical mystery formula to grapple with wider mysteries and his own more social and metaphysical speculations.

Faulkner, Auster, O'Brien, Didion, Fowles, and Marquez, in formally subverting the mystery formula, have revealed the power of that totalistic structure by its very calculated absence and yet at the same time have pursued in their different ways the framework of detective fiction, complete with investigations, interviews, and the detective himself or herself. Martin Marty's description of totalism and tribalism, as mentioned above, suggests the difference between what these authors have done and what Tony Hillerman, James Lee Burke, Amanda Cross, and Walter Mosley have accomplished. For Marty, totalism indicates a "'totalist ideology' [that] refers to any doctrine which attempts a com-plete, unified explanation of world and society" (12), as the mystery for-mula does. Tribalism, on the other hand, in challenging that idea of totalism, demonstrates that "only the peoples and groups to which one naturally belongs, or chooses to belong, or even invents as new con-structs, can provide coherence. Only these can give people an identity and then empower them" (11).

"Perhaps the most potent mode of subversion is that which can speak directly to a 'conventional' reader," suggests Linda Hutcheon (202). Hillerman, Cross, Burke, and Mosley employ the mystery con-ventions to grapple with certain peoples and/or cultural and social dif-ferences that are not usually found in the typical formulaic structure, but they also transform it because of these differences. In each case the ques-tion about such formulaic and popular literature remains: Does it merely support conventional ideologies, or can it resist them and in doing so challenge them? What exactly is the relationship between a marginal perspective, landscape, or group of people and the conventional center? Does the mystery formula stunt or empower its native American, femi-nist, southern, and black subjects? How does this affect Hillerman's Navajos and Mosley's Blacks? Whether or not these issues can be fully resolved, they certainly raise, what Brook Thomas has described as the ultimate "questions of power, domination, exclusion, *and* emancipation in conjunction with the study of [popular] literature" (ix).

Although the following chapters appear in no specific order—older writers appear first—each does grapple with certain literary issues. All four writers confront the difficulties associated with the nature of literary representation and with the presentation and construction of their own particular ideological points of view. Each faces the dilemma of sacrific-ing some of his or her concerns to the demands of the mystery genre, at the same time trying to create a recognizable mystery that remains true to its popular roots.

Hillerman, for example, must encounter both the mimetic and per-formative act of literary representation in terms of the Navajos in his fic-tion. The reader must observe them as Navajos within a distinctly recognizable and different cultural milieu of their own making and tradi-tions and as performing within the mystery formula.

Likewise in his creation of Navajo policeman Jim Chee, Hillerman uses both Navajo and Hopi myths and ceremonies not merely as a smokescreen for the necessary mechanics of the mystery formula but also as a way of creating a new sense of order and harmony that can help to heal the very oppositional and confrontational (good versus evil) aspects of the formula itself. Chee's on-going battle with himself between his policeman's role in a white world and his Navajo conscious-ness transforms the usually straightforward world of the well-crafted mystery into an exploration of different but not necessarily incompatible cultures. In effect the "white" mystery has been purified by Native American traditions. Changing Woman has had her way with, in this case, the male-dominated structure that can only succumb to Her cycli-cal patterns.

In a similar manner Amanda Cross has revitalized the popular mys-tery tradition by investing it with a decidedly feminist heroine and per-spective. In *The Players Come Again* (1990) Cross re-tells the myth of Ariadne in such a way that Ariadne determines her own destiny, as opposed to being the helpless female at the mercy of and who must rely solely upon the whims of Theseus. In the novel the revised version of the ancient myth clearly undercuts the patriarchal roots of literary mod-ernism—the mystery revolves around early novels in the 1920s pro-duced by the famous Emmanuel Foxx (a kind of Joyce-Eliot-Faulkner) and the one secretly written by his wife Gabrielle—refashions the under-pinnings and assumptions of Greek myths as opposed to the more matri-archal Cretan ones, and helps Kate Fansler solve the mystery at hand.

When Cross employs the mystery formula, however, with its clear reflection of rational and linear plotlines, themselves a product of Carte-sian logic and the patriarchal, male-dominated, objective plot, the reader may wonder whether she in any way challenges this trajectory or merely reoccupies it from the different perspective of her feminist heroine within it.

With James Lee Burke, the issue is more of a generic one. His ear-lier non-mystery novels clearly certify him as a Southern writer with their re-enactments of gothic curses, their descriptions of the weight and burden of the historical past, their pervading sense of unrelenting guilt, and their Poesque fascination with hauntings and horrors. The observant reader should consider the possible consequences when such a recogniz-able genre is re-shaped by or incorporated into the more straightforward mystery formula. Perhaps it is one reason why Burke's endings often appear to be more complex and blurred than the typical conclusions of mysteries.

With all these writers there remains the continuing problem of relat-ing a marginal group—the Navajos, academic feminists, Southern Louisiana Cajuns, blacks—to the center and including them in main-stream popular fiction, but with Walter Mosley there is also the linguistic issue. Henry Louis Gates, Jr., has discussed in great detail the role and use of oral expression in black culture, in particular both with the process of signifying and in the essential foundation of much written black literature. Can that particular style survive within the confines of the traditional mystery? Or must it be modified and abandoned in some way?

The interviews with the writers took place after each chapter was practically complete. They serve to comment upon the analyses but are not, for the most part, incorporated into them. In all cases all four writers have introduced new perspectives into and broadened the male-oriented formulaic shape of the mystery formula and have opened up the genre to newer visions of restoration, order, and harmony.

The process is still continuing with newer writers, such as Rudolfo Anaya in *Zia Summer* (1995) and *Rio Grande Fall* (1996). The first mystery is overstuffed with Chicano lore, Aztec rites, and New Mexican history and social hierarchies. All of this conflicts with Anaya's more realistic and brutally raw prose when it comes to describing characters and their crimes. In this the novel suggests Hillerman's first, *The Blessing Way*. Anaya, however, integrates all of these things smoothly and swiftly in his more vigorous and incantatory *Rio Grande Fall*.

A quote at the beginning of *Zia Summer* by Sandra West Prowell, author of *The Killing of Monday Brown*, describes Anaya in "his rightful place beside Walter Mosley, Tony Hillerman, and James Lee Burke as a master of the cultural mystery." This is the first place where I have come across their names so publicly linked. It is a noble lineage this book will examine and explore.

2

CROSSING BOUNDARIES:
MYTH AND MYSTERY IN HILLERMAN COUNTRY

What happens when Tony Hillerman incorporates his view of the Navajos and other Native Americans into the mystery formula? Can we discover differences between the "real" Navajos and Hillerman's Navajos? Since the Navajos' idea of mystery in general is not a product of the Enlightenment, must the formula distort or suppress their perceptions in order for the fiction to function? When the Navajo margin enters and apparently must work within the Anglo-Hispanic center in Hillerman's Southwest mysteries, what is lost, and what is gained? Does the mystery structure empower its characters or merely squeeze them into a popular fictional pattern? To quote Paul Ricoeur again, "Every culture cannot sustain and absorb the shock of modern civilization. There is the paradox: how to become a modern and to return to sources." How does Hillerman resolve or deal with this basic dilemma?

It may be as a self-proclaimed outsider in Sacred Heart, Oklahoma, a tiny outpost of German and French Catholics, that Anthony Hillerman, born in 1925 near the Benedictine mission that ministered to the Citizen Band Potawatomie Tribe in Indian Territory, first identified with the Native Americans around him. They both shared the ceremonies of Catholicism—"The Indians simply added Catholicism to their existing theology and kept the old ways intact" (Hillerman, "Taos" 395)—and the young white boy with his older brother and sister spent his first eight years of school at St. Mary's Academy, run as a boarding school for Indian girls by the Sisters of Mercy. The rural children always felt less sophisticated than the "townies," but young Tony enjoyed the "slow and even lifestyle . . . and what seemed like unlimited countryside to play in" (Hillerman, *Mysteries* 114). "Raised, as I was, at a rural crossroads," he also enjoyed the "social center" that his father's store in Sacred Heart became (Hillerman, "Heart" 21).

After the long illness and death of his father, August A. Hillerman, in 1941, Hillerman enrolled in Oklahoma A&M College and managed to survive a semester while working as a dentist's house-keeper, an irrigation project ditchdigger, and a dishwasher. But his brother joined the army, and after returning to farming, he enlisted as well. In C Company of the 410th Infantry, sent overseas in September 1944, he was severely wounded with temporary blindness, broken legs, foot, ankle and facial burns, received the Purple Heart, and was sent back to the States. It was in July 1945, while he was on a convalescent furlough, hauling oil field equipment to the Navajo Reservation, that he stumbled upon an Enemy Way, the curing ceremony for Navajo Marines who had served overseas as well. "I was fascinated," he recalls, witnessing "a just-returned serviceman like myself—who was being restored to beauty with his people and cured of the disharmony of exposure to foreign cultures. As it happened, it was the same phase of the same ceremony that I would use to make the plot hold together in my first mystery [twenty-five years later]" (Bulow 25).

Once back in his native Oklahoma, Hillerman never left that particular landscape again. As an editor, police reporter, and political writer he worked there, in Texas and New Mexico until 1962, becoming bureau chief in Santa Fe of the *New Mexican* in 1952, and moving up from city editor through managing editor to executive editor of the same newspaper. In 1963 he enrolled as a graduate student at the University of New Mexico and worked as a troubleshooter for the president of the university. From 1966 until 1987 he became a professor and finally the chair of the journalism faculty at the university.

Hillerman is the first to admit that his own native landscape fascinates him. Frank Nakai's advice to Jim Chee in *The Ghostway* (1984) could easily be his own: "Memorize places. Settle your eyes on a place and learn it. . . . Feel it and smell it, walk on it, touch the stones, and it will be with you forever. When you are far away, you can call it back. When you need it, it is there, in your mind" (225). Such a realm suggests the haunted presence of Wordsworth's mountains, Hawthorne's forests, and Frost's New England snowscapes, characters in their own right within the poetic and fictional texts. Hillerman loves the kind of fiction "in which the grotesque, empty landscape was as important as any character. . . . For some reason when I'm writing it's essential for me to have in mind a memory of the landscape, the place. . . . So I tend to go around looking for locations" (Bulow 27, 64).[1] And in that landscape, he came across the Navajo curing ceremony, the Enemy Way: "But from this talus slope, in the dying light, in the dead stillness of th[e] evening, the rationality of the universe was cancelled" (*Ghostway* 53).

The landscape overwhelms whatever descriptions try to encompass its vast expanse. Flat scrubby desert, dusty and endless, is broken only by occasional sandstone formations and distant mountains that rise up out of it like isolated monuments. Reddish mesas loom and glow in the hot relentless sunlight. Space overwhelms and threatens the individual consciousness with its emptiness, its waste and eroded desolation. The individual outcroppings of rock acquire an unsettling sombre presence and immediately draw your eyes to them, as if you are desperate to find an object to measure the space by or give it some sense of shape, appalled as you are by the dusty void that promises only final dissolution and oblivion. Isolated farms—a Navajo hogan, a trailer, cows, horses— lie in this sun-bleached and battered immensity, the nomadic Navajo apparently stranded in the space. Is it any wonder that such a landscape, which Hillerman also views with "undiluted nostalgia" ("Heart" 21), plays such a prominent role in his fiction and invests his plot and characters with a kind of preternatural religious aura that partakes of Navajo rites and beliefs?

"I like to describe the setting," Hillerman admits, "but it should assist the feeling or mood I want to create" (Bulow 88). That mood grows out of his own fascination with the Navajo and their landscape, akin, in fact, to the landscape of his own rural childhood and Catholicism. How could it be otherwise when he is constantly drawn to re-creating "that territory fenced in by the four sacred mountains within which the magic of the curing ceremonial has its *compulsory* effect" (*Thief* 205, italics mine).

Hillerman's story-telling abilities are also a product of his rural upbringing and landscape. In the Southern and Southwestern yarn-spinning tradition of Mark Twain and William Faulkner, he likes to tell stories, slowly, in conversational tones, whetting your appetite and taking his time to build to the climax: "People sat on front porches, or on the benches which lined the front of my dad's general store, and told tales. A lot of value was attached to being good at it. In Sacred Heart, Oklahoma, being a storyteller was a good thing to be" (Bulow 26). As he writes in *Coyote Waits* (1990), "Being raised Navajo, Jim Chee understood how human nature affected storytellers and how they worked an audience" (148). The rural boyhood, the landscape, the story-telling tradition, and the proximity to Native American culture: out of this crucible of circumstance and consciousness emerged Tony Hillerman, the mystery writer.

Hillerman was always interested in other religions and other cultures particularly in the way that they produce different perspectives: "I . . . like to explore issues of faith and people of faith, whether they be Mormon or Navajo or Fundamentalist or Roman Catholic or whatever" (Bulow 70). This lifelong interest may have been best described in terms of the landscape he wanted to conjure up in *People of Darkness* (1980): "*People of Darkness* was going to take place on the eastern side of the [Navajo] reservation: the Checkerboard Reservation, where it's all mixed up with the Native American Church and Episcopalians and fundamentalists and Assembly of God and True Gospel and Mennonites and Roman Catholics religious-wise . . . a total melting-pot situation . . . with these cultures rubbing together" ("Taos" 74). Beneath this cultural conflict for Hillerman always lay the religious dimensions and beliefs.

"It is easier to buy the Navajo view of man as part of nature than the white man's view of himself as master of it" ("Heart" 20), Hillerman has written. Perhaps because of his own separation from his family and Sacred Heart, he was even more attracted to that healing ceremony he witnessed in which the Navajo Marine "was being *restored to beauty with his people* and cured of the *disharmony of exposure to foreign culture*" (Bulow 25, italics mine). And in Hillerman's recognition that "the stark, austere, everlasting beauty of the land . . . helped form the Navajo religion [and] has helped form the Navajo character" ("Heart" 23), we may perceive his own self-recognition as well. *Hozho*, harmony, is all. "The system is designed to recognize what's beyond human power to change, and then to change the human's attitude to be content with the inevitable," Jim Chee explains to Janet Pete in *Sacred Clowns* (1993) (274). No one is punished, but all can be cured. "No penitence or plea is involved. The ritual is compulsive. The evil is eliminated" ("Taos" 383). Hillerman responded to this vision almost instinctually: "What I most value is their central goal—to be in harmony with the circumstances that surround them" ("Taos" 66).

Navajo history, however, does not seem to lend itself to this mythic vision of *hozho*. The *Dinetah*, the Navajo name for themselves as "of the people," originally migrated from northern Canada about five or six hundred years ago and may have migrated to Canada from Asia. Their loose nomadic bands were held together by an elaborate clan system, but it is their nomadic culture that one notices early on, the hunting and gathering and raiding that first distinguish them from the more settled and agricultural Indians of the pueblos, the villages, such as the Hopi. They fought the Spanish in the 1550s, the Mexicans in the 1820s, and the Americans in the 1840s. Under the leadership of Kit Carson, the Americans launched a scorched-earth policy against them in 1848 in an effort to eradicate them completely, and marched them in what has become known as "The Long Walk" to Fort Sumner, New Mexico, as prisoners and refugees. They were returned to their reservation, only to become victims yet again, this time of government policies that initiated the slaughtering of their cattle to reduce the size of their herds in the 1930s, oil companies, strip miners, and continuing territorial disputes with their neighbors, the Hopi. Today about 150,000 Navajo occupy 24,000 square miles or eighteen million acres of Arizona, New Mexico, and Utah.

Many of them live below the official Federal poverty levels. As many as 75% of them remain unemployed on some parts of the reservation, trying to support themselves on Social Security and by sheep-herding, weaving, and silverwork. Many are often reduced to hauling water and firewood to some of their more isolated hogans, having to put up with the bad roads that crisscross the arid semi-desert they occupy. Theirs remains a high land, 3,000 to 10,000 feet above sea level on the Colorado Plateau, and a region of intense heat and cold.

Navajo behavior patterns, according to James S. Chisholm, reveal, among other things, the darker side of *hozho*, patterns derived perhaps from their nomadic and catastrophic history. The Navajo often experience anxiety, depression, melancholy, and fear. They particularly fear strangers, a not uncommon response to their historical experiences, and in new situations often freeze, slipping back into their own self-possessed reserve and natural shyness (Chisholm). The pervasive belief in witches, evil spirits, and ghosts embodies this underlying feeling of dread, according to Chisholm, and the particular belief in skinwalkers encompasses the worst of those fears. It is this, the disharmony that refuses to transform "unbearable social tensions and anomalies into bearable ones" (Brady 56) that attracts both the Navajo and Tony Hillerman.

For Hillerman "the things about the [Navajo] culture that I think are negative . . . is the belief system that focuses so much on fearfulness. The witchcraft idea" ("Taos" 66). "Witchcraft pervades the confounded Reservation and it has a great negative effect on lives and you can't seem to get away from it out there. Some parts are worse than others, and I hear Shiprock is a hotbed of witchcraft" (Bulow 82-83). As Martin Greenberg has suggested, "Belief in the reality of evil, and people who deliberately cause it, seems to thrive in every corner of Navajo country" (*Companion* 411).

The Navajo rely on curing ceremonies or sings (*hataal*) led by singers or shamans (*hataalii*) as much to exorcize witchcraft as restore and uphold the cosmic harmony of the universe. And the worst of the witches are skinwalkers, witches who garb themselves in animal skins and travel at night. These creatures, who can often transform themselves into animals as well, murder relatives, commit incest, and handle corpses, all actions the Navajo regard as ultimate taboos. They participate in cannibalism and the mutilation of corpses during initiation ceremonies in caves, gather possessions for the sake of possession—a rich Navajo, it is said, is comparable to dry water!—display unbridled sexual appetites, shoot magical agents through the air, consort with predatory animals, dig up body parts from graves to wear as jewelry or use in their secret ceremonies, and track down their victims at night: "It is a deliberately learned, deliberately practiced ritual, aimed against a deliberately chosen victim" ("Power" 20). And most of all skinwalkers and witches play upon "the Navajos great dread of having anything to do with the dead" ("Power" 23). Death for the Navajo means ultimate oblivion, a return to the underworld from which the tribe originally emerged in mythic times and to which they must return. In traditional belief the Navajo will not mention the name of the dead, they will cut a hole in the wall of the hogan to let the *chindi*, the ghost, of the recently deceased escape, and then they will abandon the hogan forever. It is no wonder that skinwalkers can conjure up powers equal to the *hataalii* themselves and in many cases are more powerful than the most powerful of Navajo singers.

"The origin story of the Navajos explained witchcraft clearly enough. . . . If there was good, and harmony, and beauty on the east side of reality, then there must be evil, chaos, and ugliness to the west," Jim Chee explains in *Skinwalkers* (1986) (75). In fact the original mythic Navajo people—First Man, First Woman, and especially Coyote—were witches as well as *hataalii*. The Navajo word for skinwalker is *yenaldlooshi*, "he who trots along here and there on all fours with it," the "it" refering both to their strange powers and the animal skins in which they are wrapped ("Power" 19). Skinwalkers can climb to the top of hogans and drop pollen, which has been ground from the bones of infants, down the smokehole which is always in the center. By doing so they can cast evil spells on the people within, creating all kinds of social problems, family fights, ill health and death. Often if a Navajo hears strange noises at night, the barking of a dog, and discovers strange tracks the morning after, he or she realizes that a skinwalker has been present. And Coyote, the animal most in competition with the Navajo from the Navajo point of view, the one most supernaturally empowered and ritually protected, the animal which moves the fastest and lurks in the outside world, constantly searching for food but itself inedible, seems "locked into a continuous struggle for food [with the Navajo]—and analogically for power" ("Power" 29). Motion is power in the Navajo world, "the significant leitmotif in the Navajo universe" (29), and as mythical trickster and skinwalker, Coyote clearly represents "the spirit of disorder, the enemy of boundaries" (31). Hosteen Pinto describes him in *Coyote Waits*:

He talked of Coyote as the metaphor for chaos among a hungry people who would die without order. He talked of Coyote as the enemy of all law, and rules, and harmony. He talked of Coyote's mythic power . . . how Coyote transformed First Man into a skinwalker. (234-35)

Hillerman is obviously aware of Coyote's power and the dark designs of witchcraft as evidenced by some of the titles of his mysteries: *Dance Hall of the Dead* (1973), *People of Darkness* (1980), *The Dark Wind* (1982), *The Ghostway* (1984), and in particular, *Skinwalkers* (1986) and *Coyote Waits* (1990). While *hozho* supplies the positive view of Navajo lore for Hillerman, the dark shadow of witchcraft conjures up the more potent and more dramatic incarnations of Navajo belief.

Skinwalkers, the men who, through complicated and often terrifying initiation ceremonies, transform themselves into witches, can often be rich, elderly, political leaders, and *hataalii:* "Each of these individuals has accumulated power in a system that disdains any sort of individual accumulation" ("Power" 55). Not for nothing, then, does Brady suggest that "to be a success in the white world [Navajo children] need to act very much like witches" ("Power" xiii), an insight not lost on Hillerman, whose villains are often white academics, politicians, engineers, and archaeologists. As we shall see, the exorcism of Navajo witches and the discovery of villains within the ritual exorcism of the mystery formula are completely compatible.

Hillerman began his writing career as a journalist and investigative reporter, a method which for him seems to have led easily into the writing of mysteries: "No job exposes a writer more often to that basic raw material of fiction—people under stress" (Bulow 28). As he explained about his reporter-hero, John Cotton, in his second mystery, *The Fly on the Wall* (1971), "The investigative techniques used by Cotton are simply a description of techniques I had used to dig through records" (Bulow 34). However, his interest in Navajo lore and his desire to try and write a popular mystery revealed to him the limitations of the journalistic method: "Working with facts, as a journalist must, is like working with marble . . . . the longing grew to . . . move into the plastic of fiction" (Bulow 28). "Objective journalism allows you to give people the facts—but it doesn't allow you to give them *the truth as you see it*. Fiction does. You can paint the picture for them *as you see it in your own mind*. The facts don't allow that" ("Taos" 67, italics mine). And yet his use of factual materials and specific landscapes certainly underscores and helps create the credibility and sense of realism that we find in his fiction. As he remarks about *The Great Taos Bank Robbery* (1973), a sort of trial run for his later fictional work, "My master's thesis at the University of New Mexico was a series of experiments in descriptive prose aimed at a popular audience" (Bulow 32). And some of the factual material in these essays, such as "The Hunt for the Lost American," about Folsom Man and the splintered chips of flint he left behind, turn up later in such plots as the one in *Dance Hall of the Dead* (1973).

What Hillerman is best at as a writer and what qualifies as the signature of his particular mysteries are the ways in which he employs Navajo and/or Hopi and Zuni myths in the service of his plots: "The rule I force myself to follow is that any ethnographic material I work in must be germane to the plot. . . . I use the culture of The People as the turning point of my plots" (Bulow 39, 25). In effect "I begin with a thematic idea [such as] revenge—a white value which has no counterpart in the Navajo culture. . . . In *Dance Hall of the Dead* [I concentrated on] child-parent relationships. . . . In *Listening Woman* (1978), I hoped to take the Navajo mythology concerning the Hero Twins, and the dichotomy of human nature [the two Tso brothers in that novel, the good priest and the bad killer] reflected in the myth. . . . Finally, I have in mind some aspect or other of the Navajo culture, and usually several, on which the story will be hung" (Bulow 37, 38).

In several instances white villains use Navajo myths to protect and disguise their own plots and strategies. For instance, in *Sacred Clowns* the two swindlers and murderers use the ceremony of the sacred clowns in a typical Hopi ceremony to mask their own evil designs that result in their need to kill one of the *kachinas* (one of the masked figures or dancers who may represent anthropomorphic spirit beings or spirits of the dead in pueblo ceremonies),[2] who may discover their scheme involving faked Lincoln canes, a symbol of Hopi authority and legitimacy. In *Listening Woman* an old man has stumbled upon a sacred cave which is being used as a hideout by the villains, the perfect cover for their own murderous ends. A false crystal gazer in *Skinwalkers* turns out to be the murderer, using the Navajo lore to further his own corrupt cause. The evildoer manipulates an Indian cult to his own ends in *People of Darkness* and slowly kills off the Navajos who may be witnesses to his original crime. And as a final example in *Dance Hall of the Dead*, the murderer disguises himself as Salamobia, the harbinger of death in Zuni mythology, and in effect specifically uses the Zuni belief to eradicate witnesses. George Bowlegs, "the boy who hunted heaven" (232) and the Navajo trying to learn about Zuni lore, participates in the myth itself as he pursues the spirit of his murdered friend to the lake from where Zunis believe original members of their tribe emerged in mythic times.

At the same time Hillerman reveals the power that these myths have for true believers. These powers of belief remain intact throughout the mystery because of the effects they have on their adherents and because of the unexpected results that often occur no matter how callously the white villains use them for their own ends. For instance, in *Sacred Clowns* Hillerman explores the role of clowns, *kachinas* and *koshares*, the black-and-white striped clowns or *kachinas* (Gill and Sullivan 162), in the pueblo/Hopi culture. As Teddy Sayesva explains to Joe Leaphorn,

To outsiders, they look like clowns and what they do looks like clowning. Like foolishness. But it is more than that. The koshare have another role. I guess you could say they are our ethical police. It's their job to remind us when we drift away from the way that was taught us. They show us how far short we humans are of the perfection of the spirits. (*Clowns* 178)

Thus when a *koshare* is killed, not only is the sacred nature of the pueblo ceremony disrupted and the spirit of disorder or disharmony let loose—a spirit which is also embodied in the nature of the *kachinas* as well: "It is in this coexistence of opposites that real power to energize [or destroy] the social system lies" ("Power" 32)—but a crime is committed which necessarily has to occur in the ritualistic ways of the mystery formula. In effect sacred disruption and secular crime in a Hillerman novel often reflect one another and add that supernatural or religious dimension to his plots which both generate and energize them. Since the Hopis in particular believe that "all humans are clowns," and "all Hopis imitate the original clown ancestors by and through their weaknesses and limitations" (Loftin xxi, 113), the mythic dimension also underscores the horror of the crime and the wider consequences that it inaugurates.

As critics Ellen Strenski and Robley Evans have pointed out,

No book is exactly patterned like a particular ritual, but the detective's search for meaning and the ritual development of the [Native American] cures with their return to harmony nonetheless correspond. . . . Hillerman maintains correspondence between the "evil" of the detective story, its exorcism, and the ceremonial values of the tribal world with its essentially religious vision of the world's natural harmony. (205)

Evil, therefore, in a Hillerman mystery is both a crime to be solved and a desecration or sacrilege to be cured. And, as Strenski and Evans go on to suggest, in a novel such as *Dance Hall of the Dead* the detective formula also parallels the mythic traditions of the hunt, the death, and possible rebirth, as the exorcism and discovery of the villain in the mystery rite parallel the curing ceremony and the return to harmony in the tribal rite. In the Zuni migration mythology of that novel as explained by Hillerman, the original ancestors of the tribe emerged from *Kothluwalawa*, in English translated as " 'Dance Hall of the Dead,' or maybe 'Dance Ground of the Spirits,' " a place which embodies the Zunis' "perfect expression of . . . ecstasy, or joy, or life, or community unity" expressed in their own "ritual dancing" (Hillerman 146), which may be located in one of four mysterious lakes in the region. Since George Bowlegs, the boy and friend of Ernesto Cata who has been murdered, believes that the murder was the result of his breaking a Zuni taboo, Bowlegs' urgent desire to get to the correct lake and in doing so seek forgiveness from Cata's spirit before it re-descends to the "Dance Hall of the Dead" initiates the running plot of the mystery and compels both Joe Leaphorn and the villain to pursue him, Leaphorn to solve the mystery of Cata's death, the villain to murder Bowlegs before he can reveal what he knows. Mystery plot and ancient Zuni rite parallel one another. Both the solution of the mystery at its conclusion and the playing out of the Zuni myth become "a ritual enactment of the ideal of cooperation, harmony, and balance" ("Power" 51), precisely what Native American ceremonies are all about. The power of belief in both the credibility of Hillerman's mystery formula and the Zuni mythology remain intact, each enhancing the other. In this manner the Native American mythology emerges intact and still potent long after the mystery has self-destructed and revealed who has been up to what and for what reasons.

At the same time Hillerman does not reveal the deeper intricacies and complexities of Native American rituals. He confines himself, as most outsiders must, to the shell of the myth, the trajectory of it as viewed from a distance. Of course he must do this in order for the mystery to function. The reader is privy to the outward shape of certain ceremonies without being let into the potent and often paradoxical meanings or ultimate significance of them. The mystery formula by its very nature must repress and marginalize these deeper and more religious attributes in order for the formula to work. If the reader gets too caught up in the religious aspects of what we are reading, this could unbalance the plot of the mystery and undermine it completely, exposing it as the pre-fabricated and formulaic fictional pattern that it is. As Ernie Bulow has suggested, "Certainly one of the things Navajos like about Tony's books is the feeling that their secrets are safe. He doesn't really get into matters of substance for the most part. . . . Readers usually finish one of his books thinking they have been deeply immersed in Navajo culture, though they have not actually accumuluated a lot of factual information" (Bulow 17). All we need do is compare the source material on such cultural myths with Hillerman's use of them to discover the distance between them.

For instance the *kachina* in Southwestern pueblo culture has been described as "any masked figure among the Pueblo peoples," but it also may refer to "anthropomorphic spirit beings who mediate between the human and spiritual worlds, to masked dancers who personify these spirit beings, or to elaborately carved and decorated *dolls* of these beings" (Gill and Sullivan 147). At the same time they "may be understood as spirits of the dead. The Hopi believe that, upon death, those who have lived the proper Hopi life go to the west, where they become *kachinas*, returning to Hopi villages as clouds." In the kachina dance, "when a Hopi man places the mask over his head and wears the appropriate costume, he becomes the kachina he is representing" (Gill and Sullivan 148). The kachina dance may bring rain, which suggests that they "rather than being literally clouds, are the spirits standing in close relation to clouds and to the deities that control rain and give life."[3]

So, then, exactly what are these *kachinas*? Are they representative or symbolic figures of some cosmic force or consciousness? Are they embodiments and incarnations of these actual forces? Are they ancestors come back to life, clouds that are not literally clouds, icons in the shape of dolls, ghosts? And exactly how do the ceremonial cures or ways work with their sand paintings and chants and dances? As Gill and Sullivan make clear, "The stories are intended to *do* something at least as much as they are intended to *say* something" (Gill and Sullivan xii). From an outsider's perspective it is impossible to decipher these rituals and myths. One can only suggest how much of them must remain ultimately mysterious and how much of their paradoxical and secret nature can only be hinted at by Hillerman in order to use them in the service of his fiction.[4] He employs their outward form to shape and enhance his tale of detection and solution and in doing so necessarily can only use or freeze them according to his fictional dictates. However much they embody and help to underscore and in many cases generate his mysteries, they remain themselves the most mysterious parts of his texts. He can *say* what they appear to do to move the story along, but he cannot make them *do* what they in Native American culture ultimately can do.

In *Coyote Waits*, Hosteen Pinto explains the doubleness of Navajo myths: "They teach us that everything has two forms. . . . There is the mountain we see there . . . the *biligaana* [white people] call Mount Taylor. That is the outer form. And then they say there is the inner form, the sacred Turquoise Mountain that was there with the Holy People in the First World. . . . All living things. You too. And I. Two forms" (Hillerman 231-32). Hillerman describes the outer forms well, and it is these that create the supernatural or religious atmosphere in his fiction. We cannot see the Turquoise Mountain, but we can see Mount Taylor and recognize that it casts a long metaphysical shadow in Navajo mythology and culture which can and does affect certain characters' actions and assumptions.

In the mystery formula the binary oppositions remain clearly intact: the detective versus the villain, order versus chaos, social conventions versus crime. The very notion of a recognizable literary formula works to render such a text familiar and recognizable. If this is a mystery we have picked up to read, then of course we assume it must accomplish certain things. At the same time it must appear to be authentic. Hillerman has commented often, as have other writers, how essential it is to flesh out a story with physical details whether they exist in a particular landscape, culture, society, or wherever. Indeed, as Peter Widdowson has explained, "realism's central strategy is to disguise its artificiality" (35). The mystery, which is itself one of the most artificially constructed of literary texts, must strive to maintain its appearance of realism. Therefore it must exclude and regulate its own discourse, and one of the ways it achieves this is through its often rigid series of binary oppositions and polarized confrontations.

Such closed texts, closed in the sense that they "predetermine the reader's response" (Selden and Widdowson 49), build upon these distinctly recognizable binary oppositions. Such polarities include, among others, the white vs. the Native American culture, oppositions within Native American cultures, such as the Navajo and the Hopi, Hillerman's own relationship to his adopted culture, and the reader's confrontation with what originally appears to be an alien culture and landscape. These basic polarities help to strengthen the mystery's necessary confrontation between hero and villain and, as we shall see, are often highlighted in the career of Jim Chee, the Navajo policeman in a white world who is studying to become a singer, a *hataali*, in his own world. To keep these polarities in place becomes one of the mystery writer's prime objectives.

Postcolonial theories in literary criticism may also be of use here. In this approach critics, such as Edward Said, expose the assumptions that western thought makes when it approaches other cultures.[5] Viewing the world through tightly controlled binary oppositions or polarized confrontations is decidedly a western phenomenon and is essentially patriarchal and hierarchical. In such a binary view of things, one half of the pair obviously becomes more powerful than the other. For instance, the good detective is obviously meant to be praised and celebrated as opposed to the evil villain, just as conventional and social order in the mystery should ultimately triumph over chaos. This decided inclination in western thought must, therefore, exclude and regulate other competing philosophies, as the analytical and compassionate detective must conquer the villain. The western approach must necessarily dominate and repress other approaches.

In such a way Hillerman exploits the Navajo and their culture for his fiction. No matter how understanding he is of that other culture, particularly in a mystery it must always play second fiddle to the analytical tale of rational solutions. Besides the mythical identity of all things at the core of Native American cultures, the identity between the self and the earth and the ceremonies they each perform, ultimately threatens the bipolar nature of the detective-vs.-villain format. Therefore, coming at Hillerman's use of Navajo lore from this perspective, we can see how he must always view that lore in its outer forms. Navajo mythology must always remain subordinate to the mystery formula. Hillerman's success as a writer, however, does reveal his ability to allow the supernatural aura of these myths to color and permeate his otherwise analytical and formulaic texts.

But as poststructuralists suggest, binary oppositions usually do not remain so interminably rigid. One definition of deconstruction, the critical process of dismantling these binary oppositions and revealing both their artifice and also their powerful hold on the western mind, suggests that "deconstruction can begin when we locate the moment when a text *transgresses the laws it appears to set up for itself*" (Selden and Widdowson 147). I have already discussed this aspect of all literary texts in the first chapter, but here it is appropriate to refresh our memory about two of them in particular. First of all part of the psychological appeal of mysteries is to allow ourselves the luxury of, at times, siding with the villain's often brilliant schemes and designs:

A dramatic example is a case . . . of a boy compulsively driven to read detective stories to satisfy his aggressive feelings towards his mother by allying himself with the murderer. The stories not only took the imprint of his desires but also allowed him to assuage his guilt by associating himself with the victim and also the detective. In this way the boy was able to gratify his instincts *and* set up dcfences against anxiety and guilt. (Selden and Widdowson 64)

At the same time Hillerman and others have acknowledged the excitement of plotting their tales in much the same way that the villain would, no matter how they come upon the discovery of just who has done what to whom. In many instances the author assumes Coyote's role, as we will see in more detail when we examine *The Dark Wind* (1980) as a fine example of Hillerman's craft. The *Dictionary of Native American Mythology* defines the chief attributes of Coyote as those of the trickster or deceiver, "a complex character type known for his trickery, buffoonery, and crude behavior, but also as a *creator, culture hero,* and teacher" (308), one of the perfect roles, excluding the buffoonery and crude behavior, in which to cast the writer of mysteries. But even then the idea of the trickster "is an academic invention intended to make more comprehensible various Native American figures who share some common traits. Trickster is not a term or category used by any Native American culture. . . . all this talk about trickster is a discourse by Western culture about Western culture" (Gill and Sullivan 310). Even the very term "trickster," then, is a westernized outer form of Native American inner forms and partakes of western structuralist and postcolonial perspectives. No matter how fluid these binary oppositions are, therefore, such as that of detective and villain, or how easily one can dismantle and deconstruct them, their power remains apparent in the western mind and especially so in the artificial construction of the mystery formula. However much we try to circumvent it, which is impossible, our interpretations are always pre-determined by the system of discourse within which we operate.

In Hillerman's process of writing a mystery, we can also recognize the influence of other mystery writers. "I seem to need to sort of memorize the places in which my plots take place" (Greenberg 35), Hillerman admits, at the same time he recognizes the importance of such landscapes in the mysteries of other writers. When he wrote his first mystery, *The Blessing Way*, "I set it on a Navajo reservation primarily because I thought the Navajos were so interesting, and their reservation was so interesting, that it would make a captivating setting for a mystery novel. . . . I really thought I gave a glimpse of the ceremonial that revealed something about the Navajo culture" (Greenberg 68, 69). In this he was acknowledging the legacies of Eric Ambler and Graham Greene—"I would play out my tale against an exotic, interesting background, a la Ambler, Greene, et al." (Bulow 30)—and Raymond Chandler, "a master of setting scenes which engage all the senses and linger in the mind" (Bulow 27). At the same time he wished to "combine memory . . . with imagination [to] create garish red afterglow, slight breeze from south, smells of a desert summer, silence" (Greenberg 401). And in this he again admires Greene: "It's the master craftsman in him which builds the mood that makes the books" (Bulow 27). Martin Greenberg would also add the influence of John Dickson Carr who employed "the continuing theme of the seemingly supernatural disspelled by a natural explanation" (Greenberg 62).

We can trace Hillerman's development in terms of the way he uses Navajo lore and his deepening sense of the Navajo culture in terms of its relationship to others in his first two Navajo mysteries, *The Blessing Way* (1970) and *Dance Hall of the Dead* (1973). Each was nominated for an Edgar Award by the Mystery Writers of America, the former as the best first mystery of the year, and the latter which won the best mystery of the year. In both Hillerman creates the vivid landscapes of his fiction:

The sun was down now. The tops of the evening thunderheads over the mountains were still a dazzling sunlit white, but below the fifteen thousand-foot level they turned abruptly dark blue with shadow of oncoming night. The desert was streaked with pink, red, and purple now, the reflected afterglow from cloud formations to the west. . . . [Leaphorn] stared at the darkening line of the Lukachukai ramparts, searching out the points of blackness, the open mouths of the canyons which drained it. (*Blessing* 217)

In both he develops his tale around a specific Native American ceremony or myth, in the first, the Enemy Way (which was the original title of his first mystery), and in the second, the Zuni myth of the Dance Hall of the Dead and the Shalako ceremony. In both he describes the use of chants and prayersticks, the role of sacred clowns and prayer, and several other specific Native American objects and rituals that are used to insure a long and healthy life, the process of healing, and good fortune. At the same time Hillerman deepens the context of his story with references to relocation Navajos, a theme he will continue to pursue in later novels—"A lot of Navajos feel people who leave the reservation are no longer Navajo. It's very difficult for a Navajo to remain a Navajo when he moves to the city" (Greenberg 78)—to similarities between the Tribal Council and the white man's laws (a complicated issue of jurisdiction, political realignments, and bureaucratic turf that Hillerman will expand in later books), the Navajo sense of language, time, and the terror of death, as well as to broken taboos and the resulting penalties: "If this ceremonial was not properly done, rain did not fall, crops did not sprout, and sickness and bad luck were loosened across the land" (*Dance* 211).

I agree with Ernie Bulow in his assessment of *The Blessing Way* and its use of ethnographic material: "It was something like reading a student paper with a lot of vocabulary freshly mined from a thesaurus" (13). Much of the material remains inert, not so much a part of the plot as it is shoehorned into the book itself. A good example of this can be found in the first five pages of Chapter Five in Hillerman's description of Joseph Begay's waking and his hogan. Within three pages we learn about Mount Taylor, "one of the four sacred mountains which marked the four corners of the Land of the People" (Hillerman, *Blessing* 40), the covering of a smoke hole to prevent ghosts from bothering the living, the position of the hogan door that must face directly east, the place where Changing Woman gave birth to the Hero Twins, the traditionally round shape of the hogan, the necessary pinch of corn pollen to secure it, and Begay's singing of the song from the Blessing Way. At the same time Bulow remarked in 1991, "Of course it didn't matter that in the real world there are no Navajo policeman of the sort Hillerman invoked. In reality they are used primarily as traffic cops and for crowd control at Reservation functions and little else. This is still true today" (Bulow 14).

By the time Hillerman wrote *Dance Hall of the Dead*, we can see how much more readily he has assimilated his materials. In fact the trajectory of the plot parallels and reflects the very Zuni myths and lore that he is commenting upon and describing. The murderer actually disguises himself as Salamobia, who is the personification of anger to be exorcised, and he suddenly appears to Ernesto Cata, who is personifying Shulawitsi, the Little Fire God, in order to kill him: "And he remembered that Salamobia, like all of the ancestor spirits which lived at the Zuni masks, were visible only to members of the Sorcery Fraternity, and to those about to die" (*Dance* 5). The final performance of the Shalako ceremony "is a relay race in which the figures run back and forth betwen 12 holes" (Gill and Sullivan 267), and Hillerman's story, as we suggested above, incorporates various kinds of running which involve the flight of children—both Native American and those young adults in the hippie commune nearby—from what they perceive to be dark and probably murderous pursuers. George Bowlegs' interest in learning about the Zuni culture pervades the novel and parallels Hillerman's and the reader's own.

In *The Blessing Way* Hillerman originally created coequal protagonists, Navajo Tribal Police Lieutenant, Joe Leaphorn, and the white professor and anthropologist, Bergen McKee. But as he revised his manuscript and ignored "his one-time (anonymous) agent's notorious advice to 'get rid of all the Indian stuff' " (Greenberg 11-12), "I expanded the role of Leaphorn. Even when I finished it, I said, I've got to do another book and do the Navajo part right. That was the genesis" (Greenberg 68). McKee's role is far more accessible at first in that he displays a romantic attitude toward the Navajo culture, is interested in witchcraft as lore in its own right—"The People linked owls with ghosts, but not with witches, and gave crows and ravens no supernatural significance at all" (*Blessing* 190)—and is convinced by his own rational analysis "that the Wolf superstition was a simple scapegoat procedure" and that witchcraft gossip produces "a need for a scapegoat witch" (*Blessing* 25, 57). Leaphorn, on the other hand, insists "that there was a basis of truth in the Navajo Origin Myth, that some people did deliberately turn antisocial, away from the golden mean of nature, deliberately choose the unnatural, and therefore, in Navajo belief, the evil way" (*Blessing* 26). Hillerman slowly discovers that Leaphorn "counted . . . upon his own ability to sort out the chaos of observed facts and find in them this natural order . . . [based] on his ingrained Navajo conviction that any emergence from the human norm was unnatural and—therefore—unhealthy" (*Blessing* 212) and, with his natural tracking abilities, will emerge as a full-blown and fully created character in his own right.

Not only does *Dance Hall of the Dead* succeed as a more carefully crafted mystery in the way it includes and reflects its Native American mythology, but in it Hillerman also widens his perspective to include Leaphorn's own personal background and history, his confrontations with the FBI and the values of other white men, and the differences between the Navajo and Zuni cultures. We learn, for example, that Leaphorn's grandfather, Hosteen Nashibitti, was a singer who taught him "a reason for everything. In all things a pattern, and in this pattern, the beauty of harmony" (*Dance* 77). And the spiritual legacy lingers on in Leaphorn's "double vision" that occurs during the Shalako in the Zuni village:

He saw [the great bird] as a mask of tremendous technical ingenuity, a device of leather, embroidered cotton, carved wood, feathers, and paint held aloft on a pole, its beak and its movements manipulated by the dancer within it. But he also saw Shalako, the courier between the gods and men, who brought fertility to the seeds and rain to the desert when the people of Zuni called, and who came on this great day to be fed and blessed by his people. (*Dance* 224)

Nashibitti's tales also fill him with the tragic history of his people:

. . . of the redder side of tragedy: of two brothers with bows against a troop of mounted riflemen; of sabered sheep, burning hogans, the sound of axes cutting down the peach orchards, the bodies of children in the snow, the red of the flames sweeping through the cornfields, and, finally, the litany of starving families hunted through the canyons by Kit Carson's cavalry. (*Dance* 76)

Leaphorn is suspicious of the Zuni: "Once, or so Navajos believed, initiates into the Zuni Bow priesthood had been required to bring a Navajo scalp" (8). He feels that the Zuni think they are superior to the Navajo, that he is a much better tracker than any Zuni could possibly be, and that they lacked "the respect for privacy of a scattered rural people" (81), because they themselves lived in villages. Susanne, the woman who flees from the hippie commune, wonders why the Navajo harbor such a deeply rooted sense of loneliness in their nomadic existence as opposed to the Zuni desire to live in pueblos. Ghosts for the Navajo are to be shunned at any cost, aware as they are "of the evil ghosts of a thousand generations of Dinee who rode the night" (83). The Zuni on the other hand believe in a kind of heaven, the Dance Hall of the Dead, a concept the Navajo cannot fathom. George Bowlegs, the Navajo boy, trying to understand Zuni lore, reflects Leaphorn's own preoccupations with it and by analogy Hillerman's and the reader's.

At the same time Leaphorn is confused by white values and consciously wrestles with them. The graduate student at the Folsum dig, Ted Isaacs, is determinedly more interested in his work and career than in the woman whom he loves. "I'm trying to learn more about white men," Leaphorn admits. "You wanted all that worse than you wanted your woman. What else will you give up for it?" (241-42). He also goes on to wonder what really motivates the white men in the FBI: "He had a sudden vision of an office in the Department of Justice building in Washington, a clerk sending out draft notices to all the [white] male cheerleaders and drum majors at U. S. C., Brigham Young, Arizona State, and Notre Dame, ordering them to get their hair cut and report for duty . . . trimmed, scrubbed, tidy, able to work untroubled by any special measure of intelligence" (98). All of these perceptions broaden Hillerman's own toward Native Americans and their attitudes toward each other and white men and lead to Jane S. Bakerman's astute conclusion that "a major difference between hero and villain in Hillerman's work is an awareness of one's prejudice and a willingness to combat it in oneself" (17-25).

Throughout Hillerman's first three mysteries, excluding *The Fly on the Wall* and including *Listening Woman* (1978), he deepens Joe Leaphorn's Navajo background, a development he had begun in *Dance Hall of the Dead*: "It was the Navajo philosophy, this concept of interwoven harmony, and it was bred into Joe Leaphorn's bones" (*Listening*). At the same time Leaphorn's sense of evil, *hozho*'s Manichean opposite, clearly reveals his Navajo culture: "The Navajo Wolves were men and women who turned from harmony to chaos and gained the power to change themselves into coyotes, dogs, wolves or even bears, and to fly through the air, and to spread sickness among the Dinee. As a boy he had believed, fervently and fearfully, in this concept of evil" (*Woman* 103). "Religious values had always fascinated Leaphorn, and he'd studied them at Arizona State" (*Woman* 164), in much the same way as Hillerman had studied at the University of New Mexico. No matter how much he has become disconnected as a believer from his Navajo traditions, he still finds himself, "as he had since childhood, caught up in the hypnotic repetition of pattern which blended meaning, rhythm, and sound in something more than the total of all of them" (*Woman* 145) when he hears his native ceremonies.

When he came to writing about the Checkerboard Reservation—the more eastern expanse of the Navajo Reservation in New Mexico—with its incredible mixture of religious sects and cultures in *People of Darkness*, Hillerman found that the older Leaphorn was just not interested in or amazed by "these cultures rubbing together. . . . So I thought I'll start me a new guy. This time I'll give him a real Navajo name instead of that damned thing I called Joe. I'll try to give him a more traditional background. . . . So I came up with Jim Chee" (Greenberg 74, 75). Thus began the development and contrasting identites of the older, more cynical Leaphorn and the younger, more idealistic Chee, both with their anthropology degrees but with Chee's fervent interest in his own culture. Chee is anxiously torn between accepting a position with the FBI and studying to become a Navajo singer, a *yataali,* like Hosteen Frank Sam Nakai, his uncle: "It was Hosteen Nakai who had chosen Jimmy Chee's 'war name,' which was Long Thinker. . . . When he came to understand this white man's world which surrounded the People, [Chee] must make a decision" (*People* 84-85). Chee will continue to wrestle with this dilemma throughout the series, complicated by his later involvement with a white school teacher and a white lawyer and his own misgivings: "One defined himself by his family. How else? And then it occured to him that white people didn't. They identified themselves by what they had done as individuals" (*People* 105). Of course this also allows Hillerman both to explore in greater detail the culture that fascinates him and to deepen the character and plot development of his two primary policemen.

Hillerman amplifies the contrast between Leaphorn and Chee. When it comes to witchcraft as it does in *Skinwalkers*, Leaphorn sees only "a sick tradition—this cruel business of killing a scapegoat when things went wrong. . . . It had converted Leaphorn's contempt for witchcraft into hatred" (*Skinwalkers* 152). He easily reiterates Bergen McKee's notions about witchcraft in *The Blessing Way*. On the other hand Chee, studying to be a singer and still torn between cultures, "believed in witchcraft in an abstract way. Perhaps they did have the power. . . . But he knew witchcraft in its basic form stalked the Dinee. He saw it in people who had turned deliberately and with malice from the beauty of the Navajo Way and embraced the evil that was its opposite" (*Skinwalkers* 252-53). In the novel Chee must test his own powers against the real witch, Dr. Yellowhorse, who is trying to turn the Navajos against Chee, telling them that it is Chee who is the witch causing trouble. And in Chee's struggle over what to do with a stray cat that has crossed his path, as well as with Mary Landon, the white teacher (whom he finally decides to marry, but she moves back to Wisconsin and slowly realizes the impossibility of their union), we see his dilemma more fully: "If the cat was to make the transition—from someone's property to self-sufficient predator—it couldn't rely on him, or on any person. To do so was to fail. . . . He wanted the cat to tear itself free. He wanted *belagana* (white) cat to become natural cat. He wanted the cat to endure" (*Skinwalkers* 223).

In *A Thief of Time* (1988) Leaphorn's wife Emma has died, leaving him a sadder and lonelier soul wondering whether or not to continue with his police work. In what Hillerman considers to be his favorite novel in the series, Leaphorn looks at Chee more objectively, drawing the contrasts more greatly between them: "An odd young man, Chee. Smart, apparently. Alert. But slightly . . . slightly what? Bent? Not exactly. It wasn't just the business of trying to be a medicine man—a following utterly incongruous with police work. He was a romantic, Leaphorn decided. That was it. A man who followed dreams" (*Thief* 226-27). Leaphorn, the aging lonely widower as pragmatist, confronts Chee, the younger bachelor, the idealist. And yet because of his loneliness he asks Chee at the end of the novel to perform the Blessing Way for him, an event that is described in more detail in *Talking God* (1989): "Everything had gone beautifully. Not many of Leaphorn's relatives had been there. But then the old man was a widower. . . . But the curing itself had gone perfectly. . . . Old Man Leaphorn had, in some way difficult for Chee to define, seemed to be healed of the sickness that had been riding him. The bleakness had gone. He had seemed back in harmony, content" (*Talking*). And once again Hillerman has revealed the lasting powers of Navajo ceremonies and the culture from which they come.

Strenski and Evans have made the point that "Leaphorn is a culture hero whose concern for pattern as defined typologically by the People gives him a spiritual strength and insight not available to the alienated criminals and misfits who die without finding the appropriate kachinas" (255), an explanation that could pass for Chee as well. Also "especially happy is the coincidence in Indian culture and the mystery genre of the hero's powers of close observation" (253): "It is Leaphorn who serves both as the raisonneur, and as the mediator of human values, making the connections between the analytic or Western mind and *the idealized tribal mind* with its symbolic formulations, a kind of Hermes figure crossing boundaries that are metaphysical as well as physical" (254, italics mine). However, that "idealized tribal mind" must be reduced to simpler concepts of harmony and cause and effect in order for it to function within the confines of the mystery formula. What we are actually reading about is a westernized tribal mind, a point of view that has been necessarily truncated and shaped by the analytical demands of Hillerman's fiction. It works well but perhaps only because it is so ultimately sketchy and carefully assimilated.

This raises another question about Hillerman's work. In his focus upon the spiritual values of Native Americans, as opposed to the more consumerist and materialistic non-values of his often villainous whites, how much is there a tendency to romanticize and idealize the Navajo point of view? This is a problem which bothers Hillerman as well and has been cited most recently in Verlyn Klinkenborg's *New York Times* review of *Sacred Clowns*: "[Hillerman] chooses to portray the spirituality of the Navajos and Hopis and merely hints at the often brutal conditions of life on the reservation. Politeness is the prevailing mood of a Hillerman mystery" (Klinkenborg). One way to check this is to look more closely at the typical actions and incidents in Hillerman's plots to see how they measure up to the contemporary scene.

Betty Johnson, who is in charge of an Elderly Day Care Facility on the Isleta Pueblo, about fifteen miles south of Albuquerque, in an interview in 1996 talked about the problems confronting the tribe. Drugs, alcohol, obesity, unemployment, and diabetes contribute to the day-to-day difficulties of life in the pueblo. Public transportation between Isleta and Albuquerque does not exist. All Isleta high school students must leave the reservation for school, but many after that remain stuck in the pueblo by circumstances beyond their control. Only recently with the income from the new casino has the reservation been able to give out tribal scholarships to all students who wish to go on to college. Title Three in federal regulations covers all policies and procedures concerning the elderly, but it did not cover any Indians at all. In 1980 after much work and pressure, Title Six was created to take care of that glaring omission, but of the $25 million promised to cover the needs of *all* Indians in the United States, only $6 million was forthcoming. Every three years Johnson and others had to fight to increase the funding, which by 1996 had reached $16.8 million, still nowhere near the promised $25 million. Johnson helped to pass a bill in the New Mexico legislature to use the Isleta Pueblo as a model program for the elderly, but it took monthly meetings of a coalition between the nineteen pueblos in New Mexico and the two Apache tribes to get the effort moving. She managed to get $70,000 in operating funds for the program, a level of funding which each of the other eleven non-Indian elderly day care centers receive in New Mexico.

What made Johnson's work most difficult was the bureaucratic hierarchy and labyrinth of the law. The pueblo is sovereign territory when it comes to city, county, and state government. However the federal government exercises complete control over it. In order to function, tribal officials and local, county, state, and federal officials have to coordinate their policies and procedures, a nightmarish realm that sounds almost (but practically is not) impossible. Hillerman captures this clash of jurisdictions well with its racist overtones, bureaucratic infighting, hierarchical hegemonies, inter-tribal rivalries, and federal power plays. In effect the local tribal community elects its own council and representatives, in the case of the Navajos, to the Navajo Tribal Council at its capitol in Window Rock, Arizona. These councils were originally formed in the 1920s to negotiate with oil companies for lease rights to reservation land, were an outgrowth of the reservation system which was devised in 1868, and were finally officially recognized in the Indian Reorganization Act of 1934. Of course such a democratic structure often clashes with the traditional tribal imperative of the village chief as in the case of the Hopi.

Hillerman not only explores and exposes these jurisdictional and bureaucratic confrontations, but he also makes clear that the council system is one that has been superimposed by the federal government on the basic tribal patterns of families and clans. James S. Chisholm has described the intricate clan system of the Navajos, which involves matrilineal kinship, the camp which is a step above the nuclear family, and the outfit or residential lineage which occurs next on the hierarchical ladder of the tribe. Following the outfits comes the local clan, which may occupy one area of the reservation; the clan proper, about eighty of which are named, matrilineal, and exogamous; and the phratries that link various clans to one another and regulate such things as marriage. Hillerman has done his homework in this area, linking Leaphorn, Chee and others to their particular clans, all of which are fully listed in Greenberg's *Companion* (113-21). When a man marries, he becomes a member of his wife's family. The husband and the mother-in-law operate within strict prohibitions. In *The Dark Wind*, for instance, since "a sexual relationship between members of the same maternal clan is considered incestuous" (Greenberg 111), Chee, knowing this implicitly, discovers a lie in the story of a vanished character whom he's been trying to track down.

Hillerman pays close attention to life on the reservation. For instance, alcohol and drugs appear again and again in his novels and at times directly affect the plot. The reader sees the poorer areas of the reservation, the long barren but beautiful distances between families and their hogans, and becomes aware of all the driving both Chee and Leaphorn have to do in order to get from place to place. Relocated

Native Americans, who live off the reservation, suffer a rootless and alienated existence, disconnected as they are from the sacred land that embodies their beliefs. Grave robbers and crooked archaeologists bide their time. The business of Native American artifacts remains a brisk and often illegal one.

Hillerman is very much aware of the continuing land disputes which involve both the Navajo and the Hopi. Not only does this enter into his plots, but he also reminds the reader of the scope of the dispute and its ongoing nature. In *Talking God*, for instance, certain Navajo familes face "eviction from their lands in what had become the Hopi part of the old Joint Use Reservation" (*God* 40). In *The Dark Wind*, nine thousand Navajos must be replaced by Hopi: "The U.S. Supreme Court had ruled, and the Hopis had won" (*Wind* 144), and such victories and defeats point up the tribal differences between both peoples in terms of their religious and cultural beliefs, which Hillerman also pursues in some detail. Loftin explores this ongoing problem. The federal government had given some of the Hopi lands to the Navajo, a decision that infuriated the Hopi, since there are only 11,000 of them in existence as opposed to the c. 180,000 Navajos. In 1977 the equally divided joint-use area resulted in the expulsion of Navajo families. And in 1988 Navajo police prevented the Hopi from securing eagle feathers to use in their ceremonies, an episode that Hillerman uses in his latest mystery, *The First Eagle* (1998). While the group referred to as the traditionalists want no interference from white entrepreneurship, "the progressives see economic development, money" (*God* 108). Hillerman is right at home in this disputed territory.

Hillerman's concentration on religious and cultural values and their effect upon believers and non-believers alike diminishes his desire to paint the reservation as only a place of despair, alcoholism, drug addiction, and joblessness. These are present, but they have been marginalized by the lore, the landscape, and the supernatural aura of other lands. At one point he seems to indicate that the possibilities of coordinating Navajo and Christan beliefs may exist. In *A Thief of Time*, for instance, the Navajo/Christian evangelist, Slick Nakai, makes a decent case for Christianity's belief in resurrection and heaven as an antidote to the Navajo belief in utter oblivion after death: "Jesus didn't let Death live. . . . We don't just drift away into the dark night, a ghost of sickness. We go beyond death" (*Thief* 78). Hillerman, a faithful Catholic, may be making his pitch here in terms of some ultimately hopeful powers of assimilation and integration. It is this consistent focus that somewhat marginalizes but does not avoid what Klinkenborg has called "the often brutal conditions of life on the reservation."

The structure of several of Hillerman's plots often parallel Leaphorn's search for some missing characters in *Listening Woman*, as he investigates a series of endless canyons, one after the other, coming upon "an endless labyrinth—deeper and deeper into the sheer-walled maze" (*Woman* 206). Other characteristics of these plots include the eruption of the crime in the first chapter to get the tale off to a fast start, Hillerman's often elaborate use of disguises, the appearance of hired guns and rootless creatures distinctly different from the culture and shared values that flourish on the Navajo reservation, and Hillerman's questioning of the ethics of several contemporary disciplines, careers, and academic research. Villains often disguise themselves as mythic and ceremonial figures in order to further their plans, for instance, Chester Reynolds, the archaeologist, as Salamobia in *Dance Hall of the Dead*. Or they pretend to be someone else: James Tso as "Goldrims" and Hoski in *Listening Woman*; Carl Lebeck, the geologist, returned as the bearded B. J. Vines in *People of Darkness*. And there can be various cases of mistaken identity such as Leroy and Albert Gorman in the witness protection program in *The Ghostway* or the strange case of Joseph "Iron-fingers" Musket in *The Dark Wind*. In later books when Hillerman focuses on Jim Chee as his hero, the tensions between Chee and Leaphorn are more pronounced.

At the same time Hillerman seems very critical of modern analytical and research techniques in the manner in which they affect various characters. So many of his villains are academics or researchers, geologists, engineers, archaeologists, environmentalists, and collectors for museums. It is as if his love for the Navajo culture carries over into his attacking the very analytical values that make his mysteries possible. It is the eruption of diseased white values—urban, often mafia-driven, gangster-powered—on the Navajo Reservation that generate the most trouble. Leaphorn is especially critical of Navajos who have left the sacred land for the white world: "Just another poor soul who didn't quite know how to be a Navajo and couldn't learn to act like a white. No good for anything" (*Blessing* 70). Relocation often maims the soul.

Hillerman's consistent exploration of rootless and alienated hitmen (as well as hippies, unassimilated Native Americans, even the uneasy relationship betwen Chee and Mary Landon as opposed to Leaphorn and his thoroughly Navajo wife Emma), such as Colton Wolf in *People of Darkness*, Eric Vaggan in *The Ghostway*, and Leroy Fleck in *Talking God*, in contrast to the Navajo world, reveals his greatest criticism of our contemporary consumerist and materialistic society. Colton Wolf searches for his mother, trying to locate what fragile family roots he can, but he selects his own name: "Something simple. He picked Wolf"

(*People* 66). As we know, the wolf is the highly charged symbol of witchcraft in Navajo lore. And the name suggests his own alienation from society with his "sense of loss and confusion and rejection, and with it the bleak, hopeless loneliness" (68). Violence provides him with the only identity he knows. As it does with Leroy Fleck, the hired gun who spends his time wondering where to put his aging and obstreporous mother, since she keeps getting thrown out of nursing homes because of her ferocious and brutal behavior towards others. They both share "rage. This was what Mama had told them about. . . . About the ruling class. The way they put you down if you let them. Treated you like niggers. Like dogs. And the only way you kept your head up, the only way to keep from being a bum and a wino, was by getting even" (*God* 63). These embittered and violent outsiders, empowered by their own racist grudges, Hillerman pits against the likes of Leaphorn, Chee, and their native culture.

In the manipulation of its several strands of plot, the antagonisms between whites and Native Americans and the organization of their law enforcement agencies, and the particular qualities of its villain, *The Dark Wind* is a fine example of Hillerman's art. The very complex plot begins with a Hopi discovering a body that he will not report since that will disturb the Niman Kachina, the ceremony in which he is involved at the moment. A plane crash, which Jim Chee witnesses while investigating vandalism at Windmill Number Six on Joint Reservation land, swiftly follows. These two separate incidents are further complicated by the disappearance of Joseph Musket, who has supposedly robbed Jake West's trading post, the involvement of the FBI, DEA, and Agent Johnson because of the drugs associated with the plane crash, rumors of witchcraft at Black Mesa, the arrival of the sister of the dead pilot, the discovery of the corpse in the first chapter and the fact that his feet and hands have been skinned, and the later discovery by Chee of a dark green GMC Carryall that contains the body of Richard Palanzer, a possible drug smuggler.

Chee's continuing search for Musket takes him to the New Mexico State Penitentiary, where Musket had served time for burglaries and a drug bust, and he learns that Musket's partner in crime, Thomas Rodney West, the son of Jake West, the owner of the trading post, had been stabbed to death in the prison yard. Before he was killed, West was visited by T. L. Johnson, the DEA agent, and Jerald Jansen, the dead man found on the ground near the downed plane. Chee interviews Taylor Sawkatewa, a caretaker of Hopi shrines, and learns that the vandalized windmill had been placed near one of the shrines, thus interefering with Hopi sacred ceremonies.

The upshot revolves around Chee's knowledge of Jake West as a master of illusion because of a card trick West has performed for him. The unknown body discovered in Chapter One is really Musket whom West has murdered, and the feet and hands had been skinned to leave no fingerprints. Johnson turns out to be the other villain who is after the aluminum suitcases of drugs that had been on the plane which had been lured by false ground lights to its destruction. In the final accounting Johnson shoots West, and West knocks him off a cliff into the raging flood waters below. West had misdirected the plane and shot Jansen and Palanzer, eager to bring the drug smugglers out into the open to avenge his son's murder, which Johnson had set up at the prison, and after West's death Chee hurls the drug-filled suitcases into the flood waters to follow Johnson to oblivion.

Throughout the mystery Hillerman creates Jim Chee as a solitary and meticulous hero, with his sense of time to be used carefully and unhurriedly and his sense of the natural cycle of the seasons and life on the reservation. He appreciates the very harmonies and beauty that the white men's plans thoroughly disrupt. He is an excellent tracker and purifies himself during the Stalking Way, in order to capture West, "to put hunter and prey in harmony. . . . One changed the formula only slightly to fit the animal. The animal, now, was man. An Anglo-American, ex-husband of a Hopi woman, trader with the Navajos, magician" (*Wind* 251). Only in this way can he participate within "the Great Navajo myth of how hunting began and how man himself became a predator" (*Wind* 252). For the Navajo "someone who violated basic rules of behavior and harmed you was . . . 'out of control.' The 'dark wind' had entered him and destroyed his judgment" (*Wind* 147-48). In order to deal with this, Chee himself must undergo the healing process of the Stalking Way to align himself with the natural order and harmony in all things. And Chee's own appreciation of the natural landscape as the great part of that natural harmony contrasts visibly with the way that Johnson meets his death, hurled into the flood waters, as if nature itself has killed him and restored the natural order of things.

In *The Dark Wind* Hillerman uses Hopi and Navajo ceremonies and lore in various ways. They function within the plot itself, rather than as additions to it. First and foremost the values embedded in these cultures generate specific actions, such as Chee's manner of investigation and the protection of Hopi shrines that leads to vandalism and the choice not to report the dead body in chapter one. The importance of kinship and the elaborate relationships between tribal clans provide Chee with a much needed clue: the elusive Joseph Musket would never have presented a necklace, supposedly stolen from Jake West's store (West, of course, made up the robbery tale to keep Chee looking in the wrong direction), to Edna Mezzie, because they are both members of the same maternal Navajo clan, and to do so would be incestuous and, therefore, taboo. Fannie Musket's tale of her son and his seeking an Enemy Way, a purification ceremony, clashes with West's descriptions of him and momentarily confuses Chee's investigations. The references to witchcraft, which provide the novel with its supernatural aura and atmosphere, also turn out to be clearly related to the skinned feet and hands of the corpse.

The white villains use the cover of the Astotokaya ceremony in the village of Sityatki, which must be entirely sealed off during the period of these initiation rites, to carry out the transfer of drugs and money. One of the priests turns out to be an impostor, disguising himself so that he can make contact with the man in the Lincoln whom he stabs. In this case Native American rituals provide a smokescreen for evil designs, a process Hillerman employs often in several of his other mysteries.

Finally the mysterious landscape itself reflects the Hopi and Navajo lore, thus underscoring the importance of these ceremonies and myths that have been so easily subverted and undermined by the drug thugs. What appears symbolic to the Hopi represents beauty to the Navajo, but both celebrate the inherent and transcendent worth of the sacred land they inhabit. Hillerman animates these landscapes so that they seem like participants in the tale itself, actual sacred spaces that demand obeissance and revenge against all non-believers: "Black Mesa . . . is virtually roadless, almost waterless, and uninhabited. . . . It rises out of the Painted Desert more than seven thousand feet. . . . It is a lonely place even in grazing season and has always been territory favored by the Holy People of the Navajo and the kachinas and guarding spirits of the Hopis. . . . It is dotted with shrines and holy places" (*Wind* 133-34). The weather, too, contributes to this often eerie and spiritually charged domain: "The cloud spawned by the San Francisco Peaks . . . was huge, its top pushed up into the stratospheric cold by its internal winds. . . . The great cloud now dominated the sky, and illuminated the old place with a red twilight" (*Wind* 179, 187).[6] Landscape and people are one: "In the Hopi villages the people were calling the clouds. . . . To the Hopis, rain . . . would mean the endorsement of the supernatural. The Hopis had called for the clouds, and the clouds had come" (*Wind* 122, 179). Against such powerful forces, what chance do West and Johnson really have?

Jake West is an acknowledged sorcerer. He is expert in "misdirecting attention" (*Wind* 256), first with his card tricks, later on with the discovery of his keeping Musket alive in his tales for Chee to hide his real deeds. West had married a Hopi woman from the Fog Clan with its legendary connections to sorcery: "And of course, the sorcerers were the *powaqas*, the 'two-hearts,' the Hopi culture's peculiar version of what witches were like" (*Wind* 182). West has two hearts, his public facade and his private cunning. He like other Hopi sorcerers before him "could keep their animal hearts as well as their human hearts and change back and forth by passing through the magic hoop" (*Wind* 197). Chee has spotted a gallery of *kachina* figures in West's living quarters and among them has "recognized Masaw, the guardian spirit of this Fourth World of the Hopis, and the god of fire and death, and the lord of Hell" (*Wind* 50). It, in effect, symbolizes West himself, and this bloody-faced Lord of Hell must be exorcized within the healing rites of Hillerman's mystery in order to return all to ultimate harmony and resolution. Of course Hillerman is very much his own sorcerer "misdirecting attention," carefully revealing and re-veiling the contrived deceptions of his intricate plot. West's undoing is Hillerman's own, the unmasking of Masaw, one of the presiding *kachinas* of the mystery formula.

The Hopi and westerners, John Loftin suggests, "met and became transformed. Both are in a new world that is neither Hopi nor Western, but rather one where each is part of the other's world" (122). Such is Hillerman's world in his mysteries as well. These are permeated with and saturated by the spiritual values he has discovered in the Navajo and Hopi cultures. These values drive his plots and furnish him with both form and content in order to create them. "I use the culture of The People as the turning points of my plots" (*Mysteries* 25), Hillerman admits, but he uses it even more in the perspective and vision embodied in those plots. There are difficulties in crossing boundaries, but in his own way he is trying to unite and resolve the differences he describes and addresses. The mystery formula by its very nature may limit his abilities to achieve this, but within it he is a master of harmony and faith. Witches may exist and threaten the landscape, but they are always ultimately defeated. Family and harmony triumph over the crasser expressions of western society, such as the evils of "accumulation for the sake of accumulation" ("Power" 33). Hillerman's mysteries are themselves blessing ways in an age in desperate need of such a vision, and we as readers are left like Leaphorn at the conclusion of *A Thief of Time*: "I would like to ask you to sing one for me" (324). Ya eeh teh: "Be cool."

One of the major attractions of Hillerman's mysteries, therefore, is their revelations about Navajo life and perspectives. True, we really only get a glimpse of them from the outside looking in, but the pressures and antagonisms that plague both Jim Chee and Joe Leaphorn emphasize the dilemmas of characters stranded between two worlds and trying to operate in each. The Navajo consciousness has been simplified to fit the mystery formula—as have many of the villains, who are white—but

Hillerman's novels do introduce the reader to an entirely different way of life and its problematic position in contemporary times. In his mysteries Chee and Leaphorn are empowered to act, and their roles illuminate their own backgrounds and difficulties, as well as the particular landscape they inhabit. They do have to sustain and absorb the shock of modern civilization, at the same time that they recognize the need to cling to and deal with their own tribal origins and objectives. This is Hillerman's greatest contribution to the mystery genre (along with his wonderfully complicated plots and clever confrontations) and introduces the American public to a world we might never have known otherwise.

Epilogue: The Fallen Man *and* The First Eagle

Even though Marilyn Stasio described *The Fallen Man* (1996) as "another gripping chapter in the evocative series . . . on the vast Indian reservation that sprawls across Arizona and New Mexico" (1)—the involved and complicated plot overpowers the characters and the atmosphere. Still the relationship between the retired Joe Leaphorn and Acting Lieutenant Jim Chee and the descriptions of Ship Rock reveal the best of Hillerman's art. Chee recognizes Leaphorn's meticulous and intelligent search for patterns in what appears to be a series of coincidences, and the younger man knows that "it would be a while before he could relax in Leaphorn's presence. Maybe another twenty years would do it" (*Man* 29).

Ship Rock, that magnificent and towering pinnacle, becomes a character in the novel and overshadows all else: "At the center . . . was the great volcanic monolith that was now looming ahead of them like the ruins of a Gothic cathedral built for giants" (*Man* 227). The fact that a white man may have been left there to die has to be the result of a white man's plot, since for a Navajo, "If this is a crime it's a white man's crime. No Navajo would kill anyone on that sacred mountain . . . climbing Ship Rock to prove that man was the dominating master of the universe was also a desecration" (*Man* 99, 49).

Hillerman recognizes as Chee does that the Navajo who migrated "out of Mongolia and over the icy Bering Strait . . . brought with them a much older Asian philosophy. Thoughts, and words that spring from them, bend the individual's reality. To speak of death is to invite it. To think of sorrow is to produce it" as opposed to the western concept "that language and imagination are products of reality" (*Man* 76). This is a philosophy that Hillerman himself manages to promote despite or because of the intricacy of his mysteries, and it underscores the complex and often repetitive investigations of the past and present, of forgery, deception, and stolen cattle in *The Fallen Man*.

Hillerman's latest book, *The First Eagle* (1998), eloquently and elegantly tackles the clash between white man's science and the Hopis' and Navajos' religion and reveals a sleek, less knotted plot than the previous mystery. Again Marilyn Stasio celebrates "Hillerman's strong narrative voice and supple story-telling techniques," but she also recognizes his constant awareness "that ancient cultures and modern sciences are simply different mythologies for the same reality" (12). Here the possibility of bubonic plague and the reports of witchcraft on the sprawling reservation overlap one another and create a many-layered mystery that involves a missing scientist, an East German graduate student who may have been stalking her, a famous and obsessive immunologist, prairie dogs, fleas and mice. At the same time it seems that a Hopi has murdered a Navajo policeman at the site where a year ago the Hopi had tried to capture an eagle for his tribe's religious ceremonies. The issue is complicated by the fact that since the recent court decision about the redistribution of Hopi and Navajo lands, the place where the alleged poaching takes place, once Hopi land, is now within Navajo territory. Plague and poaching, medical mystery and murder, epidemic and religious rite eventually involve one another.

Hillerman keeps his keen eye on the various rivalries and prejudices that fester on the reservation. Besides the usual friction between Native American and white man, he explores the antagonisms between the local tribal and the federal police, between the FBI's publicity-seeking self-esteem and Chee's and Leaphorn's persistent and self-effacing investigations, and between the FBI's condescending rudeness toward the Navajo authorities and the Navajos' endless patience. Jim Chee, now the acting lieutenant at Tuba City, once again becomes involved with his former lover, Janet Pete, the lawyer, who decides to defend the primary Hopi suspect, and Chee again recognizes the differences between his own "sheep-camp Navajo" background and "the layers upon layers of social phoniness" he sees in Pete's Washington, D.C.

Joe Leaphorn has been retired for one year, but the missing scientist's niece hires him to find her. As usual Chee feels inferior when in Leaphorn's presence, even though he is beginning to feel somewhat more comfortable with the older former policeman: "He admired Leaphorn, he respected him, he even sort of liked him. But for some reason, an impending meeting with the man had always made him feel uneasy and incompetent" *(Eagle* 149).

Navajo lore that involves witchcraft and the chindi permeates the new book and lends it that quasi-gothic, forever eerie and metaphysical quality that Hillerman creates so well. As expected Leaphorn "found the Navajo taboo against talking about the dead adding to the usual taciturnity of rural folks dealing with a citified stranger" (*Eagle* 95). And "for a Navajo as traditional as Chee, digging for a corpse in a death hogan wasn't a task done lightly. It would require at least a sweat bath and, more properly, a curing ceremony, to restore the violator of such taboos to *hozho*" (*Eagle* 261). Plot and mythology perfectly reflect one another.

Because of a taped conversation between Chee and FBI Agent Reynald, the relationship between Chee and Janet Pete crumbles. The cultural distances between them have always remained insoluble, but this time it looks as though the end has come. As Chee thinks to himself before Pete returns to the reservation, "Don't come unless you can be happy without your Kennedy Center culture, your Ivy League friends, art shows, and high-fashion and cocktail parties with the celebrity set, without the snobbish intellectual elite" (*Eagle* 16). Hillerman reveals his visceral populism once again, but the clash over the taped phone conversation for both Chee and Pete may be the last straw.

The First Eagle reveals Hillerman still at the peak of his form. It is all here: the confrontation between modern science and ancient religion, the bureaucratic and racist rivalries between the white FBI agents and the Navajo policemen, the on-going strife between Jim Chee and Janet Pete as one more example of the gap between the various cultures, the dark traditions of Navajo witchcraft and the Hopis' quest for eagles that are necessary in their own ceremonies, the Navajo and Hopi lands now complicatedly interspersed between and within one another. The book also displays a seamless plot and the smooth, swift yarn-spinning of the narrator. All of these issues and practices, conjured up amid the overwhelming beauty of Hillerman's Southwest, continue to occupy the heart of his fiction.

INTERVIEW WITH TONY HILLERMAN
JUNE 1996/JULY 1997

Sam Coale: When you were growing up in Sacred Heart, Oklahoma, and you went to St. Mary's Academy, a boarding school for Indian girls run by the Sisters of Mercy, and you're a white boy: was this the beginning, looking back on it, of an initiation into assimilation with very different people? Was it traumatic? Did it foster an interest in cultures other than your own, or did you just take it for granted?
Tony Hillerman: What's important about that in forming character is that if you grew up at Sacred Heart and you went to the St. Mary's Academy and your playmates were Potawatomie kids mostly, some Semi-

noles, some whites, and you were a country boy, you were one of a little group of isolatos, and when you went to town, you saw the other culture, the more affluent, more urban. . . . Those kids knew how to shoot pool, and they had a little money in their pockets, even though it was the Depression, and they didn't have much. They wore low cut shoes and belt pants instead of overalls. There were things you could do better than they could do. You could pick more cotton, and you were a better shot, you thought. Everybody had a rifle, but you knew how to use it. I was twenty when I made my maiden telephone call.

So what I'm saying is you identified not necessarily with Indians, because Indians are not any different than anybody else, but with poor rural people. What makes Indians different is the same thing that makes me different. They were poor, they were rural, they were trying to make a living farming, and they were outsiders. We were poor, we were rural, we were trying to make a living farming, we were outsiders. So, there was us including the Potawatomie, the Seminoles, and then there was them, the town folks.

SC: So it was an almost automatic identification, because where you grew up it was the norm.

TH: That's what makes cultures. It's not your blood type.

SC: Why did you choose to write mainly about the Navajos?

TH: I found that the Indians in town were interesting people. I always liked Indians. That wasn't what caused me to choose the Navajos. As far as the Pueblo Indians are concerned, their culture revolves around the kiva, around the religion. And because the theology they follow is secretive, and the people who belong to kiva societies are not supposed to talk about it. It's very, very bad form and very rude to probe into it. The Navajos are not that way at all; they're totally different.

I wrote one book, two books involving Zunis. One was about a mother and father and some children . . . no problem. The other one was a mystery, *Dance Hall of the Dead.* They used that in their Zuni High School. The kids had to read it in their American lit. classes, and they got me to speak at their commencement. And they knew me. But my point is after I made the speech, a young Zuni told me that the Pueblo historian would like to talk to me. I went to the office and a representative from each kiva was waiting. They cross examined me: "Where did you get this information?" They just wanted to know whether somebody in their kiva was committing the heinous crime of revealing secrets. I assured them that everything I used in the book was all previously published somewhere by one of the anthropologists. Then it was okay. But they said, "If you write about us again, would you talk to us about it before you publish it?"

For example, one of the bars, the Kachina Bar or Kachina Lounge, was advertising in the paper. They had a picture of a kachina figure carrying a tray with beer on it in their advertising, and I got a phone call: "What can we do about that?" It was easy to fix. I called the ad manager and said, "Look at this ad. This is extremely sacriligious." So the ad manager called the hotel and asked them to take this ad off and, of course, they did.

The Navajos don't have that kind of theology. With the Pueblo or the kachina religions, if uninitiated people know things, then it diminishes and dilutes the power. That's the reason they don't like their pictures taken. It dilutes the power of the personality. The Navajos don't have that point at all. Their religion is purely curing. It's social. Everything about it is intended to get the individual back in harmony. They have a ceremonial because somebody is sick, or there's something wrong going on in the community. Now, your family and your clan are supposed to be there if they can. Friends are invited, too. It's kind of like a wake. You come, and if you behave yourself, and you take part in the good spirits, that's what they want, and it adds strength, you see. A lot of things are taboo, but it's not secretive. They don't have the sense that if somebody knows it, it diminishes the effect.

SC: I wonder if that has anything to do with their more nomadic quality as opposed to Pueblo societies which appear to be more enclosed?

TH: That could be. Pueblo secrecy may have started when they were trying to preserve their religion from the Spanish, some of whom were very hostile to it.

SC: Are there curing ceremonies for different illnesses? For instance, the Enemy Way was used for Navajos who had returned after serving in World War Two to restore them to harmony.

TH: They used it when there'd be a fight with the Utes or the Comanchis or the Spanish, in more recent times when somebody had been away, went to California and came back. The ceremony is to restore you to the Navajo way, to relieve you of all these foreign influences.

SC: So whatever the illness is or the sickness, there's a particular curing ceremony to go with it.

TH: Yes. The shaman knows how to reenact the proper episode from mythology. Done properly the cure is mandatory. There's no plea to it, no prayer to it, it's like chiropractice. You click it back into place, psychologically of course. If you do this properly, you're cured.

SC: Do you know where the Navajos originated?

TH: I don't think there's any doubt in anyone's mind where the Navajos came from. They came out of North China. There's one anthropologist— I don't think it's generally accepted but is a theory—who thinks that she can pretty well pin down where they came from in Mongolia and that they moved North during the disruption when the Mongolians rose and swept China, at least North China. She believes the Navajo ancestors were warrior people on the side that was losing.

SC: Why did you choose to write about the Navajo in the mystery form?

TH: I wanted to write a very important American novel. But I had been writing short stuff for years. I thought I'll try to write a mystery, first because they're short. I liked some mystery novels, I was aware of the ground that Raymond Chandler had broken, and others were using novels as vehicles. So here's a people about whom the American public is almost totally ignorant.

The traditional Navajos are people of faith, who haven't been assimilated too much. They let their religious belief affect the way they live in important ways. That is rare, and people should know about this. Americans basically just thought an Indian was an Indian. They were all alike, and they wore feathers in their hair.

Whites had the crazy ideas that they were ruled by chiefs and princesses. I don't know what it's going to take to root that out. You still see city Indians who claim that they're princesses, or they're the son of a chief. I don't think there was ever a tribe in the United States that ever had a princess. They don't have rules based on heredity. Power doesn't pass down. That whole concept that Europeans brought over is very strange to us Indians.

Anyway I wanted to write a mystery, and I thought I'll use this as a setting, a wonderful landscape and the Navajo culture. I like to write about landscape. I'll use that as a background, and then I'll write a mystery story, and maybe if the plot's not very good, the color and culture will carry it. That was what I was doing. But I didn't do a very good job of it in *The Blessing Way*. There were some good scenes. There were some spots in it that I thought I did very well. The plot was kind of a little bit on the hybrid side.

I sent it to my agent who didn't like it and told me why. And so then I wrote a letter to an editor at Harper & Row, Joan Kahn, and asked her if she'd read it. She said she would, I sent it to her, and eleven days later, she said that she wanted to publish it. I was in New York, and I called her and she said, "Yes, we want to publish it. Have you got my letter?" And I said, "No, I haven't because I've been away." And when I got back, I had a real long letter telling me what was wrong with it. Okay, so now they're going to publish it if I fix it up.

Joe Leaphorn was really a very minor character in that draft. Bergen McKee was my central character, my hero. Leaphorn was just a source of information, the guy you could work with to make it possible for

McKee and the reader to get information. All of a sudden I realize the damn thing is actually going to be published, and by now I've become aware of what I can do with this Navajo material. So when I rewrote it, I substantially expanded Leaphorn's role in it. But even then it was sort of a patch job.

Then I wrote the book that I had wanted to write, *The Fly on the Wall*. When I finished *Fly*, I decided to go back and do that Navajo thing right. And to really do it right, I'll try to make a little chip in this homogenized Indian concept. I'll put the Navajo cop on the Zuni reservation [in *Dance Hall of the Dead*].

SC: Are you attracted to the Navajos because of your own Catholic faith? Or faith in general?

TH: It's just faith in general. Let's put it this way. Let's face it. The dominant overwhelmingly pervasive religion in America is Mammon. And the dominant philosophy is Hedonism. Consumerism is also dominant. The golden calf.

But there are people whose religious faith affects their lives: The Pueblos in general, the Hopis, the Navajos, some of the other Indian religions, but I know so little about them I don't know for sure. Mormons, some fundamentialists, some Roman Catholics, some Lutherans, Presbyterians, some mainstream religions, but a good many people who answer the census questionnaire saying they're religious or belong to a church do so only as long as it doesn't interefere with the way they live. For example, they'll go down to court claiming they're Christian and clamor for the death penalty if their son is killed by somebody, even though their religion tells them not to go to bed till you've forgiven your brother. I will forgive you as you forgive . . . know what I mean? They're still for the death penalty. Or they're for religion as long as it doesn't affect their social position or their financial positon or their comfort or anything like that. Okay, but you run into people like the traditional Navajos, like the Hopis overwhelmingly, and your admiration for them is deep and broad.

I was one of those people who was raised a Catholic in Oklahoma where we were sort of a little island. Surrounded by refugees from the Civil War from the South, you learn how it is to be a minority, and I'm one of those who believe strongly in keeping religion out of the public schools, because I know what would happen. But I was watching television the other day, and this nice looking woman probably in her late thirties was being interviewed by one of our intellectually elite in New York, Barbara Walters? And Barbara Walters just shocked her. This woman had moved to some place in Washington State, and her children came back from school and told her that during the noon hour or assembly this little girl got up and prayed. And Barbara Walters said, "Prayed? What did she say? Was it one of those. . . .?" The woman said, "Oh no. The girl asked God to bless them in the name of Jesus Christ." "Were you shocked?" "Of course I was shocked." And I thought, isn't that great? I mean, of course I respect her for stopping that, because that's against the law, and the law should be enforced. But the attitude is so taken for granted by our thought leaders that we should all be shocked and mortified by a child praying aloud in school.

SC: This interest you have in ceremony, religion, and faith seems to be connected to your particular landscape. Does this landscape do that to you? In your books you describe the landscape as if it were haunted.

TH: It reminds you of your insignificance. I was putting gas in my car the other day, and a middle-aged black lady was putting gas in hers. We've been having a terrible drought this year. So far we've had four-tenths of an inch of rain in 1996. And it's really having an effect. I said something about the drought, and she said, "You know what the bright side of the drought is? It reminds us of how dependent we are on our creator." It sure does, doesn't it? And I thought if you want to find religious strength in this country, you find it in the little islands I mentioned. But you also find it overwhelmingly in the strength of Christianity in the United States, in black churches. Of course there's not just Jesus but other great religious teachers, such as Buddha.

SC: You capture that religious presence in your books. There's something there that obviously has to do with your faith and your growing up in the Southwest.

TH: My dad ran a little store, but we had a farm, and it was during the years of the dustbowl. When you wake up in the morning, the first thing everybody does is look at the sky. Nature is so important to your life, and you never get that out of your system.

SC: Were your parents religious at all?

TH: Yes. Both were, and not just on Sunday. My father was a Christian in the sense that he was the guy everybody came to when they were out of luck, or out of money, or needed somebody to take them up to Shawnee to get a problem solved. I don't know how he kept that store out of bankruptcy, because the down-and-outers relied on it. We were practicing Catholics, the family was, but being a religious person doesn't have anywhere near as much to do with going to church as it does to listening, believing the words and following the instructions.

SC: I don't mean to belabor the religious point of view, but there seems to be no real break between that sense of faith and religious values you had as a child and those you have as a writer. It just seems like one and the same thing. It's intact.

TH: I hope it is, I think so, yes. Let me put this in a different way. I'm going to use a specific example of this. I was watching a program on astronomy on the BBC, and a young woman was interviewing astronomers in the United States and Britain, mostly Britain, about the origins of the universe, the origins of life, the origins of everything and comparing it in some ways with religion. But anyway, she's talking to one of the authors of the "Big Bang" theory, an old man, and he explains it to her, and she says, "But what was there before the 'Big Bang'?" And, kind of startled, he says, "Young lady, that's a non-question." And I thought, it really is in a sense a non-question, because we don't have the evidence to answer that, but it's a question that religious people, my Navajo friends and the Hopis I know, are asking. They're going beyond the Big Bang into the ultimate question. Not everyone's intelligence allows them to be happy with the limitations physics tries to put on us.

SC: You talk about Navajo harmony, and in your books you relate it to Anglo-American justice. They're very different concepts in terms of revenge and punishment. Jim Chee is wonderfully situated in the middle, caught between being a policeman and a shaman.

You also describe the darker side of Navajo culture, their mythology of witchcraft, in *Talking Mysteries.* Why do you think that there's so much about witchcraft? It permeates your books and adds to that sense of a haunted presence. It also adds to the suspense of the mystery. It gives a supernatural flavor to things. And even though the mystery is solved, the flavor is still there. Do you have any idea why this is such a part of Navajo culture?

TH: I've got two. I've got just my own guess based on just two things. I think the Navajo brought it with them when they crossed the Bering Strait. I think their religion grew out of the form of Buddhism, call it Taoism, that was prevelant in that part of North China and Mongolia. It is full of, what's the word for it, bad spirits, that are offended in various ways.

The other thing is that being a people without antibiotics and surgery and all that stuff, being subject to so many diseases and all the things that will kill you—I think that those two things combined to give them a taboo system that really makes you be very, very, very careful about a hell of a lot of things. It's full of scary stuff, the taboo system is. So then how do you understand evil? You make it a mirror, a reverse image. Some people just can't understand why mean people are mean, so they call them witches. I mean, they explain evil with witchcraft as the Pilgrims did.

SC: And this still goes on?

TH: I don't know. Who knows? Do they actually initiate a witch anymore? I suspect that some of the people do. It's in their mythology; it's in their tradition. It pops up in murder cases.

SC: In *A Thief of Time* Slick Nakai, the Navajo-Christian evangelist, gives a sermon for about four pages in which he tries to integrate both the Navajo religion and Christianity. He suggests that the Navajo religion ends in oblivion after death. Christianity takes you into the possibility of something else happening.

TH: I present Nakai not as a Jesuit. He didn't study Plato and isn't deeply into the philosophy of theology—but here's a fundamentalist, you know, the true gospel, and that's the message he's preaching. It never occurs to me that most of the guys you see on television are actually Christians. When I wrote that stuff, those questions you're raising were in my mind, but I'm trying to show the character and not the religious factor. What the Navajos say about life after death is that "We aren't sure."

SC: I've read a little about Navajo child development, about the anxiety, the depression, the melancholy quality of the Navajo which James Chism linked to the pervasive belief in witchcraft. Does that make sense?

TH: Yes, it does.

SC: Because on the one hand you celebrate harmony and family values. But on the other hand there's this darker side of thing.

TH: One book reviewer once very astutely noted that you could read my books and not get the image that he gets of the Navajos—of drunkenness, poverty, broken lives—that he sees when he drives down Railroad Avenue in Gallup, that I am painting a much brighter picture of this Navajo culture. I said that the press when it writes about the Navajos almost invariably writes about that: the bad, the drunks, the losers. It is a very important problem, but those few border town drunks aren't the Navajos I know.

SC: They're just publicly visible.

TH: And highly visible. It's in the border towns. The tribe has prohibition, of course. So the drunks go to the border towns. Those aren't the Navajos that I'm writing about. You guys are writing about drunks all the time. I'm going to write about the other 95% of the tribe. Those who don't drink. I don't really know any Navajos who drink.

SC: Is there that tendency in writing about metaphysical issues, the mythology of another culture, that you could romanticize it without meaning to?

TH: I don't think so. But again I don't know. Here's my problem. I'm selling an unlikely story, a plot. To make that plot believable, I try to make the background just as real as I possibly can, so you believe in the people, and you believe in the dent in the Chevy's fender, and you believe in the dust on the bowl and the paper cup blowing across the parking lot. You believe in all that stuff, you know. So you also believe in the plot. I make a point that the Navajos I'm writing about are usually traditional. I sometimes have my sheep-camp Navajos talk in uncomplimentary terms about the city Navajos. I'm trying to make it as real as I can without romanticizing. A lot of Navajos, when you first meet them, will deny that they believe in witches, and when they know you better, they tell you of their encounter with one. A lot of my Navajo friends have told me their own witch stories. They're embarrassed about it in a way, because in the surrounding culture the people look on them, as I look upon people who read their horoscope every morning or like the New Agers with their Tarot cards and pyramid power and their "om" chants.

SC: You said at one point that you found plotting, the writing of plots, the most difficult of the things to do. Is that true?

TH: I know I say that, and that's what I'm worried about all the time, but I write incredibly complicated plots. I guess I just demand more of a complex plot. I try to make seamless plots, melding subplots and the central story.

SC: One thing I admire is how when you present the Navajo attitude toward a particular ceremony, you also set up your white villains to use these same ceremonies as disguises to promote their own designs. You also use the Navajo myths as a way to plot the story. So on the one hand, the plots are very elaborate, but the myths and the mysteries reflect each other, play off each other.

TH: I try to make that work. It doesn't always.

SC: Do you consciously do it?

TH: I sometimes consciously do it.

SC: When your wrote *Dance Hall of the Dead*, did you discover in that book how you could follow a particular Navajo myth and at the same time write a mystery plot in which one reflects the other? Because that book holds together so well, because it plays off the religious tale about going to the lake, and at the same time it is also perfectly symmetrical with the mystery plot.

TH: Well, the religion, of course, is what you have here. You have a Navajo who knows a little bit about the Zuni religion of his neighbor tribe. He's an anthropologist who tries to solve a mystery. To do that he has to understand the Zuni myth. What is this Dance Hall of the Dead? And how do you find out where it is? Zunis aren't going to tell you. The kid he's hunting is a Navajo, too. He doesn't have a relative in any kiva. So Leaphorn knows he has the same information about where the lake is as would the boy. Even though it may not help him find the lake, it will help him find the boy. Where's the lake? I don't know. Neither would Leaphorn, and neither would the boy.

SC: Do you set yourself a puzzle in those first chapters where you don't have a clue what's going to happen? Do you like to put yourself in as tight a corner as possible?

TH: No, no. I don't do it on purpose; it happens. I've never been able to plan a book all the way through. I don't know how it's going to work out. I keep changing things. *The Fallen Man* changed drastically from when I first started it. I sent the editor the first three hundred pages with a note on what's going to happen in the last three chapters. I get his letter back complaining about a character named DeMott climbing Shiprock. The editor doesn't think he's adequately motivated to do what he does, and there must be another way to solve this. I thought, "What the hell is *he* talking about?" because DeMott's not going to climb the mountain. DeMott's got an entirely different role. Then it dawns on me that when I sent him those pages about a month earlier, that's what DeMott was doing. Meanwhile I had already forgotten about that and come up with a better ending.

SC: Do you consciously set yourself up at the beginnings of your books? For instance *The Dark Wind* begins with three different plots. I mean, you just kind of say let's see how I can run with this and see what happens. That must be the fun of it.

TH: Well, somebody once said that if you outline a book, it wouldn't be any fun to write. That's true. Of course it's a lot of work. Take that windmill, for example, in *The Dark Wind*. I was stuck in that book. I thought, "What the hell is Chee doing?" He had to be out there by that arroyo to see all this, but I couldn't think of how to motivate him to be there. So I was stuck in the book. My wife suggested, "Why don't you go out on the reservation and poke around for ideas?" So I asked her if she'd go with me, and she said she would. The first storm of the winter caught us out there. We get to the Hopi reservation, and while we're there, I picked up a copy of the Hopi weekly newspaper. It had a story of a vandalized windmill in it. It's a minor misdemeanor with probably $80 worth of damage to it, but I think, "Why would anyone vandalize a windmill in a desert country?" And the more I thought about it, the more I began seeing how I could use it to make that book work. The subplot became more important than the plot.

That gave me a chance to play off the differences between Cowboy Dashee, the Hopi cop, and the Navajo cop. Here they are two totally different religions, really very different religions, but they both believe in God. They both have faith, and the old man guarding the windmill recognizes another believer.

SC: You also obviously have your journalist side, like your master's thesis on the great Taos bank robbery. Do you think maybe that's why, whether you chose to or not, that's why you decided to write in the mystery form, because it is like a journalist seeking the facts, the answers?

TH: I didn't consciously do that. I consciously chose the mystery form because it had a skeleton; you know, it was narrative. And it wasn't the kind of stuff that Thomas Pynchon was trying to write. It was a straightforward tale. It was a yarn spun, and you had a structure you could follow, and I thought I could do that. And you could wrap up a mystery much shorter than you can most novels, although there are some short novels, so that's what I was up to. I thought I could do it. It wasn't that, well, maybe I did, though. It was a way of using the skills you learn in seventeen years as a reporter.

SC: One of the many reasons the books work is because of the series of interviews and investigations, which give them an anchor. Would you ever like to not write a mystery?

TH: I am rather soon, I hope, going to write a sequel to *The Great Taos Bank Robbery*, a series of essays. I think the name of the book would be *Who Killed Cricket Coogar?* I've probably mentioned it somewhere before. On Good Friday morning, a cold winter morning, three kids are hunting rabbits out in the desert down at Las Cruces. They're cold, and it's a windy day, and they're about ready to quit, and one of them sees a little cavity where the wind has blown the sand away, and there's a little girl's hand sticking out.

SC: Is this a real story?

TH: Yes. Cricket was seventeen years old. But before the uproar her death aroused was over, the Democratic Party organization that ran the state was wrecked. The Democratic organization had been in the saddle. John Miles was going to be the new governor. The Republicans had picked their usual sacrificial lamb in the form of a former FBI agent whose father was a distinguished and honorable judge. But when the votes were counted, the G. O. P. had won. Practically every county in the state had a grand jury in session, the state police chief was in the federal penitentiary, the DA investigator's in the federal penitentiary, and a sheriff in the federal penitentiary. The president of the League of Young Democrats was indicted, and so forth.

SC: It was like a blood bath.

TH: Oh, it was. The people of the state just rose up. It started with a student protest, imagine! And this was in 1949, I guess it was . . .

SC: It sounds like Watergate.

TH: The guy who built the big casino in Las Vegas and made Vegas our gaming mecca bought this bunch of land in Santa Fe County. The Mafia was moving into New Mexico instead of Las Vegas. Santa Fe was a wonderful tourist town, much better than Vegas. In those days Vegas was nothing, and Santa Fe attracted the tourists. We already had gambling going on all over the state, illegal, but going on. But the clean Republican said he'd solve the Cricket Coogar murder case. He got elected, and the Mafia went away.

SC: Did he solve it?

TH: No. I'm going to write a whole series of such essays. Most of them are going to be light. That will be the heavy one.

SC: Joe Leaphorn, the older pragmatic policeman, is wonderfully developed after Emma's death, that sense he has of his own loneliness. And Chee, who is much younger and is torn between two worlds, is the idealist. And I could see how that would naturally happen. Is there any way to relate Chee's own dilemma, between being a shaman and a cop, to your being torn between journalism and fiction at one time?

TH: No, I don't think so. One thing that leads a journalist into fiction is the fact that sometimes there's so much difference between the facts and the truth.

SC: I know at one point you talked about influences on your fiction, such as Graham Greene and his entertainments. Many of his mystery and spy novels are entertainments, but they also have their serious side. Haven't you tried to achieve a similar synthesis?

TH: I just wanted to be an author. I wanted to see if I could write a book and be an author, and I made it, and I was delighted. I got a $3500 advance. That's for three years' part-time work. But it got good reviews, and there's just nothing that matches the thrill when they hand you that first book. I wanted to be an author. I didn't have any social purpose beyond that when I started writing.

SC: Even before you got into the newspaper business, you wanted to write?

TH: The newspaper business *is* writing! Listen, when you grow up in the cotton patch, you don't believe that real live human beings write books. Authors are some kind of magical super people. Books are a kind of magical stuff.

SC: Do you think much of this has to do with the whole Southwestern sense of spinning yarns and telling tales? In *Talking Mysteries* you talk about your father the storekeeper, not necessarily him, but the farmers who would come there, a place where people would talk and spin yarns.

TH: Sure. That was respected. And my mother was a good storyteller. She would make up stories to tell us kids. I had a neighbor from Vermont once, and it took him about eleven years before he'd say hello, you know. There are exceptions, I'm sure, in Vermont . . . but generally, you know, out in the country you don't see a lot of people. You're not running into people and getting elbowed, getting in traffic jams. You tend to be interested in people. I think there's more of an oral tradition.

We had a movie theater in Konawa which showed movies on Saturday. I went to one movie there in my boyhood. It was "Gone With the Wind." And I went to two movies in Shawnee. There wasn't much to compete for your attention. Obviously you didn't have television. Radio was in fine flower, but we didn't have electricity, so we had a battery-powered radio, and sometimes the battery would run out.

SC: Is anyone left of your family in Sacred Heart now at all, or all they all scattered?

TH: I have a few cousins still there.

SC: Were they both Oklahomans originally?

TH: My mother and father?

SC: Yes.

TH: My mother was born migrating down to Oklahoma territory from Nebraska, and her mother died before she got there. My dad was born in Missouri and came down to explore, farmed a little and taught school in West Texas. And then he was a cowboy and shoed horses and mules in a coal mine. He started a store on the Cherokee strip in Indian territory. Then he ended up running that little store in Sacred Heart, where the Benedictines had built a monastery and a school for the Citizen Band Potawatomies. The railroads decided they wanted that land at Shawnee Mission up in Kansas that the government had given to the Potawatomie. So the Pots were moved down into the territory and given an allotment down there. The railroads got the good land. The Benedictines had been operating a school there and moved with them. They were French mostly. And so when the land rush came, the only Catholic church in the whole territory was right there.

I know a priest who was the brother of our next door neighbor, and he came home. He'd gone to Pakistan when he was in his thirties; he wanted to go up there. Now he's in his late seventies, and something had gone wrong with him, and they sent him back to the States to have surgery. And we were sitting out on the front lawn drinking Scotch and talking, and I asked him—it was the first time he'd seen his family in years—how he felt about going back. "I can't wait," he said. "I can't wait to go back to Bangladesh. Living surrounded by a pagan culture like I've been here in America is depressing!"

SC: In *The Dark Wind*, the villain is very much a trickster, a con artist. And I began to think that part of a mystery writer's delight must be that he's the one that initiates the crime. You're the culprit, but you're also the magician. Witches tend to misplace direction, to make you look a different way. And you're doing that also. Do you get a kick out of this? I don't want to paint you as this socially correct, politically correct paragon.

TH: I would hate to be considered politically correct. Because, well, for many reasons. That *Dark Wind* thing was funny. I ran into a real life private detective in California at a writer's conference. So I think I'm really going to grill this guy, find out all the poop, so we talked a lot, but I don't remember a darn thing I learned from him except for that card trick! And that card trick was incredibly useful in that plot.

SC: Do you make notes of that kind of thing?

TH: I never make notes.

SC: You must have a good memory. Is it part of your journalist's training?

TH: Yes. When I was interviewing, I never used any of the notes I took. I would pretend to be writing things down because the guy would want me to. It was actually a very particular quote I was writing down. Then I would take the notebook and put it alongside my typewriter, and I'd never look at it. Your mind conditions itself to remember certain things. I don't remember ordinary things. I park my car with the lights on and end up with a dead battery. I couldn't tell you the license plate on any of my cars or any of my kids' telephone numbers. I've always got to look them up. I don't remember when I was a kid thinking that way. I trained myself that way, recognizing what they call significant details in journalism school.

Look at *The Fallen Man*. One of the subplots involves Chee who gets promoted to acting lieutenant at Crown Point. And the captain there hates cattle rustlers. There's always a little cattle stealing going on. There's a saying out here that nobody eats their own beef. And so, Chee is head of the criminal investigation; the junkyard dogs they call themselves at Crown Point. I'll show you a picture of them. So here comes an inspector from the Cattle National Sanitary Board. He and Chee don't get along, he looks on Chee with disdain, and he doesn't take him seriously. Chee doesn't like the son of a bitch anyway. But I had him show Chee a trick. He wants Chee to come along with him, because he's caught this guy with five what they call slick calves; they've just been branded. And he doesn't like the looks of this guy's bill of sale. He thinks he knows who just had five calves stolen. To nail the thief he wants Chee to go with him to this pasture where the mother cows are, because he wants a witness. Chee says, "Why me?" The inspector says because most of the people on the jury for this case are going to be Navajo, you're a Navajo, and they're going to pay attention.

So they stop at this holding pasture, where the mother cows have all been branded. There are about a hundred of them there. What he's looking for are wet cows, cows with bulging utters. So he lies down on his back on the ground and puts his hands under his head, and just lies there, still talking to Chee. The cows are extremely curious and start looking at him, and pretty soon he's surrounded by this great circle of Hereford cows. What's this? Somebody's lying down on the ground? What's going on, see? He's counting off five wet cows. Of course the cows are scared. Chee is impressed, and he tells the inspector that he's impressed, and the guy says, "Do you know where I learned that?" And Chee says, "No." He says, "I had to go get a root canal done by a dentist in Farmington, and he had a *New Yorker* magazine on his counter there. And I was reading this piece in *The New Yorker*, and this man named John McPhee had gone out and done this very same thing while investigating cattle rustling in Nevada." And I thought that it was the kind of detail that makes the story work. I'm not going to play with McPhee without giving him some credit.

SC: When you created Chee, when he first makes his appearance, he seems so much more developed than when Leaphorn first appeared. Is that just because you were further along in your own development? Do you see yourself developing from book to book? Since you know what you can do well, do you try then to do something differently?

TH: I try not to repeat myself. So many mystery writers repeat themselves. For example, one of my favorites is Ross Macdonald, a really good writer. He's great with metaphors, but he used to use the same plot over and over again, yet you still like to read his books. I try not to repeat myself if I can help it, but I can't always help it. In a way, you get caught in a kind of trap when you write a series. You say, "I can't do this, because I covered this so well in *The Blessing Way*." I'm presuming that everybody has read all of these books. But some haven't, you see.

SC: You introduce such characters as Mary Landon and then Janet Pete. There's the cat who makes an appearance in several books. Chee also gets promoted. Does that just kind of happen because it's a series?

TH: Chee does get older, of course. You'd be amazed how many people know what these characters look like better than I do. They're disappointed when they don't get married or do get married. I got a letter from a woman who said she had a perfect match for Chee. She was a school teacher, and she gave me all of her facts and figures.

SC: How are they going to consummate this relationship? Did she give you the details?

TH: No. but, boy, it did sound like she was a perfect match! You know, she liked the outdoors, and she loved nature. She had a good sense of beauty.

SC: How did the development of Leaphorn after his wife's, Emma's death get going?

TH: It started when Emma was in an accident. In *Dance Hall of the Dead* she first appeared. I had Leaphorn talking on the radio to the dispatcher, I tried to make it seem real, and so the dispatcher said, "By the way, Emma called and wanted to remind you about your dental appointment." That's how you come to see that Leaphorn is married. I didn't ever intend to use her again. That was going to be it.

SC: Leaphorn seems to be such a more interesting character when she's dead. The sadness in him. . . .

TH: It was an unintended byproduct. I know people my age, and I'm seventy-one. Before long you know people who have lost their wives or their husbands, and you understand the horrible gap that it leaves in their lives.

SC: Do you find in some of the later books that you take on some very current social issues? In *Talking God*, for instance, you tackled the question of Indian bones being dug up and sent to museums. When you write different books, do you choose such specific issues?

TH: It's amazing to me how often I'll say, okay, I'm going to do this, I'm going to write this book, and I'll start writing it and get about half done, sometimes almost done, when what I'm writing about blows up in the news. Repeatedly that's happened. I was reading about a man at Harvard who hauled a lot of stuff off to their museum. He didn't keep good field notes. It's fine if they know what they're doing and approach it not as treasure hunters, like the Harvard guy did, but as serious scholars. But anyway, that's what was on my mind. And of course if you're out there a lot, you run across people who are upset by it. Then it becomes a big issue. I'm always reading a lot, and people are always sending me clippings.

SC: Are you always, when you're winding up one book, ready to start the next? Does something always pop into your head?

TH: Usually. You wish you could finish the one you're working on quickly, because you think the next one is going to be a lot better.

SC: Do you think there's any chance of Oklahoma becoming more homogenized? Do you think that could happen between the Navajo culture and the white culture?

TH: They do, in a way, already. In Oklahoma the Chief Justice of the Supreme Court was an Indian. The law school was swarming with Indians. Saying "Cherokee" is almost like saying "lawyer," you know. One of my adopted kids is part Indian. One of my brother's adopted boys was Indian, and when he wanted to go to Notre Dame, he'd get a better scholarship deal. It's useful to be an Indian now with affirmative action, but then that's keeping it alive. Nearly all of them, though, the Oklahoma types, the Eastern ones are pretty much assimilated.

SC: So, assimilation really does take place.

TH: Yes. They may be different in pigmentation and in bone structure in some cases, depending on the tribe. But the only difference is cultural. There was this woman in Maine who found out she was a Navajo. She just came back here to learn how to be a Navajo. Well, she's got no more chance of being a Navajo than you and I do. I mean, she's a city girl. On television you got all of these Indian dance troops; they're all city Indians. Maybe some of them went out and visited an aunt on the reservation once. And certainly they had nothing to do with the way Navajos really dance. What it had to do with was the dances that the Santa Fe Railroad brought in and taught the Indians to do when they were trying to get a lot of tourist business for the hotels.

SC: Is that true about that famous episode in the film, "Cheyenne Autumn?"

TH: Yes. They'll all go back and look at it, because they see their kinfolks.

But they can see how the whole thing was misrepresented on the screen. I was talking to a guy once. He'd read the book, and he was laughing about it. He said, "You know when I was a boy, a friend of mine and I decided we'd go up to Denver and get a job there, see what we could see in the big city. So, we went up there, and we got a job at a filling station. We went out to a movie. It was a Tarzan movie. Well, we're sitting there at the movie, and Tarzan and Jane had just escaped from these cannibals. The cannibals were hiding in the bushes beside the river, and they're singing hunting songs. And what they're singing was one of the chants from the Mountain Way ceremony! I don't know where they got it," he said. "I guess they got it in an archives somewhere taped."

SC: I wonder if a hundred years from now people will be reading your books to get real information.

TH: You mean the way it was a hundred years ago? I don't know. Now we're having this terrible drought. They haven't had any rain on the reservation, and they already have a horrible over-grazing problem. They've been talking about some kind of enforced stock production program. Boy, that's anathema.

SC: The government tried that in the 1930s.

TH: They did.

SC: And that was a disaster.

TH: The two hells of the Navajo people were the Long Walk and stock reduction. They rank them together, the two most awful things that were done to them. The stock reduction program not only destroyed their livelihood, but it also broke the reservation up into grazing districts, which meant they couldn't follow their old nomadic ways.

SC: Are people still very bitter about that in general?

TH: A good Navajo isn't bitter about anything. You don't find many people, at least the ones I know, that tend to be bitter There's some real fierceness, however, about the Hopi and against the Hopi.

SC: Because of the dispute over their lands. And that's still ongoing and unresolved, isn't it? It's one of those issues that sounds impossible.

TH: They've been moved and pushed around so much. Leaders from both tribes want the same land. For example, the Navajos recently arrested several Hopis for stealing eagles. The politically correct position of the liberal Indian is that neither tribe can do anything wrong. They are the anointed ones, they are the minorities, they are the perfect people, they are Rousseau's Noble Savage. So somebody else must be causing this trouble. Well, the government screwed up in the first place, and that's obvious. But we can't blame it on the Hopis, we can't blame it on the Navajos, so we blame it on the capitalists. They blame it on anybody else, and they really believe it.

The Indians I know don't really like to be called Native Americans. That is too big of a term for me to say. "Native American" is too long. Well, I was on a panel once with a man who was opening a new wing at the Smithsonian. There were seven people on the panel, and I was the only white guy. And somebody in the audience said, "What do you want to be called, you know, indigenous people or Native Americans or what, Indians?" They went down the row, and every one of them said, "I'd rather be called a Hopi or a Seminole or a Cherokee. But since most people don't know what a tribe is, then we'd rather be called Indians. Because that's what we call each other. Or Ind'ans. That's what they say in the southwest, Ind'ans. But don't, for God's sake, call us indigenous people. Thank God Columbus wasn't looking for the Virgin Islands!"

3

HEILBRUN AT THE CROSSROADS:
THE FEMINIST WEB

By now we can easily recognize the traditional mystery formula. Its patriarchal roots in enlightenment analysis, its polarizations between good and evil, its carefully concocted craft of investigation and interviews, the authority of the isolated detective figure, the linear trajectory of its form, the autonomy of separate selves and suspects: all of these, and many more, make up the traditional mystery. Solution brings salvation; cause and effect triumph; order is restored in all its psychological, religious, and moral dimensions; and society can return to its business of social conventions and logical ordinary life.

But what happens when a feminist academic pursues miscreants and murderers? Since many feminist critics would argue that the entire structure and assumptions of the mystery are forever male-biased and male-dominated, linear, objective, and straight-forward in terms of the hero interviewing various suspects, how can they accommodate such a decidedly different main character? As with Hillerman's Navajos, how much must Amanda Cross compromise and distort her feminist perspective to squeeze it into so conventional a literary form?

Carolyn Heilbrun, of course, as Amanda Cross responds to all of this. The economy of the mystery at first reveals a sense of order that is "threatened by chaos; but order is then restored. Basically, that is the pattern of the detective novel that interests me. Plus the chatter along the way" (Cooper-Clark 190). And the formula itself provides the essential order: "The chaos of modern life," Heilbrun continues, "is such that, as Eliot said, it is easier if you start with a scaffolding or a structure for what you are doing. . . . I need all the help I can get" (188-89). The fact that paperback editions of her works sell about 80,000 copies each suggests that the public enjoys her scaffolding.

However, Heilbrun, who has gradually evolved as a feminist over the years, both in her scholarship and in her mysteries, has other fish to fry. She likes the mystery formula because she can also use it, infiltrate and subvert it to a certain extent with her own social and political perspectives. "With the momentum of a mystery and the trajectory of a good story with a solution," Heilbrun has explained, "the author is left free to dabble in a little profound revolutionary thought. . . . Formula fiction has almost alone and with astonishing success challenged the oldest formulas [of gender roles and patriarchal traditions] of all" ("Keynote" 7). Critics disagree over the boundaries and success of her endeavor—as we shall see, some applaud the "profound revolutionary thought" and others belittle the "dabbling" and the "little"—but her own agenda is clear. She is determined "to articulate a self-consciousness about women's identity both as inherited cultural fact and as process of social construction." The interesting questions occur as a result of the collision between the male mystery formula and her distinctly "female" designs upon it, within which she must clarify whatever distinctions may exist between male and female detectives.

Heilbrun succinctly states her perspective on gender roles and issues, derived as they seem to be from specific psychological and biological truths. Males grow up recognizing their separation from the mother. That is the primal fact of their development of consciousness and self: "Boys and men defined themselves, from their first separation from the mother, as not feminine, not womanly. . . . Their masculine personality comes to be defined as the denial of relation" (*Reinventing* 33, 193). They desire to see themselves as autonomous individuals in a world of other autonomous individuals: confrontation is the key, since "men fear, perhaps, having nothing to define themselves against" (33). Hence the male detective remains an essential loner at odds with his society and estranged from it. Females on the other hand "do not fully separate from the mother. . . . Women define themselves by their lack of separation, of selfhood" (192). The problem in social and cultural relations has arisen because "men have monopolized human experience, leaving women unable to imagine themselves as both ambitious and female" (192). Or as one friend of mine summarized it in relation to "women's films" in the 1940s: "Men act. Women react."

Maureen T. Reddy in her astute analysis of Heilbrun's fiction supports this argument:

Men tend to define themselves through individuation and separation, valuing autonomy over connections with others and perceiving relationships in terms of rules and procedures . . . whereas women tend to define themselves in terms of relationships, valuing affiliations with others over autonomy and perceiving relationships in terms of balancing needs and negotiating responsibilities in order to maintain the relationships. (9-10)

Such a point of view questions the entire trajectory of the male mystery formula with its solitary detective and undermines its traditional procedural narrative. As we will examine below, this perspective must create new forms, must violate older assumptions, and must subvert the older authority as established by the single male detective with his apprehension of logical solutions. If it is successful, plot and discourse, character and action, text and texture will reflect one another and propel the mystery toward its resolution.

If we can use the *war* metaphor as an analogy to describe the traditional mystery—good versus evil, detective versus villain, analysis versus the (at first) obscure contours of the crime and the perpetrator's motive for committing it: the binary opposites of the conventional male perspective—then perhaps we can use the *web* metaphor as an analogy to describe the female point of view, recognizing the fact that this oversimplifies very complicated and complex issues but may be a way of getting at the initial clash between Cross' idea of mysteries, say, and James Lee Burke's. In the web pattern, Cross focuses on several nonlinear issues—family affairs, feminist aspirations and perceptions, the bonding between female friends—that involve the characters as they interact among themselves and may not appear to be directly linked to the linear mystery plot. Clearly this is what Heilbrun-Cross is up to in her assault on the prisonhouse of socially constructed genders and her recognition of an essential human soul or self that is ultimately androgynous (*Toward*). Her own autobiographical account of her evolving feminism, *Reinventing Womanhood* (1979), amplifies and explores these views in greater detail.

At the same time Heilbrun recognizes the contradictions inherent in her own point of view and in her writing mysteries. Of *Reinventing Womanhood* she writes

There will appear to be, at the heart of my book, an inherent contradiction. On the one hand I deplore the fact that women of achievement, outside the brief periods of high feminism, have become honorary men, have consented to be token women rather than women bonded with other women and supporting them. On the other hand, I find that those women who did have the courage, self-confidence, and autonomy to make their way in the male-dominated world did so by identifying themselves with male ideals and role models. I want to tell women that the male role model for autonomy and achievement is, indeed, the one they still must follow. But if women's best hope of accomplishment is to follow male examples, am I not encouraging the very thing that I deplore? (31)

Women must, therefore, "claim the male model and . . . deny its maleness"; they must "appropriate the male model without giving up the female person" (*Reinventing* 140, 142).

Several feminist critics find difficulties with this approach. "Heilbrun tends to undervalue women's past and present endeavors," Sara Ruddick suggests. "At the same time, she accepts too uncritically concepts of achievement and adventure which are both male and privileged" (551). Reddy views Heilbrun as accepting "both the masculinist definition of achievement as outward success in the existing hierarchy and the popularized, liberal reduction of feminism to merely a process of adding women in to preexisting institutions" (52). In both cases Heilbrun's feminism becomes suspect, especially in the guise of the mysteries she concocts. Can one create a web in a formula that is essentially a war zone and re-invent that formula to allow that web to take precedence over the war? Even Heilbrun was aware of the discrepancies: "One realizes that to worship the totem of superiority [in this case, the penis] is to protect it" (*Reinventing* 187).

Part of Heilbrun's dilemma comes from her own biography, since the contradictions we are grappling with arise clearly out of her own life and expectations. Her own father provided her with the kind of indispensable role model that her mother could not. The poverty of her mother's childhood, her place as the oldest of seven children in an Austrian-Jewish family, and her working as a stenographer only until she was twenty-three and married limited her possibilities. She was the only member of her family not to practice Judaism and determinedly cut herself off from it as she did from everything "common." According to Heilbrun, her mother was aware of the futility of women's roles and the imprisoning conventions that surrounded and underscored them in the 1930s, but she was never able to act on it: "She achieved the status she sought, but never denied the burden of futility she carried with her until her death" (*Reinventing* 17).

"My mother never ceased blaming circumstances for her life," Heilbrun acknowledges. "Even now I cannot think of the emptiness and futility of my mother's life without pain" (*Reinventing* 56, 57). In 1936 on her fortieth birthday she was struck down by a car and killed, and the money she had carefully squirreled away—"It was as much evidence of her fear [of poverty] as of her love" (59)—came to Heilbrun. But the legacy of futility never changed: "As I look back on my mother's life, at least in the years when I shared it, I can see it as entirely organized to avoid suffering, her own and others'. . . . She managed to insulate herself. . . . I remember her despair, her depression. . . . I have a sense that my mother's terrible failure, as I saw it, and more importantly, as she saw it, helped to make me more feminist than most other women of my generation" (*Reinventing* 68, 65).

Heilbrun's father was a different story. He also had lived with poverty in his childhood, spent in a Russian-Polish village before he came to the United States. "His mother had never spoken English. His sisters had been doomed. He had been saved only by an occasional teacher, here and there, and by his own brilliance and determination. He was early disenchanted with the whole culture from which he had come, with its ignorance, its illiteracy, and what he considered its rigid, distorted beliefs" (*Reinventing* 21). As a Jew he renounced his background. His older sisters preceded him to the United States and started sewing for $2.50 a week at the Manhattan Shirt Company: "From this they saved enough for tickets to be sent back to the old country for their mother and brother and the third sister" (Heilbrun, *Gift* 195). He left home at seventeen, became an expert typist and taker of shorthand, a CPA, and at age thirty achieved a partnership in a brockerage firm where he made his first million. In 1928, however, the head of the firm suffered a heart attack, Heilbrun's father had a nervous breakdown, and he underwent two and a quarter years of psychoanalysis, five days a week, that finally cured him. But with no money and no job during the Depression, his prospects were slim. In 1932 he moved to New York City, remade his fortune, and when he had achieved the money he wanted, he quit.

What drew Heilbrun to him was his determination to succeed: "My father was the only possible role model. . . . Perhaps the most important aspect of this which he passed on to me was his conviction of the efficacy of will and destiny. You could do what you set yourself to do. . . . *My Gatsby sense of self-creation* [was] acquired from my father" (*Reinventing* 52, 64, italics mine). The Gatsby analogy stuck with Heilbrun: "My parents' roots consisted precisely in their severing of them. My father and mother had cut themselves off from their past. Like Gatsby, my father had been his own creation" (23). From such experiences grew her invention of Amanda Cross who then invented the old-money graciousness and security of her amateur academic detective, Kate Fansler.

Heilbrun's sense of self-creation "became a recognizable pattern. Her father "sprang from his Platonic conception of himself. He was a son of God. . . . So he invented just the sort of Jay Gatsby that a seventeen-year-old boy would be likely to invent, and to this conception he was faithful to the end." Heilbrun's creation of Kate Fansler suggests a similar invention: "If personality is an unbroken series of successful gestures, then there was something gorgeous about [her], some heightened sensitivity to the promises of life" (Fitzgerald 2). Heilbrun's Anglophilia parallels Nick Carraway's Midwest with his nostalgic evocation of lost worlds and romantic settings, much of which, in Fitzgerald's novel at least, avoided the more piercing vision of "what a grotesque thing a rose is and how raw the sunlight was upon the scarcely created grass" (Fitzgerald 162). Is it any wonder, therefore, that Heilbrun has wrestled with both the male role models in her life and with "the attempt of women to become protagonists in their own stories"? (*Reinventing* 123).

The web of contradictions and self-inventions both limited and nourished Heilbrun's own sense of a developing self. Her Jewishness which, while not an issue in her childhood—her parents had more or less renounced the patriarchal ways of their Jewish pasts—made her aware of her own outsider status in the predominantly Anglo-American culture of her youth. And that background probably contributed to her developing sense of herself as a feminist: "Being an outsider as a Jew made me somehow better able to bear, or to accept as inevitable, my status as outsider because I was female" (*Reinventing* 61), both during her undergraduate years at Wellesley in the late forties and later on during her graduate years at Columbia, where she eventually became a full professor in 1972. Out of the 325 tenured professors at Columbia, only fourteen were women.

In the era of the New Criticism, where literature was studied apart from its cultural and social roots, Heilbrun thrived: "This criticism nicely reinforced my need for impersonality. . . . That I managed to keep my personal and professional lives so separated permitted me to survive" (*Reinventing* 23). Her love for England and all the cultural skills and possibilities it offered—"England for me is a country of dreams, long established in my mind and heart" (*Gift* 89)—allowed her to dissociate herself from "the worrying, self-pitying passion of the Jews" (*Reinventing* 61), even though several years later she discovered "the essential deadness at the heart of the proper Anglo-Saxon demeanor. . . . As I came to understand its coldness I stood amazed, as before a great revelation" (*Reinventing* 61). Yet her constant self-invention or at least the mask of impersonality helped her succeed in the male-dominated academy, where at Columbia and elsewhere, Lionel Trilling reigned as the critic of the day, wrestling with the issues of selfhood and culture in *The Opposing Self* in a way that at the very least downplayed his own Jewish background. Heilbrun became convinced "that male adventure may indeed be translated into female adventure . . . [that] a woman might convert the materials of her male-centered education into a guide for female accomplishment" (*Reinventing* 132, 138-39). In such a way she both validates the female detective and re-assembles the Golden Age forms of such writers as Margery Allingham and Dorothy Sayers.

What Heilbrun constantly needed in all of these guises and shifting masks was "to create a psychic space for myself," the creation of which became her pseudonym, Amanda Cross (*Life* 113, 121). Women had trouble enough being taken seriously as scholars and teachers in the academy in 1964 without her making public the fact that she had begun writing and publishing mysteries. Her creation of an alter ego seems to have coincided with another instance of self-creation: "Women come to writing, I believe, simultaneously with self-creation. . . . Women transform themselves only after an awakening. And that awakening is identifiable only in hindsight" (*Life* 117, 118). She knew all too well that "only the female life of prime devotion to male destiny had been told before," and it was time to strike out anew (*New York Times* Book Review 24 June 1984: 27). She was also very clear about her goals and Kate Fansler's initial role: "I created a fantasy. . . . [Kate] set out on a quest (a male plot); she became a knight (a male role), she rescued a (male) princess. . . . She leads the alternate life [Cross] wished to inscribe upon the female imagination" (*Life* 115, 119). At the same time, she readily admits that "the other thing that interested me is the combination in Kate of liking the manners of another era while also being rather revolutionary socially. This intriguing characteristic is something I share, and it's totally contradictory. I like manners and courtesy of a certain sort very much but I understand the price is too high and a lot of it is silly. And, at the same time, I can't bear the frozenness of that world" (Cooper-Clark 194-95). Contradictions, yes, but surely we can view them as part of the threads in a wide and shifting web as opposed to polarities constantly and only at war with one another. The characterization of Kate Fansler, therefore, carries with it a fundamental irony, which is embodied in Heilbrun's attitude toward the kind of manners she writes about. The trick, of course, is seeing if this can be adapted successfully to the mystery formula.

To sharpen Kate Fansler's identity, Heilbrun made it clear early on in her first mystery, *In the Last Analysis* (1964), that Kate had a mind "too finely tuned to moral dilemmas which more sensible people happily ignored." The influence of Henry James on this characterization Heilbrun gratefully acknowledges, particularly in Kate's recognition "how few people there were who understood morality apart from convention" (*Last* 47). "Henry James had said that . . . the morality of one's actions . . . depend on the moral quality of the person who was going to do the action and not on the moral quality of the person one was doing the action to" (*Last* 70). Thus, as Reddy explains, Kate Fansler emerged in 1964 within "a male role in a patriarchally constructed text: the detective functions as an exemplar of inviolate reason, restoring order to a chaotic world while resisting personal entanglements" (Crime 54-55). And thus have we come full circle, returning to where we began in considering the attractions of the mystery formula. However, as we can also see, more is at stake here than mere plots and solutions.

In terms of her use of the mystery formula, Heilbrun herself has summed up her critics' attacks: "These can be summed up, fairly enough, by saying that my mysteries, aside from having no plot, too many political opinions, too few bodies and (to quote a disagreeable chap from 1980) a 'veneer of educated allusion,' are 'fairly simple-minded.' . . . This all seems legitimate to me."[1] The veneer is obvious enough. Dazzled by the dialogue in Dorothy Sayers' mysteries, Heilbrun has always readily acknowledged that particular debt: "The only direct influence is Sayers. Sayers, Josephine Tey, and to some extent Ngaio Marsh. . . . Forster and Woolf have been an enormous influence. . . . They like to talk. And they like to talk with intelligent people and they like to explore ideas. And to have time for conversation, you need leisure, so you tend to have people from the upper class. Obviously you need a certain kind of person; that's another reason for the academic setting" (Cooper-Clark 196). But Heilbrun's is no mere veneer as we will see. Conversation creates the web, the various points of view, whether or not these appear in conversation or in journals and letters. The characters may speak the same language, but they see things very differently and in doing so help to undermine that solitary and isolated authoritarian view of the male detective.

The second literary problem that Heilbrun has dealt with is the character of Kate Fansler. One must remember, as Heilbrun constantly reminds us, that when Fansler made her appearance in 1964, there was only one publicly recognized female detective in circulation, Agatha Christie's Miss Marple. And *The Feminist Mystique* had just been published. Both Roberts and Reddy are eager to attack Fansler's "male" position, although Reddy modifies her point of view and accurately acknowledges Fansler's growth as a feminist. Reddy first views her as "the image of the classical [read male] detective . . . a reinvention of [Heilbrun] without complications or pain" (Reddy 53, 66). And Roberts bolsters that argument: "The conventions of masculine mystery stories and of romance have obscured Heilbrun's goal of depicting the autonomous woman" (Reddy 53). Heilbrun consciously admits that Fansler began as a "fantasy figure," but she also makes very clear that she has developed, enlarged, and deepened her over the years.

Finally, however, the most problematic issue remains the mix of feminism with the mystery formula. Does the feminist message weaken the mystery trajectory? Can complex social issues be explored within the contours of that popular form? Why do many readers often express profound disappointment when they learn that a suicide has occurred instead of a murder or when they discover that the motive of a murderer turns out not to be the old stand-bys: money, lust, revenge? Have formulaic expectations curdled the abilities of readers to accept a subverted or expanded mystery form? And is this somewhat of a red herring to begin with? Why must the mystery formula rest on its polarized foundations? Why can't it prove to be elastic enough to incorporate more consciously ideological issues within the various complexities of literature and language themselves which, in these post-deconstruction days, have been revealed as always compromised and always contradictory?

Heilbrun has always maintained that within the trajectory of the mystery, the author can create a clearly defined feminist perspective. At the same time this parallels Heilbrun's own interest in social issues that deepens as her mysteries succeed one another: gender roles, tenure in the academy, the relation of the individual to the institution, the problems with the authority of all authorship, battered women and murder as self-defense, Watergate, Vietnam, and the process of aging. Also Heilbrun's love of literature and her grappling with textual issues in the academy expand to encompass all kinds of initial questions, speculations, and doubts from the most basic Greek myths to the roots of literary modernism in our own century. "Literary criticism teaches you to be on the watch out," Fansler explains. "We deal in subtexts, in the hidden story" (*Fools* 210). "One ought to have some faith in the revelatory powers of the text," she muses (*Winifred* 126). All of these issues, of course, permeate her work, for, as Heilbrun insists, "Only stories . . . serve as models. And it is a hard thing to make up stories to live by. . . . We live our lives through texts. . . . These stories have formed us all" (*Life* 37).

Kate's first appearance in *In the Last Analysis* fulfills the traditional detective's role: "In books, Kate thought, detectives were always enthusiastically interested in their work, rather like knights on a quest" (*Last* 9). In her discussion of Freud in the novel, Heilbrun mentions his discovery that many Victorian women's revelations of sexual relations with their fathers turned out to be, in fact, fantasies, but "the fantasy had an immense importance of its own" (*Last* 53). Kate clearly embodies Carolyn Heilbrun's fantasy of Amanda Cross' fantasy of a bright, witty, old-moneyed academic with flair and perception. Her past affair with the initial suspect in the case, psychiatrist Emanuel Bauer—"theirs was far more a meeting of minds than of passions" (*Last* 47)—lends her a certain social panache, but her unusual methods of solving the crime appear to be a bit fanciful: "I began with one of the great modern novels, and a scene in it, indelibly impressed on the mind. . . . I began with a punning association in a dream" (*Last* 150). The mystery bristles with fine conversations and the recognition of such but is fairly straightforward in its unravelling.

Mary Bradford, the victim in *The James Joyce Murder* (1967), is a self-righteous and obnoxious creature whose murder is applauded by nearly everyone. Heilbrun titles each chapter with the title of a story from Joyce's *The Dubliners*—"Ivy Day in the Committee Room," "The Dead," and "Araby," for example—there is much made of a possible manuscript by Joyce never before discovered, and there are a plethora of references to writers' names in a self-conscious, whirlwind manner,[2] but the mystery itself moves straightforwardly to its conclusion, despite one character's complaint about traditional mysteries and the present dilemma: "How unlike life those stories really are. Their whole point is that so much *happens*. . . . they're so full of *events*. We have had a murder, now, but all we do, of course, is talk about it. . . ." (*Joyce* 95). Kate's friend Grace more or less solves the crime, and Kate's friend, Reed Amhearst, winds it up. Kate drifts along in a bounty of wonderful academic chitchat and maneuverings but hasn't yet taken hold as a dedicated detective. At one point she speaks about the "only three possible lives" that women can expect to lead: "You can marry and continue to function professionally, even with children. The number of this sort increaseth. Or, you can marry, seeing a clear choice and choosing to work. . . . Their number decreaseth. Or you can be one of that third group, much less publicized, which requires and enjoys the love of men, usually more than one man in a lifetime, and scorns the role of homemaker" (*Joyce* 117). In 1967 these seemed the probable choices, but if this is any indication of Fansler's feminism, it gets lost amid the characters and plot of the mystery at hand.

Heilbrun accomplishes a kind of exorcism in *Poetic Justice* (1970) by creating a villain whom many critics have suggested resembles the academic *eminence grise* at Columbia at the time, Lionel Trilling.[3] While other such types of patriarchs, such as Max in *The Question of Max* (1976), several of the professors at Harvard in *Death in a Tenured Position* (1981), Canfield Adams in *A Trap for Fools* (1989), and the fustian reactionaries at the law school in *An Imperfect Spy* (1995), follow in a more or less similar pattern, as if Heilbrun were killing off or triumphing over a certain kind of patriarchal authorities of her generation and the preceding one, Frederick Clemance embodies the contradictory feelings that she felt for Trilling. On the one hand he was a model for Heilbrun, "the first Jew given tenure in a humanities department at Columbia" (*Reinventing* 130), and his New Critical approaches to literature along with his vision of the self in opposition to the general American culture underscored her own textual values of the time. On the other hand, he thoroughly ignored women in his work but left her hopeful "that male adventure may indeed be translated into female adventure" (*Reinventing* 132). She realized then, as she had had inklings before, that "I want to suggest how a woman might convert the materials of her male-centered education into a guide for female accomplishment" (*Reinventing* 138-39), a lifelong ambition that obviously began to seep into her Amanda Cross mysteries and propelled her to grapple with such issues in *Toward a Recognition of Androgyny* (1973) and *Reinventing Womanhood,* among others.

In *Poetic Justice* Kate takes on the battle, one of her many yet to come, to rescue the adult education program, the University College, of the university at which she teaches, and she does this amid all the tensions and moral dilemmas that have arisen from the student take-over of campus buildings and the Vietnam War. She is angrily opposed in this by Professor Jeremiah Cudlipp, who means "to bounce the University College off the campus altogether" (37). And Cudlipp, merely the chair of the English Department, is joined in combat by Frederick Clemance. Admits Kate to Reed Amhearst, who wants to marry her, "I don't want to get close enough to Clemance to discover he's not as great as I prefer to suppose he is. . . . I've been hero-worshipping him since before I got into his special seminar as a student, and that, God help me, was nearly twenty years ago" (*Poetic* 43, 44). Kate's dealings with Clemance are in many ways a replay of Heilbrun's dealings with Trilling, which is a more dramatic instance of her own desire to model herself after her father's less complicated and more celebrated guidance and example.

Clemance invites Kate to lunch, an invitation about which she is both pleased and terrified. They share their appreciation for Auden's poetry—Auden, indeed, is the residing prophet of the entire book with his notions of the relationship between freedom and authority and with Kate acknowledging his greatness as "the best balancer of all" (*Poetic* 156)—and then Clemance explains his opposition to the present state of affairs: "I find I am offended by the manners, by the lack of culture in the deepest sense of the word, prevalent today. I think in order to give everyone an opportunity, we are sacrificing our gifted people" (*Poetic* 57). Kate responds in her own truthful manner, consciously aware of her own contradictory impulses: "I can't bear bad manners . . . yet I also realize that superficial good manners may cover the most appalling nastiness and hostility" (57). She is also wittily aware of "the inverse correlation between moral outrage and sentence structure: apparently one could be radical or syntactical but not both; a disturbing thought" (118). Her search for balance challenges Clemance's reactionary but heartfelt views. He suggests that she is accusing him of prejudice in favor of male undergraduates, and Kate agrees: "Professor Clemance, I have often wished for the opportunity to tell you that you taught me more—about literature, something I can only call morality, and about the honor of the profession of letters—than anyone else in the University. But you seemed to wish only for young male followers, and I did not wish to burden you with an older female disciple" (59). Clemance admits that the student revolution has broken his heart in terms of his love for the university, while Kate stands her ground: "I love talent, but do not care for privilege which takes itself for granted" (60). Such complex arguments—both Kate and Clemance are privileged souls in their academic distress—lie at the heart of Heilbrun's life and fiction.

Clemance's accidental killing of Cudlipp, who dies because of his fatal reaction to the aspirin Clemance has surreptiously given to him (a reaction Clemance is unaware of), results because of Clemance's recognition of Cudlipp's increasingly visible and vocal paranoia, which is undermining the department and the concerted attack on the University College. Clemance wishes only to "immobilize" him for a time. Clemance, however, also recognizes his own blindnesses: "I expect I was so drawn to literature from the beginning because it is the only way in which man can create worlds: his godlike faculty. The only mistake is not to understand the necessary distinction between the laws of the primary and secondary worlds—the primary world being, of course, the actual one we inhabit. . . . But we are not gods, and the laws of the primary world inevitably operate" (*Poetic* 157, 160). The University College is spared, and so is Clemance, but he remains distraught: "There is a terrible need to demand punishment . . . but it seems to me that since I destroyed Cudlipp for the sake of the young men in the College, I ought to stay to serve those same young men—those, at least, who care for what I say. Yet . . . there is never a half hour together when I do not relive that moment of handing him the aspirin" (166). His feelings remain in a kind of psychological limbo, as do Kate's: "Kate felt an aching need to offer comfort and knew no comfort existed on earth" (166). If the penalty seems too easy, the dilemma does not. Kate's institutional victory assured, she marries Reed Amhearst at last, but the confrontation between manners and matter will not leave Heilbrun alone, for she will return to it again and again in her later mysteries.

The Theban Mysteries (1972), overwhelmed by Heilbrun's discussion of "Antigone," forcefully raises all of her issues, but the mystery gets bogged down in such analysis. It is as if, for the moment at least, Auden's sense of balance had deserted her. At the same time it could be because Heilbrun was beginning to mine the deeper issues that were beginning to attract her: "Love versus tyranny, for actions of a woman against a male-dominated world" (*Theban* 12); the Theban School's nurturing and cooperative atmosphere for young women that still manages to find itself "to have been revolutionary without ever losing its reputation for conservatism: a neat trick" (19); the effects of the Vietnam War, draft dodging and civil disobedience on the culture and body politic: "Creon as tyrant or hero is one subject" (54-55); "the question of obedience, whether to the state or a father on the one hand, or to oneself or divine dictates on the other" (79). Kate realizes "that man only learns at a terrible price and there are no easy answers" (85), but such overarching agonizings overwhelm the mystery. Contradictions continue to demand their price. Angelica Jablon has hidden her brother at the Theban School in his attempt to avoid the Selective Service, and her grandfather cannot understand why: "Like many of his generation and his experience, he had lost the connection between his personal morality and the national morality of his beloved country, on whose behalf he was willing to defend offensive practices on the grounds of national necessity that he would never for a moment have endorsed as personal actions" (157). The issues remain clear cut, but the mystery seems an afterthought.

Heilbrun's discussion of sexual polarization and the imprisonment of gender in *Androgyny* clearly indicates her growing interest in such issues which help explain her attraction to and contempt for Max in *The Question of Max,* a man whose manners are impeccable and values despicable, especially from a feminist perspective. Whereas Clemance stood for a distinctive type of academic and critical outlook confined to the academy that she had had to deal with in her own life, in Max and St. Anthony's School Heilbrun broadens her criticism of gender and other social and political issues. St. Anthony's, with its slick public relations and jet-set patina, prides itself on its young men, the "already initiated male. . . . their self-absorption was absolute, their arrogance of status palpable," as is Max's (60). Each reflects the other. A cheating scandal breaks out, conjuring up the mentality of Nixon's Watergate, winning at all costs. "That's why the good guys won over Watergate," Kate decides. "They minded being lied to" (*Max* 96). Kate's friend Phyllis, a wife of a scholar at Oxford, bemoans her fate there: "I've never seen a place where women are such slaves. . . . It's the hideously masculine quality of life here that's undoing me" (134, 148). Cecily Hutchins, a student at Oxford in 1919 and writer, "never doubted that to be a boy was to have won the better part" (108), and her friend and confidant, Dorothy Whitmore, wrote in one of her letters that Kate comes upon: "Men know nothing of life and have kept women shut up for centuries lest women discover this. . . . I shall have the baby . . . and please God, let it be a boy, with his destiny clear and sharp before him" (191).

All of this culminates in Maximillian Reston, a professor of art history, at once urbane, lively, charming, brilliant, and refined as well as snobbish, sexist, prejudiced, and authoritarian. Did he kill someone to keep the fact of his lower-class birth a secret? Can he be the best biographer for a rediscovered feminist writer from Oxford, her papers left to his mother? Kate admires his lively chatter and company, the manners if not the man, but slowly other matters intrude—just as they do upon Kate's Anglophiliac and nostalgic celebration of Oxford and England: "the hub of the scholar's universe," with which she had been "besotted . . . all her life" begins to reveal its true, anti-female colors (129, 86). As does Max despite the Noel-Coward-like urbanity and civilized demeanor: "Who would want for a mother, however goddesslike, a feminist, a freethinker, a socialist, and a pacifist? It's everything I loathe" (181). Appalled at student behavior, he rails, "It's all because of a lack of discipline, student rioting, a loss of all values," to which Kate thinks coolly, "That's just what Nixon would have said" (119). The facts of Max's misogyny leads to the solution of the mystery.

In *The Question of Max* we can see the development of Heilbrun's textual web with its series of lively conversations, asides, and apparent tangents. Her interest in early British female writers opens up new possibilities in her plots and concerns, paralleling similar issues of the present day. The duplicitous and clever mystery itself plays directly upon conflicts of interest, biographers and scholars, men and women. In traditional detective stories, Kate muses, "the detective would set out to discover. All sorts of other things would then happen, leading to one suspected criminal after another, not to mention other murders, attempted or achieved" (117). This suggests the mysteries of Dick Francis to Kate, the more typically masculine trajectory of the formula. In this, Heilbrun's fifth mystery, she begins to create her own patterns, pausing to create the web of interlaced lives and often dangerous crosscurrents as opposed to the bipolar wars of the past.

All of this comes to a head in Heilbrun's next novel, the one that won the Nero Wolfe Award for Mystery Fiction in 1981, *Death in a Tenured Position*. Just before this in 1979 she had published the more academic *Reinventing Womanhood,* a treatise on the creation of characters in women's fiction, on the search for models, including her own revealing autobiographical search, on marriage and the family, the claims of women and a marvelous re-interpretation of the Oresteia. In the latter, which she describes as "the great misogynist tragedy" (*Reinventing* 153), she claims that the overthrow of Clytemnestra is not the overthrow of woman or parent but the overthrow of motherhood as an institution: "Its establishment as an institution, must be demythologized and ritually destroyed" (154). Motherhood as institution suggests the male control of childbirth: "Orestes, in the Greek version, murdered motherhood to destroy what he feared would be female domination. A female Orestes today must undergo the same rite. . . . The male destruction of the mother must now be reenacted by the female, not for the assumption of dominance, but rather for the sake of equality" (162, 163). The institution and all its social and gender stereotypes must be "done in" by a new belief in the powers of the individual, female as well as male, and the Furies "transformed into the defenders of a new order, where individuals are more kindly and institutions of kinship less inevitable" (158). It doesn't really matter if we accept Heilbrun's argument or not, but it does display her new concern about the capacity of all kinds of institutions, social and cultural as well as academic, to coerce, sabotage, and overwhelm the individual androgynous spirit.

In *Death in a Tenured Position* Heilbrun takes on Harvard, the outgrowth of St. Anthony's and Oxford, the all-male bastion of privilege and power—the title itself betrays Heilbrun's rising sense of anger and coercion—amid the welter of racism and sexism and the death of yet another reactionary curmudgeon, Professor Canfield Adams. At Harvard a woman's place is definitely in the attic. "Warren House . . . spoke loudly of long-held power and patriarchal attitudes. . . . Harvard's general attitudes toward women were not badly represented by this room" (*Death* 27), Kate concludes, having come to Harvard to solve the apparent murder of the recently hired token feminist, Janet Mendelbaum. Kate recognizes how much of a token woman she has become, sitting on committees at her own university. Here lurk Allen Adam Clarkville, a milder version but of the same ilk as Clemance, Cudlipp, and Max: "Our chairman is not exactly amenable to the idea of women's studies" (*Death* 138). And student Howard Falkland who helps precipitate the catastrophe: "So you've got me trapped in a room of women's libbers. . . . I hate lesbians. . . . [They] blamed men for everything that was lousy in the world, and I lit into her. These women horrify me" (114, 117). Agreeing with the brother of the dead victim, Janet Mandelbaum, Howard Falkland in all his Midwestern self-assurance declares, "I'm all in favor of women working, of course, provided they put their homes and children first. . . . Janet wasn't made for marriage . . . and then when she got married she went and married a Jew. Not that we have anything against Jews, but after all, it does show something" (122, 123). True, Andrew Sladovski represents the more liberal, open-minded professor, and "Moon" Mandelbaum, Janet's brother and a former lover of Kate's, in his laid-back

Sixties appearance has a wider view of circumstances, but these two are outnumbered by the claustrophobic bastion of Harvard Yard.

Into this maelstrom of masculine mores comes Janet Needham Mandelbaum, an excellent scholar who thinks she has been given a position at Harvard because of her scholarship. To her shock and dismay she learns all too quickly that she has been selected to be the token woman to run the Women's Study program, a sop to political correctness. She herself is essentially an "honorary male," one who believes firmly in her own individual success as distinct from any female movement or solidarity, "telling herself that any woman with qualifications could make it" (*Death* 49): "She thought of herself as a full-fledged member of the brotherhood of professors, males all." Adds Kate grimly, "I think she died for that" (82). She refuses to teach Women's Studies, "scared to death of being unconventional but seething underneath" (33). Her death highlights the many facets of feminism; had she been a feminist, she wouldn't have died but, of course, had she been a feminist, Harvard wouldn't have hired her.

Maureen Reddy has clearly described the ramifications of feminism in the novel, arguing that "this novel fictionally works out the theoretical heart of *Reinventing Womanhood* by setting a woman who consents to be a token woman (an honorary man) against both women who refuse to participate in the male world and women who achieve in the male world while bonding with and supporting other women" (64). As an imitation of a man, Janet's failure has proved fatal. The entire mystery reveals the dangers of her position. Avoiding men, as the lesbian cooperative chooses to do, remains possible but ineffective. Kate cooperates with patriarchal institutions and bonds with other women,[4] but at the same time she and her friend Sylvia wonder about other ramifications of feminism in general. Sylvia, for instance, attacks Joan Didion's feminism as a "particularly narrow and cracked determinism [in opposition] to those of us who remain committed mainly to the exploration of moral distinctions and ambiguities" (*Death* 63-64). Kate's visit with the sisterhood at the "Maybe Next Time Coffee House" in Cambridge prompts her own concerns about the with-us-or-against-us mentality of the lesbian group: "Being here, one defined oneself too sharply: either one was an observer from the outside, automatically 'other,' or else one qualified to be a member of the club, which limited one in a different way" (*Death* 66). All of these perspectives of feminist issues are not as simple as they might first appear to be,[5] but here she has begun that expansion of them with her inclusion of Janet's perceptions, the lesbians' perception of events (and their being set up and used by ruthless male academics), and Kate's own musings about feminism, Harvard, and the direction of both.[6]

The critical response to *Death* proves interesting. Jean White delights in Cross' "wicked fun with Harvard's entrenched male establishment" and her "not espousing militant feminism" (256). But Katha Pollitt describes her as "a better feminist than mystery novelist" (257). And John Leonard refers to the novel as "a good mystery and a very angry book. . . . the mood is generally bitter; Miss Cross seeks less to entertain than to revile. She not only makes her point, she also hammers on it, leaving a nail in our skulls" (256). Heilbrun suggests a much wider and more personal approach in that "it occurs to me now that as we age many of us who are privileged . . . are in danger of choosing to stay right where we are, to undertake each day's routine, and to listen to our arteries hardening. I do not believe that death should be allowed to find us seated comfortably in our tenured positions" (*Life* 130-31). Near the conclusion of the book, at the 1979 Harvard Commencement Exercises, Kate is reminded of a Commencement of 1969 in which a law student spoke out about the necessity for law and order: " 'The streets of our country are in turmoil. The universities are filled with students rebelling and rioting. . . . And the republic is in danger. . . . Without law and order our nation cannot survive.' After wild applause, the law student continued: 'Those words were spoken in 1932 by Adolf Hitler.' Kate would have given a great deal to have heard the silence that followed" (*Death* 162-63).

Heilbrun's focus with all of its feminist perspectives and complications coincides with Fansler's "morbid fascination with institutions, the army, the church, the prestigious universities, they are so implacable. I can't take my eyes off them" (*Death* 58). And from such a perspective even the institutionalization of feminism may be suspect. Kate's developing feminism is still coupled with her wariness about an either/or position that in a novel seems far more plausible than it might appear to be in an ideological discussion or analysis. Heilbrun's moral discriminations, though muted in her mysteries, nevertheless take into account the possible injustices of choosing sides too vehemently. Rebellion in the academy is finally a good thing, but exclusionary power politics can only result in the further institutionalization of rigid positions. Perhaps Heilbun's feminism and Fansler's will never ultimately satisfy the feminist ideologue because of those distinctions. It may be contradictory, but it also may be truer to experiences in everyday life than in ideological battles. The personal and the political in Heilbrun's own life are complexly interwoven, and her choices may indicate the price of each and the continuing development of both.

The unresolved issues brought out into the open in *Death in a Tenured Position* energize both the novel and the issues themselves. "The fact is," Kate exclaims, "women, at least around here, live in a never-never land, not certain where they belong, where their allegiances lie, not even what their hopes are" (63). Janet Mandelbaum desired "to be a collaborator with destiny. She wanted to fill some marvelous role that had been set out for her by God Almighty" (147). It is this unsettled vision with her sense of personal despair and suicidal agonies that Heilbrun continues to pursue and in doing so enlarges the mystery formula with her concerns, contradictions, and conversations. This territory may reveal and make use of the truly androgynous dilemmas of the human condition. As Gertrude Stein once wrote, an epigraph Heilbrun uses at the beginning of chapter one, "Disillusionment in living is the finding out nobody agrees with you" (*Death* 4). Heilbrun quotes Samuel Johnson at the beginning of chapter six: "Inconsistencies cannot both be right, but imputed to man they may both be true" (61).

Both *Sweet Death, Kind Death* and *No Word from Winifred* are rich, multi-layered mysteries, enriched by the journals of the murdered Patrice Umphelby in the first and the journals of the missing Winifred Ashby in the second. Both explore the depths of feminism and anti-feminism, the first at Clare College, a women's college in western Massachusetts that remains staunchly single-sex and antifeminist, the second in the broader world of women's friendships as a threat to the male-female dynamic and the world of Oxford in long-ago summers which reveals the limitations of boy-girl gender roles. Both explore the roles of biographers and biographies, approaches and conceits, strategies and angles which raise all kinds of complex questions. In the former Umphelby writes about the need at age fifty-eight to reinvent oneself, particularly in a world when older women might as well be invisible. And in the latter Heilbrun continues to search for plots that women writers and characters can create, even though at times more ardent feminists may feel that she is only feminizing the male quest. In both the mysteries are tied in directly with the issues, a further reflection of Heilbrun's increasing skills and power as a writer.

"When she realized she would be alone, she threw away every assumption she had learned and began at zero. . . . Then she tackled the problem of trying to decide how she wanted to live." This quotation by Toni Morrison in *Song of Solomon* begins the third chapter of *Sweet Death, Kind Death*. After reading Umphelby's journals Kate is reminded of "a motto of Isak Dinesen's Patrice liked: 'It is necessary to sail; it is not necessary to live'" (*Sweet* 100). At fifty-eight Umphelby seems obsessed with death and may have killed herself by walking into a lake at Clare College, but her true interest, which Kate divines, is in self-creation, re-creating a self to steer by, an issue close to Heilbrun's heart who coincidentally was the same age as Umphelby when the novel was published. Umphelby clings to no false nostalgia about her past and, in wrestling with the inevitability of death, tries to find a reason for moving on, curious as to "how death gave intensity to middle age as passion and hope gave intensity to youth" (*Sweet* 25). Her identity crisis pitches her forward not into resignation—or the lake—but into discovering the possibilities of growth, of life's intenser moments yet to come: "If only I were artist enough to convey the incredible sense of possibility I feel, of wonder. . . . What do I want now? Only to be gloriously fifty-eight, and to write if I am so blessed" (97, 98). Kate realizes in such lines lie no resignation or suicidal impulse.

When Kate is brought to join a Gender Studies task force at Clare, she recognizes how many patriarchal attitudes and values still thrive, even if Clare is a women's college: "If women's colleges aren't concerned with women's advocacy, what are they doing, except protecting the male idea of womanhood?" (147). Her concern about Umphelby's death leads her into a fascinating conversation with the deceased's daughter, Dr. Sarah Umphelby, who acknowledges how difficult it was for mother and daughter to come to terms with one another. Muses the doctor, "She didn't understand, I think, the effect of just her presence, of her slightest word" (94). The woman who thinks Umphelby might have been murdered turns out to be Veronica Manfred, a self-proclaimed virgin, who once sued Umphelby over the co-authorship of a book. The two men writing her biography, the witty and seemingly frivolous Archer and the more dour and earnest Herbert, cannot decide whether or not Umphelby was suicidal or a saint or both. Kate wonders what it would have been like to have a mother like Patrice, a full-grown daughter like Sarah, thus wandering more deeply into the interrelationships between women, between youth and age, and into the realm of the detective story in which "the discourse focuses on the bringing to light of a crucial event, identified as a reality which determines significance" (111).

Heilbrun broods intelligently within this novel, worrying the details of and approaches to biography, age, detection, and death. Kate realizes that "it is in the telling, more exactly in the writing down, the language, the ordering of events together with the way those events are expressed that constitutes authorship" (78). And she also understands the problems with writing biographies: "We never know it all; we only make up stories about it, and sometimes our characters seem fully developed; but they have only fooled us again. And if we call ourselves biographers, we call the stories and the characters we have invented biography" (96). Kate identifies wholly with this process, which obviously reflects and parallels Heilbrun's own and embellishes her sense of writing mysteries with a deeper social awareness and more troubling focus. The mystery's solution involves the various life cycles with which the novel is fascinated and results in a tightly knit tale. But we are left with more complex issues, expressed most precisely here in Heilbrun's epigraph to chapter nine from Ralph Waldo Emerson: "In silence we must wrap much of our life, because it is too fine for speech, because also we cannot explain it to others, and because somewhat we cannot yet understand" (93).

These same concerns emerge again in *No Word from Winifred,* products no doubt of Heilbrun's more academic book, *Writing a Woman's Life,* published two years after this mystery, and in which Heilbrun deals with her own musings on the need for women's narratives and the invention of Amanda Cross. In that 1988 book Heilbrun recognizes her need "to create a [psychic] space for myself" (*Life* 113) and discover new stories for women, along with the development of Kate Fansler in more outspoken feminist terms. Heilbrun admires the confessional poetry of such women as Sylvia Plath, Madeline Kumin, and Adrienne Rich: "They thought of women as 'we'" (*Life* 72), and at the same time praises Toni Morrison's remark that "Friendship between women is special, different, and has never been depicted as the major focus of a novel before *Sula*" (*Life* 75).

Winifred Ashby confronts such issues in her journals, in her chosen solitary life on a farm, in her developing interest in the works and life of the writer Charlotte Stanton, yet another of Heilbrun's Oxford-educated authors. At the same time she becomes sexually involved with a married man and develops an intimate friendship with his wife, a relationship the man cannot stand, since it seems to be a threat to his autonomy. He then advises her to leave the country. "It was Winifred I felt betrayed by," Martin Heffenreffer, the husband, admits. "She was a spy in the enemy country" (*Winifred* 244). Stanton wrote novels about Greece in which men were prominently featured. They are "on the whole idealized, harsh fighters but loving, with intense loyalties to one another" (129). Is this merely a betrayal of her sex, as Winifred's betrayal of Heffenreffer is supposedly of men in general? Kate zeroes in on the problem: "It may be that . . . she had despaired of women . . . insist[ing] on centering their lives on trivialities, domestic virtues, and the admiration of men. . . . Why struggle with female characters and love plots, when you can write of everything else if you will only write of men?" (129). Winifred seems trapped in a male-centered plot, and flight is her only way of dealing with it. The crime lies in the system, not in the soul.

What Heilbrun explores alternatively in warm detail is the very real friendship that can develop among women: Winifred's with Stanton's old friend, eighty-year-old Harriet St. John Meriweather, who still lives in England; Winifred's friendship with Mary Louise "Biddy" Heffenreffer, her lover's wife; Kate's with Biddy's, and Kate's with her Watson-like ally, her niece Leighton. All these friendships cross generational and international lines. "We—women, I mean—are beginning to tell each other about things," Kate discovers, "and we have to find the language; it's not always easy, the words have been overused for other purposes" (196). Biddy is convinced that what bothered Winifred most about the complicated relationship—the husband's lover, his wife's best friend—"was that it was a situation there weren't any stories about; we didn't have any rules to go by; it was a new game. . . . I haven't got the right language for it, and I didn't then either" (197). The web of female relationships replaces the war between autonomous male egos.

This is precisely what Heilbrun has achieved in these two mysteries. Kate is not the ultimate authority, though she guides the reader through the voices and the evidence and the texts. Social issues expand the focus of the investigation-interviews-solution form of the mystery. The several voices—biographers, at times competing biographers, letters, journals—increase the depth of these issues and reveal subtexts and undercurrents that fascinate and reverberate long after the mystery is solved. Heilbrun, like Kate at committee meetings, wishes to leave "space for the routine out of which meaning grows" (*Winifred* 204), and when her niece Leighton asks her if she has been treating Winifred's life as a text—we have the journals to peruse—Kate responds, "I wouldn't put it so grandly . . . but yes, that is what I'm doing" (227). The liberating effects this has on Heilbrun as a writer are apparent. Kate recognizes the fact that "most people like to fit things into stories they already know; it makes them feel a bigger part of life than they are. Writers do this more than most people" (35). Heilbrun would, of course, agree in her use of the mystery formula. But in these two mysteries she enlarges her scope and unfolds newer possibilities. The layers and levels of the text overlap and unfurl, as characters and author celebrate the need for women to escape the separation of each from the other in separate homes and discover the need to talk to one another. Kate gets it right: "We have a friendship between women, each involved with the same man, and not acting like Cinderella's stepsisters. There's a new story for you" (206).

All of this culminates in Heilbrun's masterpiece to date, *The Players Come Again* (1990). By now feminism is so deeply ingrained in her consciousness that it needs no introduction or explanation. It permeates the tale. In this mystery the complexity of family trees, relationships between male and female writers, friendships between women as opposed to the sexually exploitative relationships between men and women, the origins of literary modernism and patriarchal Greek myths: all of these reinforce and interpenetrate one another in the hands of an author so certain of her craft that the whole thing seems seamless and effortless. Veils are lifted, disputed origins exposed, assumptions uprooted, and timeworn myths are discredited, all within the confines of a (more or less) formulaic mystery. The feminist web emerges triumphant.

The levels and layers tantalize and spill over effortlessly into one another. First of all family and its interconnections take precedence over the more elaborate plots of writers such as Hillerman and Burke. In doing so Heilbrun invests her tale with greater personal stakes and attitudes for her characters. Emotional ties and female bonding occupy center stage as old family myths are exposed for their inaccuracies. Warm relationships transcend the harsher, more businesslike confrontations of the male mystery. Secondly Heilbrun explores and exploits the pop-fiction glamor of romance and flight in her Romeo-and-Juliet tale about Gabrielle Howard and Emmanuel Foxx. Emmanuel Foxx, celebrated modernist icon, has written one of the most heralded modernist novels, *Ariadne,* in which a modern-day woman reveals her own secrets and longings, the narrative carefully paralleling and playing off of ancient Greek myths (one thinks of Joyce, Eliot, and Faulkner). At the same time it is discovered that Gabrielle has written her own novel, a "counter-novel" that questions the veracity of that myth and the modernist mythic methods that her husband has used. And finally Heilbrun investigates Greek myths themselves, speculating about how they have set the tone of western civilization for years and wondering if, indeed, there are different ways to examine such myths and invest them with meaning.

The story begins straightforwardly. Simon Pearlstine invites Kate Fansler to consider writing a biography of Gabrielle Foxx, wife of the famous Emmanuel, author of *Ariadne* in 1927. Mark Hansford has written a biography on Emmanuel, complete with photographs that Dorinda Goddard Nicholson possessed and some by the yet unknown Anne Gringold. Pearlstine owns Gringold's memoirs, which he had purchased from her, and she owns the rights to Gabrielle's papers. The memoirs make up the second part of the novel.

The patriarchal family tree is fairly straightforward as well. In 1905 Gabrielle Howard, daughter of a wealthy father in England, at the age of sixteen first sees Emmanuel Foxx and falls in love with him. Fleeing from England to Paris with her lover, already pregnant with Emmanuel's child, their son Emile, she is disowned by her family. Emile later marries Hilda Goddard, who gives birth to their daughter Nellie. Hilda turns out to be a rich, spoiled and promiscuous woman who eventually goes mad. We also learn from Gringold's chatty and romantic memoir, from a girl who is "quiet, unobtrusive, observant, full of longing" (*Players* 32), that

Hilda had a brother named Sig who wed his secretary Eleanor and that they had a daughter, Dorrinda Goddard. Anne Gringold's life in her own eyes is "more like a romance than a realistic biography" (67), and she envisions Gabrielle and Emmanuel as fated lovers such as Romeo and Juliet had been. Adopted by the Goddards and with her mother as the housekeeper in their home, she immerses herself in descriptions of the glamorous Goddards on the New Jersey shore, the "Jewish Newport" of its day in the Thirties and Forties. She spins yarns about rich, spoiled, adventurous Dorrinda, of Nellie Foxx coming to live with them to escape the war in 1941, and of the three girls' romantic yearnings and comraderie. The Goddards pay for Gabrielle's upkeep after Foxx's death in 1942, while Emile heroically disappears into the Resistance in 1944.

In 1955 Anne, twenty-nine, finally meets Gabrielle, sixty-six, in England and finds papers lying everywhere. Gabrielle had written several letters to Foxx about her sexual fantasies, but the next day she's taken ill and bequeaths all her papers to Anne for safe-keeping. Though a romantic at heart, Anne sees herself as sensible and conservative, along the lines of Eleanor Goddard, both working-class women who have survived intact, and juxtaposes the richer, more glamorous lives and loves of the Goddards and the Foxxs against the paltriness of her own.

Kate interviews Mark Hansford, Foxx's biographer, and finds him a self-satisfied male chauvinist whose wife Judith tells her that she thinks Gabrielle wrote most of Foxx's famous novel. Slowly Kate is drawn into the family conspiracies and secrets by interviewing ninety-two-year-old Eleanor, whom she admires immediately, and Dorinda, long wed to a dull surgeon having given up her escapades long ago, although she did have a sexual fling with Hansford. Working together Nellie, Anne, and Dorinda set Kate up to write the biography or prepare an edition of Gabrielle's letters. They also agree to sell Anne's memoirs to Pearlstine. Kate and Anne team up together in London and go through Gabrielle's papers, discovering as they do another *Ariadne,* the subversive counterpart to Foxx's original book. In the end Kate decides to edit Gabrielle's novel, which Pearlstine will publish, and keep all the revelations she has stumbled upon a secret.

This tale, necessarily elaborated here to reveal its basically straightforward manner and presentation, is completely false. So is the family tree. What Kate discovers is that Nellie is really the daughter of Emmanuel and Hilda; Hilda had seduced and married son Emile both for revenge against his father and as a cover-up for her true passion for the older man. Anne is really the daughter of Sig Goddard who had an affair with her self-effacing housekeeper-mother. Thus, the female relatives are much closer than first imagined: Nellie and Anne are first cousins, Nellie and Dorinda are also first cousins, and Anne and Dorinda are half-sisters. Theirs is a friendship and companionship based on genuine love for one another and long hidden blood ties. The legitimate patriarchal lineage may be complexly compromised—male passion demands an outlet; even Dorinda's grandfather, old man Goddard who made the family fortune, tries to seduce his granddaughter—but the strength of the first-cousins-half-sisters axis is unmistakeable and triumphant. Emmanuel is compared to a sex-crazed genius like Rodin or Augustus John, Emile becomes a weak alcoholic, Gabrielle's father cuts her off without a cent when she runs off to Paris, and Anne's publisher-boss in London is an adulterer. Despite all of that, however, Anne, Nellie, and Dorinda discover one another, feel as if they all have had a second chance at life despite their obvious setbacks, and come to realize, as Kate does, that "it all seems to go to prove how little difference fathers make." "Except to the fathers," Anne adds (*Players* 159).

Gabrielle Foxx's *Ariadne* contradicts and subverts Emmanuel's *Ariadne,* as her perspective on the original Greek myth undermines the traditional interpretations of it. At the heart of literary modernism lies "man's fascination and obsession with woman, as well as his terror of her newly empowered voice" (14). Emmanuel's "heightened prose describing sexual experiences" (38), itself another facet of modernism, also differentiates his heroine "from Joyce's Molly Bloom by her high intelligence, her allegiance to her women friends, her ambivalence toward men . . . and her sexual attraction to women" (29). And like Eliot and Joyce before him, Foxx relied upon the knowledge of Greek myths to shape and empower his story of a single year in a young woman's life, "only Foxx had decided to put his woman in the middle, to make her consciousness the center of his masterpiece" (123). Gabrielle's novel threatens to expose "the whole masculine bias of high modernism. . . . it will bring gender to the foreground of what had previously been a rather reactionary and male literary period" (208, 216). The revelations of the true nature of the Foxx and Goddard lineage not only reflect the actual origins and designs of modernism but also reveal the problematic status of Emmanuel's and Edith Hamilton's interpretations of Greek myth. And at the center for Emmanuel and the rest, "Gabrielle . . . remained this enigma . . . of this great phenomenon of high modernism. Surely she had a right to be heard" (145). Lest we misunderstand the direction of Heilbrun's unveilings, she reminds us that "T. S. Eliot took his wife's very words and phrasing in *The Waste Land*" (92).

Gabrielle Foxx's *Ariadne* speculates that the Minoan civilization and religion on Crete, defeated by the Greeks, was essentially matriarchal. Luxury and delight took precedence over weapons, as goddesses did over gods. The Greeks introduced walled cities before which there were none on Crete. The labrys, the famous double axe, was also the symbolic weapon of the Minoan Mother Goddess, and the labyrinth in the tale of Theseus, Ariadne, and the Minotaur, the palace at Knossos, forms a double ax. This newer, highly speculative myth—after all Cross is writing fiction not anthropology and is the first to acknowledge that there is no evidence to prove the matriarchal basis of Minoan culture— pits a hostile, violent, and patriarchal Greek culture against the athletic artistry and gentleness of the Minoan. Therefore the reason the patriar- chal Greek myths survived in their particular form was a direct result of the Greeks conquering Crete.

Heilbrun skewers the traditional interpretation of the myth. As you look back into these mythic tales, you find that reinterpretation is indeed possible, as Heilbrun herself has reinterpreted the anti-motherhood-as- institution designs in the *Oresteia* as opposed to the traditional anti- female response. In the traditional myth Theseus is the great Athenian hero. Before his particular feats in this phase of the Ariadne myth, Minos, the king of Crete, had sent his son Androgeus to kill a bull in King Aegeus' (Theseus' father's) kingdom, but the bull killed him. Minos invaded, captured Athens, and demanded tribute, which included the contract that every nine years Aegeus would send to Crete seven maidens and seven youths to feed the terrible Minotaur. The Minotaur is the offspring of Minos's wife Pasiphae and the white bull that Poseidon had given to Minos to be sacrificed to him (Poseidon). Minos instead had kept it, so Poseidon made Pasiphae fall in love with it. Daedalus, the great architect, built the labyrinth to house the Minotaur, hence the nine- year sacrifices. Brave Theseus offers to be one of the seven youths, Minos' daughter Ariadne falls in love with him the minute she lays eyes on him—Gabrielle and Emmanuel?—and extracts from him a promise to marry her and take her away to Athens, if she rescues him.

Notice: the men and the male gods control events: Minos demands tribute, Theseus offers himself up as a heroic sacrifice, poor Androgeus though heroic dies, and Poseidon manipulates his revenge. The women are mere victims of their own passions or male manipulations of those passions, either in Ariadne's case exploding from within, or in Pasi- phae's directed from without by Poseidon. It is a decidedly male version of events which Heilbrun underlines: "Women longed to help men, to be loved by them, to be carried off to ancillary destinies" (*Players* 124). Ariadne's fatal love for Theseus foreshadows Phaedre's for Hippolytus. Emmanuel Foxx believed "that Theseus had deserted her because her powers frightened him, or because he recognized Dionysus as having a greater right to Ariadne" (124). In doing so Ariadne's lover becomes a combination of Theseus, Dionysus, and by analogy Emmanuel Foxx. In fact Foxx names his daughter (Nellie) Artemisia, the name he chose to call his Ariadne in his novel. In all of this "all women contrived their own passions, and all men used them for their own ends" (124).

After Theseus pummels the Minotaur to death and escapes with Ariadne, he mysteriously deserts her on the island of Dia or Naxos where she is found and comforted by Dionysus. Questions remain about why and how this happened. Did Dionysus abscond with her? Did she become seasick? Did a violent wind carry Theseus away, and when he returned did he find her dead on Naxos? Did the god Bacchus command Theseus to abandon her on Naxos? Did Theseus just forget her, his triumph complete? Later Theseus marries Phaedra, Ariadne's sister, who fell hopelessly in love with Theseus's son Hippolytus whose mother was the Amazon Hippolyta. Phaedra's old nurse discovers all and tells Hippolytus, after which he exclaims, "Oh, women, vile women—every one of them vile,"[7] Phaedra kills herself, leaves a note behind suggesting that Hippolytus did her in, Theseus reads the note, and exiles Hippolytus who then rushes off in a chariot which crashes when a monster rises from the sea. In another account of the ending of the tale, a bull rises from the sea, Hippolytus gets caught in the reins of his chariot, and is dragged to his death.

Gabrielle's assessment of all of this is that Ariadne was no unsuspecting maiden deluded by her love for Theseus to be dumped when he should decide to desert her but a calculating and powerful individual who knew the Greeks would sooner or later destroy Crete, foresaw Icarus's death as a prophecy that Greek men would be self-destructive, and accepted Daedalus's ploy to let Theseus think that he has conquered her because she lusted for him. "Once on the ship, [Ariadne] must sufficiently horrify [Theseus] to force him to put her ashore at Dia, a Cretan island, where Dionysus would come to her rescue and assure her survival and her eventual return" (205). She decides at the last to stay on Dia/Naxos because it represents the furthest limits of Cretan culture, and should she stray beyond that point, she would lose her priestly powers. She would then allow Phaedra to cause Thesus to kill his son, Hippolytus, to avenge Hippolyta. In this reinterpretation of the myth the women are as equally manipulative as the men and can fool them as easily. From such a perspective Theseus did not forget to hoist the white sail on his ship when returning to Athens to signal his father Aegeus that he had triumphed over the Minotaur. Rather he had planned to forget to change the sail, thus leaving the black sail in place, which Aegeus spied and presuming his son dead, leapt to his own death in the sea. Thus did the perfidious Theseus become king.

Emmanuel Foxx has thus usurped the traditional trajectory of patriarchal Greek myths and pointedly ignored his wife Gabrielle both in terms of her assistance with his novel—the letters of her sexual fantasies and her conversations with him—and in terms of her own artistic endeavors. She has been as summarily effaced as have the matriarchal Minoans by the patriarchal Greeks. And therefore, for example, "the whole story about Pasiphae was just another male version of making women either monsters of lust or pure queens of heaven" (192). Only Theseus kills the half-bull Minotaur. The man-hero slays the earth-god, and thus Theseus comes to represent "a self-moving power greater than the force of any earthbound serpent destiny . . . a protest against the worship of Earth and the demons of the fertility of earth" (Campbell 24). Thus did the Greeks conquer Crete, Emmanuel conquer Gabrielle in the publishing world, and romance as pop-fiction for a time conquer the true tales of the Foxxes and the Goddards. And thus does Heilbrun use speculative feminist myths to subvert and discredit the accepted ones, as her own feminist strategies subtly and skillfully undermine the male mystery formula. No wonder Gabrielle felt that "the time for the revival of the Micean civilization" was at hand (205). Which, of course, empowers Kate, underscores the comraderie of Anne, Nellie, and Dorinda, and helps transform the originally spoiled sexual adventuress and later conventionally wed and imprisoned Dorinda into a fully realized human being, slowly emerging from "a dreaming sleep . . . disguised as sex object, mother, hostess [and] housewife" (224). As Dorinda discovers about the entire process of female restoration and recovery in the book, as women, "We got back in touch, we began to talk, we rekindled our friendship" (224). Thus the three co-conspirators have worked on Kate "to revive Gabrielle without reviving her as wife and mother: on her own, you might say" (164).

As Kate discovers in talking with Dorinda, Anne, and Nellie, "Each of you seems to have a cover story, and when that is removed, there's another story underneath" (164). Heilbrun as Amanda Cross punctures all the cover stories and veils ingeniously to reveal countless possibilities. The spy operation engineered by Dorinda, Anne, and Nellie snares Kate and restores Gabrielle's manuscript. That manuscript undermines Emmanuel's long-celebrated tome. Reinterpretations of traditional myths, upon which much of literary modernism and Emmanuel's novel were based, reveal a possible feminist perspective. The linear surface of the typical mystery, the war at its polarized core, has been peeled back to reveal the true web and revelations within it.

The only loose end is the almost gratuitous revelation that Emile had poisoned his father and survived to re-marry in France. Kate comes upon this circumstance with no prior warning. Though Gabrielle supposedly told Anne in 1955, and it would make sense because of what happened to Hilda, still this last disclosure appears awkward and unnecessary. In this instance only, it seems as if Heilbrun insisted on one more "regulation" revelation to satisfy the mystery formula.

In her review of *The Players Come Again,* Antonia Fraser praises Heilbrun's skill and tales within tales and adds, "Ms. Cross, in allowing Fansler her own logical development from 1964, has managed to chronicle the history of women . . . and women's education in the United States since the 1960's . . . in the most accessible way as well as to provide volumes of literate, witty entertainment." In doing so she has created her own kind of mystery (36).

An Imperfect Spy (1995), while eminently readable, reveals a falling away from the labyrinthine powers of *Players*. Battered women's syndrome and the death of a woman, clearly a victim of the all-male institution that is Schuyler Law School, are feminist subjects, but they tend to overwhelm the machinations of mystery in the novel. The battered woman, Betty Osborne, imprisoned for murdering her husband, realizes at last that women cannot submit to victimization, which she finds embodied in Thomas Hardy's Tess of the d'Urbervilles, from his novel of the same name, her example of the woman who is destroyed by the male circumstances and decisions that have tragically engulfed her: "Tess was a victim because she never thought about escaping. . . . what I thought is maybe I should think of ways to escape" (*Spy* 189). Kate's and Reed's infiltration of Schuyler is wittily conceived and smoothly executed, but issues override the mystery. Still there is much to admire here, including the exploration and reinvigoration of Kate's and Reed's long and successful marriage, the wonderfully believable character of Harriet Furst, the imperfect spy of the title, an older woman working undercover at the school toward her own ends, and Heilbrun's sharp observations of a patriarchal institution's power structure.

An Imperfect Spy allows Heilbrun to pay tribute to one of her favorite authors, John Le Carré, and reflect about the art of spying, its governmental status and "dirty frame of mind" as opposed to the "disenchanted romantics," Kate and Reed (214, 226). In doing so she has once again re-invented the mystery formula, which, like marriage, reveals its best side when "everything is debatable and challenged; nothing is turned into law or policy" (*Life* 95). She clearly agrees with the epigraph to chapter nine in LeCarré's book: "I invested my life in institutions—he thought without rancor—and all I am left with is myself" (*Spy* 166).

That has always been true of Heilbrun as well in her concern with the androgynous self at the heart of all institutional considerations and confrontations, however necessarily feminist its declared principles. Hers has been a feminist art with a human soul, realizing as we all must that "we live our lives through texts" (*Life* 37). And thus, Le Carré in the epigraph to chapter eight: "So it went on, one argument predicating another, until the only logic was the fiction, and the fiction was a web that enmeshed everyone who tried to sweep it away" (*Spy* 148). Within that fictional web Kate lives and thrives, recognizing as Heilbrun does, that "we have to make myths of our lives. It is the only way to live without despair."[8]

Several feminist critics think that Heilbrun has surrendered too much of the feminist perspective in her creation of Kate Fansler and in accommodating her too readily to the mystery formula. Fansler, however, does develop throughout the novels into a more outspoken feminist, so much so that at times the issues override the calculations and machinations of the plot. The pattern imprisons her in many ways, but at the same time it allows her to grow, comment on gender relations in general, and act on her beliefs in trying to correct the still male-oriented world she inhabits. She is no revolutionary, but she is empowered within the conventional mystery, and that formula does respond to her concerns, her concerted networking among women, and her consistent assault on conventional gender values. For the most part and in her best work, Heilbrun manages to achieve a balance between the two. She uses the formula to provoke very real issues and in doing so alters a popular literary pattern to make room for her way of thinking.

Epilogue: The Puzzled Heart

In *The Puzzled Heart* (1998) Cross sets up a marvelous and timely scenario: Kate's husband Reed has been kidnapped by a right-wing group that wants her to publish an article renouncing her feminist views. Kate is both appalled and terrified. She opposes the promulgation of "all the old family values and old-time morals, which mostly add up to supporting the rich, the male, and the white, though that's probably not the right order" (44) and at the same time acknowledges, "We walk in fear, while the radical right trumpets its lies and delusions. Someone has to do something" (88).

Cross' plot involves a St. Bernard named Bancroft or Banny, an attempt to seduce Reed for possible photos and videos, a daring rescue, a murder, and a convoluted but clever resolution of the mystery. Harriet Furst, a kind of alter-ego for her creator from *An Imperfect Spy,* returns as a private eye in league with Toni Giomatti, her younger partner. As Toni explains, "Harriet can go on being the invisible old lady who can get in anywhere, and I'll go on being the sexpot who uses the magician's trick of making you watch one hand while the necessary business is accomplished by the other" (95), a description which proves to be more than prophetic.

Kate runs into several colorful characters as well, with their diverse opinions, not to mention her own witty asides on Hitler, John Grisham, Garrison Keiller, "Thelma and Louise," Ronald Reagan, William Bennett, Philip Larkin, *Little Women,* Gore Vidal and Edith Wharton. "Moon" Mandelbaum returns as a sympathetic hippie friend and former lover from the Sixties who becomes involved in a plot to halt one of Kate's wealthy brothers from marrying a golddigger. Morton Weldon is a self-declared gay student who has been sent bullets; Emma Wentworth is a law professor whom Kate responds to immediately—"She wore a dress, fitted on top and at the waist, but with a full skirt, a dress that said: I'm wearing a dress, but I am not wearing a power suit" (114); and Nathan Rosen is a professor who worries that Kate may be anti-Semitic, which leads to yet another glimpse of her view of the world. When Rosen asks her of whom she'd be more afraid on the New York subway, "a group of adolescent black males [or] a group of guys from a yeshiva," Kate responds, "Right at that moment, the group of black males is likelier than the group of Orthodox Jewish males to frighten or even molest me. But in the long run, I fear the boys from the yeshiva more" (126, 127). And her reason? "Do I really have to pretend to admire fundamentalist Jews any more than fundamentalist Muslims or the Christian right?" (128).

Reed's kidnapping has rendered Kate strangely passive and helpless. Others refer to her "zombie state" (33) and "mental stagnation" (136). She herself is stymied by the fact that "she was out of control; nothing she might do, at least nothing that occured to her at this time, could alter these events. Regret joined with powerlessness induces despair" (152). She realizes that "to be paralyzed as I was, to be stricken into such passivity, that was terrifying" (90) but recognizes that this might indicate even deeper self-doubts:

What had threatened her, if indeed she had ever felt truly threatened, had been not violent emotions, but from time to time a sense of the purposelessness of existence, of the lack of reason for so much that occurred. It was a sin of the spirit, she knew; a failure of faith in the rightness of the universe—of God, in short. Yet she doubted that acedia was limited to agnostics or to those who had lost their faith. Indeed, she knew it was not. This sense of the pointlessness of life was far likelier suddenly to assault those whose lives were, on the whole, satisfactory. . . . It was what someone she used to know called divine discontent. (175, 176)

This kind of existential self-recognition, which is never very far away from Kate's perspective and Cross' vision, lies at the heart of Kate's puzzled consciousness. Emily Dickinson in the epitaph may have been able to "contemplate the journey/With unpuzzled heart," but Kate cannot.

This brooding awareness seems to permeate the novel and creates a Kate who seems strangely disembodied and other-worldly. Cross' string of wonderful conversations remains intact, but for much of the time, conversation replaces action, or as Marilyn Stasio suggests, "Having dispensed with what serves as the action sequences, Cross . . . frees up her characters for the intelligent chitchat that has sustained this literate series since 1964" (20). Even murder does not seem to undermine the witty smooth prose and veneer of manners that Cross maintains. Characters often gather to talk, trying to figure out what is going on and what to do, which can often feel airless, repetitive, and claustrophobic. Such gatherings often reflect Kate's own ennui. These pale discussions, neatly laced with single malt and overt political polemics, overwhelm the action in a way that reminds one of *An Imperfect Spy*. The politics and points of view are wry and astute, but the "juice" is missing, as if the mystery were as enervated as Kate's more passive and troubling moments.

The Puzzled Heart is a decent mystery without the complexities and layered voices of earlier works. Kate may be reconsidering her interests and her direction, as Cross may be. We are left with Reed looking out a window and seeing Kate and Banny entering Central Park: "He could only guess at Kate's feelings, although his was certainly an educated guess. Banny's feelings, however, were simple and evident as she ambled along beside Kate, the plume tail swaying" (257). Banny's plume may be more visibly active than Kate's self-doubt, but like most readers we await the next episode in her life to see if she can triumph over acedia, overcome her present passivity, and direct her feminist "divine discontent" toward solving her next mystery.

INTERVIEW WITH CAROLYN HEILBRUN
JANUARY, AUGUST 1997

Sam Coale: Why did you choose to write mysteries? You could've chosen to write anything. Was it just because you had this appetite to do it?
Carolyn Heilbrun: Going back, it's hard to say. I don't know if you've looked at *Writing a Woman's Life,* but the last thing is all about how she started, Amanda Cross. I loved English mysteries. And I read them all, and there weren't any more coming. I mean, not just the women, but Michael Gilbert and so on. Michael Gilbert is terrible on

women, but it's interesting. C. D. Lewis as Nicholas Blake had wonderful women characters until he suddenly turned. The same thing has happened to Robert Parker incidentally. He was great on women, and now suddenly he sneers at feminists and is back to the same women to whom he can give a ten. At his best, he sometimes honored character in women.

Why I did this: Well, it never occurred to me to do anything else. You know, novels are very hard to write, but I liked the trajectory of the mystery and so forth. Also I started with a male detective, and I discovered I couldn't get inside his head at all. I mean, I could obviously in certain ways. If I'd made him a rapist, I could've got inside his head. But when it was a just an ordinary person. . . . What actually threw me in the end was sex, not that I have much sex in the books, but that's where I had trouble. This was back in 1963, so I stopped and made my detective a woman. And she wasn't very feminist. In the beginning she also believes Freud! She was, apart from Miss Marple, the only female detective in print.

SC: Was it hard to find a publisher?

CH: No. I was very fortunate. I knew someone who was a writer. No one knew about this, but I just asked his agent, and I sent it there, and they sold it.

SC: It sounds so easy.

CH: I know. I have had an easy time in my field, but then I feel bad about this.

SC: Why?

CH: I comfort myself with the fact that I've not won any prizes.

SC: There was the scroll for *In the Last Analysis* and the Nero Wolfe one for *Death in a Tenured Position*.

CH: The first one I was praying not to win, because it would've blown my cover.

SC: I know your cover was finally blown. Exactly how did that happen? Did everybody sort of know? Or you had gotten tenure and decided the hell with it, I'm going to spill the beans?

CH: No, it totally leaked out. But it was after 1972. And it was Jacques Barzun who was doing a big thing on detective things, and he and I were friends at that time, and he said, did I know who Amanda Cross was. And I told him it was me. And I'll never forget: he nearly fell off the couch in the Cos Club. In 1972 I published *Poetic Justice,* which takes place obviously at Columbia. And everyone began to think it was a Columbia person. And they hit on a woman colleague of mine, more or less my age, because she smoked. Everybody then, as it came out, would assume I smoked and drank!

SC: You don't like Laphroaig?

CH: I love Laphroaig! I adore Laphroaig! But at the time I wrote these, I drank wine, which is what I mostly drink now, but I do like single-malt scotch, I have to say. Another colleague at Columbia, he was then at Yale, Edward Mendelson, who was Auden's literary executor . . .

SC: So they suspected him because of all the references to Auden in *Poetic Justice*?

CH: No, they didn't suspect him, but I used a lot of Auden in that book. So he went to the Library of Congress where, of course, you can find out who anybody is. Maybe it's the copyright office, I forget, but you can find out. So he found out. He then came to Columbia. He turned out to be terribly nice and useful to me, because when they were doing the German translation of *Poetic Justice*—and this is like 1988 or something or 1990—they called up and said, "We have wonderful German translations of Auden, and we'd like to use them, if you can tell us what poems these quotes came from." Of course by this time I would have had to go through all of Auden again. So I called Ed, and he was marvelous. He could identify every one of them.

SC: Was there a formal moment when you "came out?"

CH: No. There are people who are still just discovering it, because now the books are all copyrighted in my name. It just leaked out. It just sort of dribbled out. And then I told my children. And then I told a number of my friends.

SC: Your children didn't even know?

CH: No. The way you keep a secret is to keep it. Jim [Heilbrun's husband] knew, my agent knew, and the editor knew. And that was it. No one else knew. Because I never would have gotten tenure at Columbia.

SC: What attracts you to the mystery form? Is it the formality of it? I mean, it can be seen as a morality play with religious overtones dealing with the scapegoat. There are certain psychological patterns. . . .

CH: The guilt. . . .

SC: Are there any of those things that appeal to you?

CH: Probably if they did, it was subconsciously. I wasn't Dostoevsky. I liked the trajectory. It never occurred to me to try to write a novel, because what could you write about? Your own life, which I thought was terribly boring and still do! Mine, I mean all these memoirs now coming out. They're wonderful. They have got a new approach, which didn't exist before, but that's another subject. And it just seemed what I wanted to do. So I did it.

SC: Was the choice of "Amanda Cross" to cover your tracks in the academic world?

CH: Oh, yes, definitely.

SC: You write about "Amanda Cross as "psychic space" and as a secret, the power of the secret. . . .

CH: I tell the same tale about it. It's amusing in its way, I guess. Jim and I were in the darkest part of Nova Scotia and got stopped, and we saw this sign, saying "McCharles Cross." And Jim said it would make a great pseudonym. Some woman came up to me in a bookstore in Tucson, Arizona, in a store called, "They Were the Tracks of an Enormous Hound," from Sherlock Holmes. And they had an Irish wolfhound whom you had to cross. This woman came up to me and said, "I come from Nova Scotia, and there's no place like that there. There is a place known as Charles Cross." So I said, "Well, I'll go home and ask my husband, who remembers places." My husband said it wasn't a place; it was a sign. So I wrote her back, and about two years later, I got a letter from her, including one from the prime minister or whoever he is of Nova Scotia. There is indeed a crossroads sign, and she was honorable enough to send it to me.

SC: But it's not a town . . .

CH: It's not a town. We were in the middle of nowhere. And then I used it, but the publisher of the first book said it was obviously written by a woman. . . . I don't know why I thought nobody was named Amanda. There was an Amanda Cross some years below my daughter at school. But fortunately she was born after my first books.

SC: I noticed that whether it is Watergate or whatever, each of your books grapples with a contemporary social issue. Was that intentional? Also, in *Sweet Death, Kind Death,* Patricia Umphelby was the one who supposedly committed suicide by walking into the lake. She was fifty-eight when she did this, as you were at the time, and there was so much about the acknowledgment, the presence of death, middle age, the chance to set sail. Were personal issues like that something you had to wrestle with?

CH: Yes, there's no question, always. At the time I was writing my book on androgyny, I wrote the one on *Antigone.*

P. D. James, whom I know, describes everything. She does it well, unlike [Sue] Grafton, who does it kind of automatically, because she writes a book every year. But I find too much description tedious. You can't get into a room without knowing where the ashtrays are. So I sort of made fun of this in the last one [*An Imperfect Spy*]. And to my horror they—I keep trying not to get blurbs—sent it to P. D. James. She must have known it. But she was gallant as always and gave it a blurb. I'm really indebted to her. She's a grand person.

SC: When James talks about mysteries, she describes its power and sense of order. You both like Jane Austen, for instance.

CH: I like order, too. There's no question. I think we've both come to see that you can't restore order any more. You just restore order in a tiny place. You don't change institutions. I mean, it used to be, you know [in traditional mysteries], the old order thing. Everyone was innocent except one, and they all felt guilty, and then you restore order. But you can't restore complete order any more. She knows that. And I know it.

SC: In *Sisters in Crime,* Maureen Reddy makes the case that Kate's relationship to institutions starts off as fairly benign, but it soon becomes more complicated. In *A Trap for Fools,* you could see Kate's attitude shift.

CH: There's no question. Because so much has changed. You have to remember I wrote that first one in 1963, which was the year of *The Feminine Mystique,* a book that did not really affect me, because I was working. First of all I was one of the only women put on every committee, and I began to see how institutions worked. I was very, very benign about Columbia. The Sixties, you know, really turned me around. And I know there was a lot to be said against them—drugs, silliness, and so on—but it just changed me, totally. I mean students who would say to me, "The CIA is lying to you about what they're doing." I would say, "Oh, no!" But they turned out to be right. Watergate did it finally. I mean after that. . . .

SC: You have written about your relationship to Lionel Trilling. There are several curmudgeonly or reactionary and at the same time very well mannered people—men of a certain age in your books—who are almost always exorcized. There's Canfield Adams in *A Trap for Fools.* He's dead before the book opens, which is fine because you'd never want to meet him. Or Max in *The Question of Max.*

CH: But that isn't Trilling. . . .

SC: I know, but Kate thinks of Max as urbane and civilized. She's very much in favor of good manners and civility. At the same time what she opposes is the conservative or reactionary stasis that good manners can mask. If you have good manners, you can also be a horrible person like Max.

CH: Well, that's why the shifts happen. I still like manners, unfortunately. . . . I still don't understand why we can't at least still walk on the right and holds doors for older people. . . . That has no connotations of any sort. . . . My Anglophilia was the thing. It was heaven. That's why I tried in the Winifred book to suggest that one discovers what went on in those schools: big boys are raping little boys.

SC: Phyllis at Oxford for a year in *The Question of Max* finds that it's like being a slave there. It's awful. And then Kate goes to visit her and finds at first that Oxford is beautiful.

CH: So that conflict is still there. I mean, there's no question. Although I still like England. In a book of mine called *The Last Gifts of Time,* there's an essay on England. It's still my favorite foreign place.

SC: In Malcolm Bradbury's *Dangerous Pilgrimages,* which is about the different myths that America and Europe have of one another and have created in terms of one another, he wrote: "The world of Europe and America now mirror each other almost exactly. Neither is the cultural or moral superior of the other." Do you essentially write British mysteries in American settings—the closed, upper-class society, the leisure necessary for a certain kind of wit?

CH: Yes. Obviously. But I never did England without having Americans in England. I'm very suspicious about English speech. If you notice in my books, everyone who talks in England is American. Otherwise you can make too many mistakes. As Somerset Maugham suggested, even Henry James made mistakes.

SC: Do British readers respond to Kate Fansler?

CH: To some extent, not as much. The *huge* audience is German. Just huge. Go figure, as they say! They're read in Japan. They're read in Italy. And they do rather better in all those places than in England.

When we came up with the term WASP, which is just another racist term really, what it did for us was to characterize that kind of behavior of the English gentleman which is good manners and all of that underneath. . . . Kate is a WASP. I want to keep the manners and lose the rest, but of course it's impossible. I think civility is something that comes out of a person's personality.

SC: Kate's belief in manners and civility is very much like the mystery form, which has a very definite trajectory.

CH: And which can be used for other things.

SC: Right. But within that she doesn't accept the kind of things such manners have allowed people to get away with in the past. You take the mystery form, and, as you say, "dabble in a little revolutionary thought."

CH: And of course Max is like the best schools where they cover up cheating and such.

SC: In terms of some of your other female characters, is Harriet Furst a kind of self-portrait?

CH: That, of course, was based on personal experience, as every elderly woman knows. No, I actually created her in trying to write a spy book. I always loved Le Carré's Smiley. I think he's gone down hill since, but slowly. The last one I couldn't read. And it offended everyone in Panama. It's a rewrite of Graham Greene, which he admits.

SC: At one point you write that analyzing literary texts provides great practice for a detective. And Kate is very aware of her own moral sense of things, as though her study of literature and texts refines it.

CH: It's very Jamesian.

SC: Is that conscious on your part?

CH: Yes, I think so. I wanted to make her that way because I am, too. Henry James had a marvelous influence on me. William, too, but William's totally different. It was always the idea that the moral way you act has to do with you, not how you treat others. And I take this very seriously.

SC: In library talks it never fails. The audience is split right down the middle. Gender doesn't make any difference. There are those who think your books are wonderful, because they deal with social issues, but others will say, "All they do is talk. There's no mystery. There's no murder here."

CH: You have to have a following. That's it. You can't please everyone. A lot of the people hate the books, and I can only say to them, "Don't read them." I mean, I do not like Stephen King. I'm sure he's a lovely guy, but I can't read him. I just don't like to be frightened.

SC: Some critics are upset because Kate isn't feminist enough, and others see her as a kind of isolated masculine detective, for instance, in *In the Last Analysis*. But she does develop a more feminist consciousness.

CH: This is the reason also why I think I have never won a prize, apart from the Nero Wolfe thing, which was very nice. I don't want to win any prizes, but the fact is feminists don't win prizes. I did a study of the Pulitzer prizes, and it's just extraordinary until you get Joan Hendricks' biography of Harriet Beecher Stowe, which of course is a feminist biography. I don't think they knew it. I read a lot of this stuff by women, because I get sent it, and I like it, and I buy it. Yet a women's group of detective writers recently gave a prize to the most awful book that was anti-lesbian and anti-feminism.

SC: How has feminism, as it developed with you, affected your mysteries in terms of form and content or affected you as a writer in general? We can see the progress in terms of how Kate develops and becomes more aware.

CH: It affected me only as is evident in the books. The first one is unfeminist or non-feminist. The second one has more female characters. What is true of these books is true of my life. When feminism came, it seemed to me I'd been waiting for it. It was like a huge light that went on. It's as though you were in a darkish room, and suddenly a light went on. It doesn't really become a theme until quite a ways along. And then when feminism began to lose its initial and incredible excitement and began to have problems, some of that gets reflected. It does in the new one [*The Puzzled Heart*], too. But it didn't affect the way I wrote or the form.

SC: Do you set out to write a book every few years?

CH: No. It's about every three years. I've only done eleven of them. I see an end in sight very clearly. I mean I'm getting on. . . .

SC: You do a lot with journals in your books and many characters who write biographies and letters. Is that just to alter the mystery form?

CH: No, there's much less intention in all of this. . . . It's what interests me, I suppose. It's texts. Writing narratives. I mean, that's my life. I also do that to get another voice in. It's almost always with Kate. It's James' third-first person. That allows you to get another point of view in. I wanted more voices. I wanted to try a first-person narrative. I just wanted other voices.

Everything seems just to have happened. In fact it's the story of my life, I think! I think writing involves a great deal of the unconscious. I think your unconscious works if you're writing regularly. My unconscious became very devoted to feminism, so it seems inevitable. And I wanted to bring in voices that hadn't been heard. For example, in *No Word from Winifred* you have the friendship between women who matter more than the men do. That is a theme, of course, which I subsequently found in Toni Morrison. I hadn't read *Sula* at that time. I think that's a very interesting thing about friendships between women. It isn't just turning Eve Sedgewick around. She said that if you have two men arguing over a woman, they're really involved with each other, which I think is a brilliant insight. But I don't think it ever works to take a male pattern and just apply it to women. I think the context of women's emotions is much wider than a man's.

SC: So it is sort of like a web, a wider interweaving of emotions and friends.

CH: That's right. I just received an honorary degree from Brown, and what intrigued me was that the two graduating seniors made speeches, a young man and woman. He used the metaphor of weaving in his speech, and she used the metaphor of hypertext for hers. And I thought, "Great!" Men look at women, and they think they're so attractive, and they go after them. And certainly women will look at men that way, but it's not as serious. What I'm trying to say is that you can't just reverse roles and expect it to work. Feminism never works, I think, by reversing patterns that have been set up by men with other men in the world. They're different.

SC: It seems to me that in arguing for androgyny, aren't you suggesting that anyone's individual self is finally not completely female, not completely male, but is its own being? You can't define it that narrowly.

CH: Right.

SC: Androgyny is your way, then, of disconnecting that notion of the self as merely male. It is different from that simple or one-dimensional categorizing.

CH: There's the active male sports figure and the pretty young woman who doesn't know what to do unless somebody tells her. Now the woman is the result of socialization, but the man I now think is terrified and to some degree aware of the female mind in himself, which society won't let him express in any way. And I don't mean the desire to wear clothes and be a drag queen, though that's all right.

SC: In effect Kate has an essence that she couldn't discover unless feminism made it possible to see herself differently from the way women have been traditionally considered.

CH: I think feminism has certainly done this. I do think there is some following the male model, and there has to be. It's been there for millennia, and we don't have to re-invent the wheel. It's a little subtler than the way you're putting it. I tend to think of a spectrum, and you go where you want. But what has happened to athletics because of Title Nine? We are discovering both how athletic in a male way women can be, but they've also changed the sport in every case. Men weren't hugging each other across tennis nets when I was a girl. Baseball players weren't wearing gold chains. They would've been beaten to death! Also in basketball now the women play as a team, while the men are playing as big individual stars. So I think there's so much that has benefited men and all of us that women have done.

SC: How do you relate the writing of mysteries to literary criticism to your using yourself as a kind of female example or model of the way things have changed?

CH: I'm not using myself as a model or an example. What you're doing is saying, I will not, as in the male model that I went to school with, speak from Olympus. I will not speak as though there is no author. I am a person, and if I am going to speak to you, you have a right to know something about me. I want to change that authoritarian mode and offer to women a chance to speak for themselves. I'm never a model. I have to keep saying this. I was talking to audiences, and they all asked if I expected women to dress like me. And I said, for God's sake, no! I'm just a comfortable old fat woman. What you have to do is dress the way you want to dress! It's being open.

Diana Trilling wrote a book about Jean Harris, the woman who shot the diet fellow from Scarsdale. The great flaw in that book to me was that she takes a moral stance, which is all right. Jean Harris at the end is wrong. But Trilling never tells us anything about herself. Now I don't think you've a right to do that. And she got this, of course, from Lionel Trilling and all the men she was with. You don't just announce that so-and-so is immoral. You have to say, "Of course had I been in love with him, I don't know what I would have done." Or, "I would never fall in love with such a man." That's the way women speak to each other.

SC: It's advocating an openness and then applying that to your own life and saying, "Look. This is what I've done with these ideas."

CH: Or this is what I found being in my sixties is like. I'm not prescriptive. And the implication is if this interests you, maybe you want to think about what being in your sixties is like.

SC: But it's very liberating, maybe because your voice is so personal, and I begin to think, well, maybe I can do that.

CH: That's it, Sam. Judging from the letters I get, that is the effect it's had. I got one wonderful e-mail: "My husband and I enjoyed your book. He's taken up e-mail, and I got a dog!"

SC: My favorite book is *The Players Come Again*. Taking literary modernism and exploring its roots in terms of gender and literature. Alternative novelists. The matriarchal Cretan, within which Ariadne may be a priestess.

CH: But it is historically unsubstantiated. There is no evidence.

SC: But does it matter in terms of myth?

CH: No, I don't think so. Besides it's inference. If you look at the tremendous maleness of both Judaism and Islam, where even the man is giving birth and so on, this has to be in opposition. And it's clear what the Greeks were fighting against. I think Jane Harrison and Gilbert Murray and others have, as far as the Greeks go, established this. And of course Knossos was an amazing place. There's no question it was. But I get, you see, letters or books. Someone just sent me a book in which someone is writing about Mary Renault and argues with me for what I say about her in that novel [*Players*]. And then someone else wrote me and said I am writing a book on Ariadne, and you say that Daedalus built a dance floor. And could you tell me more about this? As far as I know the only reference extant about the fact that he built a dance floor is in Homer. Most of the mail I get is from people wanting to know: could you tell me where a quote comes from? I can't remember now.

SC: In several of your books there's a guiding author or vision, whether it's Freud or Auden or Le Carré, Joyce. Sometimes it's stronger than in others.

CH: It comes out. It's in my head. You see, Le Carré was in my head because this whole idea of spies—everybody's spying and fooling everyone else and everybody's a mole and so on—it totally came to me that this is true. And it's particularly true of children. They become spies. They figure things out for themselves, and often they're wrong.

SC: It's interesting in *An Imperfect Spy* that even Harriet for all her spying has a very sound political and moral position.

CH: Harriet comes back in the new book. Yes, I was very fond of her.

Because of course Kate started out my age and ages about one year to my seven. But I did want her to age. I think of her in her fifties now.

SC: In *An Imperfect Spy* she's going through a kind of crisis in her marriage.

CH: I got a terrific letter from a man who said it was the only thing he really understood. I couldn't believe it! It went on for three pages, and he is a male feminist who could talk about all of the problems you have.

SC: Does it amaze you what chords you strike in your readers?

CH: Yes. You never know. But you see I'm very aware of the whole group of people. . . . I get letters from someone who'll say I'm glad I read this book in the library and didn't have to pay for it. It's the biggest garbage I ever read, because they don't like it. . . . They're furious right-wing people.

SC: You get caught in the crossfire.

CH: All the time. Being between two stools describes my life. I've become a revolutionary, I suppose you'd have to say in terms of gender.

SC: Do you feel you've gotten pigeon-holed?

CH: Oh, once they call you a feminist. . . . Columbia would always say, "Oh, she'll just let any woman through. She has no standards." At the same time we get a man who is "neutral." I mean, this is what I so object to. It's still a real problem. It's very hard, because it's assumed that you hate men. I don't know any feminist, I don't know any lesbian, who hates men! What feminists are fighting against is the patriarchy which puts men at the center of every order. But who hates men? It's ridiculous.

SC: One thing that really struck me in *Gift,* was your references, both pro and con, to loneliness and solitude. Is one of the reasons you write to relieve that loneliness? By putting Kate through her paces or devising these plots, do her actions become an antidote to it?

CH: It's a way of finding your own space, as I've put it. I mean, there was Jane Austen writing in a room full of people. I think most writers were probably lonely as children or outsiders in some way and made up stories, whereas the non-lonely ones may not have needed to or whatever. In the end I think if one is a writer, you obviously want solitide, and you don't play bridge or go dancing, both things my parents did. I stay home and write. I do find this passion for solitude and the recognition of its cost. It's very important to me, but that's never come out in my novels. That came out in my studies of May Sarton.

SC: You quoted her once: "We have to make myths of our lives. It's the only way to live without despair." That may be too heavy a notion with which to describe the Kate Fansler mysteries, but Kate Fansler is a fantasy, and she moves in this rarefied world. And in a way that does counteract solitude.

CH: The thing I've learned since is that you can be slim, gorgeous, and all the rest of it, but whereever you get to be, there are problems. You can live as I now live, an absolutely ideal life, in the sense of having my health and enough money. But there are problems. You don't say, "Ho, ho!" The minute you're anywhere, there are other problems to face. It's the hardest thing for women I talk to to realize. Young women today say, "You told us it'd all be wonderful, and I've got a job, and I've got a child, and I've got a marriage, and I'm hectic, and it's terrible, and you lied to me." It's never perfect, because wherever you are, there are other problems. What was horrible was being home all day with a three-year-old. That's a problem! The other is just life. Kate does suffer from despair, acedia. She does. And the new book is actually rather dark, *The Puzzled Heart.*

SC: At one point in *Gift* you talk about the atmosphere at Columbia being poisonous, nasty, and tense, which may be the definition of academia in general.

CH: Everyone seemed to think so. There *must* be better places.

SC: In creating the whole academic aura of your books, are you trying to exorcize it?

CH: No. The one thing mysteries aren't is a personal thing to me. It was Jacques Barzun who taught me that. In a seminar he said that whenever you see something in a book that stands out, it's because someone is making a point that they're angry about against someone else. And I don't do that in those books. I often do when speaking my mind. What interests me is institutions, and in regard to institutions, there are one of two things you can do. You can get out of them or try and blow them up, or you can try to change them. Somewhere I used the phrase, "the long march through institutions." And what Kate does is not much, and she doesn't reform the institution, but she changes it a little. That's what happens.

SC: Institutions are very self-serving by definition. Is there such a thing as institutional morality? Or is that an oxymoron?

CH: It's true of every other business. It's the free market. And while it's not great, it's better than anything else that we know about. I think occasionally you get administrators with some moral sense, but everything now is money. How do we get it? If you've got money, they're interested in you.

SC: What comes out so often in your work is a fierce anti-nostalgia. You fiercely oppose the idea that somehow the past was better and worked and that the present is a falling off from that golden era.

CH: Yes. But you see all of the things that you see there, which is very clever of you, I didn't put in necessarily, but since I have an unconscious, and I write. . . . You know, Coleridge once said that every meaning you attach to a word—he was talking about poems—that word has to bear that meaning. And so what's there is there.

SC: Are you surprised when some people will come out and say I saw this there and this?

CH: By now I'm not surprised at anything! My mysteries are often called elitist and snobbish. That is not because I want to be elitist and snobbish. It's because that's all I know. Just in the same way that I could never make Kate a man. One of the things that I have done is stuck to feminism in all my aspects. It has grown very heavy on race, class, ethnicity, and sexual orientation. And I think a lot of us have been tempted away from the terrible anxiety of feminism to do these subjects, which are totally worthy. But I'm probably not only the oldest living academic feminist but the only one for whom it's still pure feminism. To me I'm talking about feminism. And that's where my heart is.

SC: Perhaps one of the most important successes in your novels is that you have made feminism less frightening to people who would automatically react negatively to it.

CH: No question. *Death in a Tenured Position* helped many women see what they were up against. Let me try to say this in different terms. Even though the enormous influence on me was the British detective story, the fact is that I and everyone else who is an American is influenced by the American private-eye types. The one thing they had in common with female detectives—independence and again loneliness, if you want—they didn't belong to a little village or something. But the difference between them and your feminist detective, I think, is that the feminist detective recognizes a world of women with whom she will connect. The male detectives didn't have male friends. They had partners—as Sam Spade said, "If someone shoots your partner, you're supposed to find out who"—but they're alone walking down these mean streets, a man who is not mean. Chandler or somebody said that. In a sense that's true of the woman, too, except she now is aware there are other women. Kate, who began before feminism, did not have that. Peretsky has always had that woman doctor and other women friends, but Kate slowly began to acquire female friends. But that's an influence that we female detectives have to accept, because we're American, and it's American. Even though I didn't want any of it, I had to recognize it, it's there, that lonely fighter for however little justice you can manage.

SC: In *The Players Come Again* you get to experience the genuine excitement of Kate discovering Ann discovering Dorinda discovering Nellie. They all get into what really went on and what were the real family connections. You can see the four of them coming together with Gabrielle.

CH: But you see the point is they all turn out to have the same father, which we all do. We all inherit patriarchy, but if you connect with women, it doesn't matter so much. This is the sort of thing that I'd discovered I'd done after I'd done it, but I never thought of it at the time. I mean, I knew they all had to have the same father, but I didn't give it any symbolic weight.

Did I ever tell you about when Hillerman and I were on the same panel? Someone asked the question, "Do you make outlines, or do you know what the plot will be?" Hillerman said, "Well, no, not really. Suddenly there was a car, and there was a driver, and there were a pair of eyes in the back seat. And I said, now, whose eyes are those? And I looked in the back seat, and it was a dog. And I went on from there." That is certainly closer to what I'm doing. P. D. James does use an outline. She has it so outlined that she can write any section when she feels like it. Of course you have to go back and revise when you make mistakes. One time a free-lance editor told me in my latest book, "You have Kate holding a class on Saturday. I don't think classes are held on Saturday!" So I had to go back and squish two days into one! I made it a Friday, which is not likely but at least not impossible.

SC: What is it, then, that gets you started?

CH: I don't know. I don't know how it happens, but suddenly it's there. For instance, in *An Imperfect Spy* I was intrigued by spying, how we all spy, and I'm very intrigued by Smiley. So that was there, I guess. And wanting to write about a place like Harvard was there [*Death in a Tenured Position*]. It's totally different. I'm sure Hillerman would agree. I told you that he and I are the same age.

SC: Have you started a mystery and stopped dead and thrown it out?

CH: Oh, yes. Three times. You just know that it's not going anywhere. Very early I wrote a whole one which was really rather feminist, outspokenly so. The editor told me it was much too feminist and would never sell. So I buried it. In fact I've lost it. Men do read them. The ones who like that world like it because it's a little radical, but it's comfortably radical. I don't head any organization to blow up anything.

SC: You seem to be very at ease with yourself as a writer. Is this something you have worked at to achieve? Is this the myth that you're creating?

CH: Again, all I can ever say, Sam, is it's all there. In the one about the law school [*An Imperfect Spy*] I really set out to say something about these people and the law, who think everything is wonderful. The Clarence Thomases. And that's why I put a black character in there who talks like him. But very rarely do I take on something so directly. A colleague described me as half Kate Fansler and half Janet Mandelbaum.

I'm not remotely like Janet. I never have been and never would be. I might have been in the beginning, before feminism.

I almost never say mean things about anyone. What I respond to most viscerally is unkindness. Now to call a concentration camp "unkind" is a little silly, so clearly I'm in another world in my mysteries. Sometimes you have to be. There is no question. As a teacher it may be necessary at times.

When I was very young on a ranch, a very young thirteen, socially speaking, I was riding out with one of the guys who took care of the horses, and he said to me, "I've never heard you say a mean thing about anyone." And it was the first time that anyone had noticed this. Now since I've grown up and been a feminist, I've learned to say a lot of mean things. I'm very unkind about a lot of people, but it's gratuitous unkindness that bothers me, when there's no reason for it.

SC: The approach to feminism in your mysteries is never offensive or threatening.

CH: Wayne Booth told me this in Chicago that he and a lot of men ate lunch around a table, and said that one of them said, "I never understood what feminism was about until I read *Death in a Tenured Position*." So it happens, but, of course, not as often as I'd like.

SC: You mention in *Gift* about the way religions define themselves in terms of opposition to others, purposely excluding them.

CH: Clearly Kate Fansler has no place in that world. And occasionally I get a letter from someone in that world who mistakenly took my book out of the library, and they write me the most abusive horrible letters: "I'm writing to your publisher to tell them that your writing should not be allowed!" I don't get many of those, but I get some. They're right-wing. And they can't stand this liberal propaganda, which we all know is all over the airways. I've yet to see it. I do think it is a nice point that Hillerman found his Indians, and I found feminism. Neither of us found them, of course, but in a sense the world made it possible for us to do that. And so many people read him and love him, I assume, because of the Indians. I've read quite a number of his books, and I admire them. He's just a lovely man.

4

THE DARK DOMAIN OF JAMES LEE BURKE:
THE SOUL'S DEPTHS

James Lee Burke has been described by Joyce Carol Oates as a writer of the American hard-boiled mystery, and she has included him in the company of such fellow writers as Raymond Chandler, Dashiell Hammett, James Ellroy, and Robert Parker (20). This may situate Burke generically but does not take into account the rich Southern tradition of fiction from which he comes. In fact Burke began as a Southern writer in terms of his geography and characters and later switched to writing mysteries. One wonders what happens when one tradition collides with and is incorporated within another. Has the mystery formula limited Burke's vision in any way? Have generic considerations distorted and stunted his earlier perspectives? Does the formula subvert his talents as a writer, or has he managed to transform the mystery in such a way that can accommodate his own imagination?

Houghton Mifflin published Burke's first novel, *Half of Paradise,* in 1965, when he was in his twenties. Scribner's published *To the Bright and Shining Sun* in 1970, Crewel published *Lay Down My Sword and Shield* in 1971, and Burke sold *Two for Texas* as a paperback in 1982, but from 1971 until 1985, he was almost unable to publish anything. This phenomenon has even been pointed out by a fellow mystery writer, John Dunning: "It defies logic. . . . it takes a real writer like Anne Tyler half a career to catch on, and James Lee Burke can't even find a publisher for ten years" (61). It wasn't until Louisiana State University Press published *The Convict and Other Stories* in 1985 and *The Lost Get-Back Boogie* in 1986 that Burke's writing career began anew. Until 1986 *The Lost Get-Back Boogie* had been in circulation for almost eleven years and was rejected by one hundred New York publishers, according to Burke. When it was finally published, it was nominated for a Pulitzer prize. Burke published *The Neon Rain* in 1987, his first mystery with Dave Robicheaux, the Louisiana Cajun cop, which launched his career as a mystery writer.

Throughout this period Burke survived in various guises. Born in Houston in 1936, the son of an itinerant pipeline worker, he published his first short story at nineteen, attended the University of Southern Louisiana at Lake Charles from 1955 to 1957, went on to earn both a Bachelor's and a Master's degree from the University of Missouri in 1959 and 1960 respectively, and returned to Southwest Louisiana as an English instructor. But without a doctorate he didn't get tenure. He worked as a social worker on skid row in Los Angeles (1962-64), as a reporter in Lafayette, Louisiana (1964), a pipeliner in Texas, a land surveyor in Colorado, as an oil lease negotiator in Louisiana, in the United States Forest Service in Kentucky (1965-66), and taught reading to Job Corps students in Kentucky's coal country. He drove trucks and succumbed again to the lure of academia as a teacher of English or creative writing in five colleges, including Miami-Dade Community College in Florida, Wichita State University in Kansas, and finally the University of Montana in Missoula. A Bread Loaf Fellowship in 1970 and a Southern Federation of State Art Agencies Grant in 1977 helped him make ends meet. His triumph over alcoholism by 1977 through the twelve-step program at Alcoholics Anonymous proved a very real personal victory during his publication drought. And simultaneously he and his wife, Pear Pail, had and raised four children.

When we consider Burke's fiction, therefore, we can conjure up a bifurcated career. During the first half he wrote five novels and one collection of short stories. And so far in the Dave Robicheaux series of mysteries, since 1987 he has written ten books. One day on a fishing trip in 1985, according to Burke, a friend, Rick Dimarinis, suggested that he try writing a crime novel: "He began outlining an idea, and about a week later in San Francisco, I started writing the book in long-hand on a legal pad, and I knew it was going to be a winner" (McClurg E8). This turned out to be *The Neon Rain,* and a new mystery series was launched. In 1989 he was awarded a Guggenheim Fellowship and for *Black Cherry Blues,* his third Robicheaux mystery, was awarded the coveted Mystery Writers of America Edgar Allan Poe Award in 1989. The drought was clearly over. As a result Hyperion published all the earlier novels in handsome paperback editions in 1995.

The earlier novels, interesting in their own right, also suggest what the Robicheaux series would become in terms of themes, points of view, the complexities of Burke's finely honed moral vision, and style. His is a very Southern perspective, because of his own background, and suggests the dark domain of Faulkner's greatest works in terms of his lyrical style, his confrontations with race, class, and family background, and his over-arching fascination with the past, both in its gothic haunted atmosphere and in its compelling moral dilemmas. "The past is always with us," he has commented. "Unless we confront the mistakes we made and atone for them, we can never extricate ourselves from the misdeeds of our ancestors" (McClurg E8). This driving, almost demonic force and point of view Burke has developed in all of his books. It fuels the best of his fiction.

Faulkner described his vision as "the human heart in conflict with itself," and certainly Burke works in the same vein with his Manichean confrontations between good and evil, between damaged goodness and energetic evil, the legions of light and the demons of darkness. His characters, too, feed on rumor, gossip, legends, and their own distorted and often rigid explanations of events. Burke's plots often approximate the fluidity of Faulkner's world, employing at times individual streams of consciousness, dreams, and the more Hemingwayesque cinematic presentation of "hard" images and sharp details, although, of course, the plot must be resolved and preserve the basic goodness of the protagonist. Past battles present; a vanished moral code confronts its continued violation, as if it can only be known by its absence. White opposes black; the "New South" often stands as a withered bitter outrage in contrast to the urgently nostalgic sanctuary of an "Old South" that may never have existed. Biblical and mythic patterns of justice and retribution intermingle with mob violence and sudden murder, as if the present constitutes a falling off from some irredeemable, more moral past, a diminishment, a tragic, inexorable loss of some deep, abiding kind. Indeed the dark domain of Burke's South reveals its distinctive connections to Faulkner's outraged territory. "I was raised here," Burke explains,

and I've always subscribed to Faulkner's statement that "I will never be able to exhaust that small postage stamp of experience I learned as a child" . . . But in addition, there's just no place more intriguing than southern Louisiana. It belongs much more to the Latin and Caribbean world than the Anglo-Saxon South. And it has every contradiction, every kind of European, African and Caribbean influence—as well as Indian—extant in the Western Hemisphere. It's French Catholic and very religious, but right in the middle is this pagan ambiance. People who don't know the word "existentialism" have been living that ethos for 200 years. (Ringle D10)

Clearly the mystery formula came late to Burke's work, and this raises several questions. Has his earlier fiction helped him in improving, changing or deepening the mystery formula? Can the earlier work be seen as a prelude to the later mystery series? These and other issues I hope to examine closely from *Half of Paradise* to *Cadillac Jukebox* (1996), from *To the Bright and Shining Sun* to *A Stained White Radiance* (1992), and from *Lay Down My Sword and Shield* to *Burning Angel* (1995). How much of a change is there from *The Lost Get-Back Boogie* to *In the Electric Mist with Confederate Dead* (1993) and *Dixie City Jam* (1994)?

Half of Paradise is perhaps a too schematically, overtly designed first novel in its conscientious craftsmanship that interweaves the lives of three male characters who figure as pawns in the multi-racial, class-conscious landscape of contemporary Southern society and are consequently doomed. In three sections, "Summer's Dust," "Big Midnight Special," and "When the Sun Begins to Shine," Burke juxtaposes the stories of Avery Broussard, a white man whose family has owned the same land and farmhouse in Martinique parish for over a hundred years and who winds up in prison after a failed bootlegging scheme; J. P. Winfield, a white hillbilly who succeeds as a popular country singer but must sell his soul and body in order to do so; and Toussaint Boudreaux, a black fighter who ends up in prison with Broussard, escapes, and is hunted down and shot. Burke's South surrounds and destroys them all. Avery remembers his father's monologues, tales of "the agrarian dream of Thomas Jefferson . . . destroyed by an industrial revolution that pierced America to its heart. . . . Mr. Broussard had been raised to live in a society and age that no longer existed. By blood and by heritage he was bound to the past. . . . Only an inborn memory remained, a nostalgia for something that had flowered and faded. . . ." (*Half* 76). Nostalgia hangs over the landscape like a dense fog.

Throughout the novel Burke paints a dark domain of segregation politics, easy sex, available drugs, superstitious backwoods preachers, and gullible country folk. Con artists, convicts, sadistic prison guards, whores, would-be alcoholic writers, and New Orleans drunken revels exist side by side, often in dazed humid stupified villages. And everything transpires within a beautiful heart-breaking landscape often ravaged by oil rigs, soulless politicians, and fraudulent roadshows. In such a world the individual self is forever imprisoned within the claustrophobic and dangerous cells of race, class, caste, politics, and crime. Burke's French Quarter becomes "rows of stucco buildings that had once been the homes of the French and Spanish aristocracy, and which were now gutted and remodeled into bars, whorehouses, tattoo parlors, burlesque theaters, upper-class restaurants, and nightclubs that catered to homosexuals" (*Half* 185).

Underscoring all of this is Burke's own love for and use of folk songs and country music, which act as a kind of choral accompaniment and cultural background throughout the novel, with their own nostalgic mix of pain and platitude, loss and melancholy waywardness. J. P. Winfield remembers Woody Guthrie, "an Okie who bummed his way across the Dust Bowl to California . . . to ride the roads with never enough to eat and to get thrown in jails by town constables who feared a man with a hole in the bottom of his shoe. . . . And there was Joe Hill, who had belonged to the I. W. W. and sung the songs of the working class that fought outside the factories with axe handles and lengths of pipe when striking was considered Red . . . so he was stood against a wall in the Utah penitentiary and shot to death" (*Half* 210). Burke's own populist perspective in this instance easily separates the soul of his fiction from the more "doomed-aristocrat" perspective of a Faulkner, aligning it more closely with the people and worlds created by Carson McCullers, Flannery O'Connor, and Cormac McCarthy. We can also glimpse Burke's own fascination with and love for the underdog in a dark domain that has inevitably been rigged against him or her, a perspective that will grow and deepen in his other novels and in the world and character of Dave Robicheaux.

In this first novel, written in the third person, we can clearly see the influence of writers such as Hemingway on Burke's precise and detailed style with its insider's descriptions of jail cells, penal camps, the docks, and other realms:

The men dropped out of the back one by one and walked in single file behind him. The truck was parked by an irrigation canal that was being dug into a flood basin. The canal ended abruptly where yesterday's work had stopped. Two long banks of dusty red clay were piled on each side of the ditch. The pine trees were green and sweet smelling in the morning air. The trees stretched away over the loam down to the river. The breeze from the river blew through the woods and scattered the pine needles over the ground. (*Half* 103)

This earlier style is crisp and clean, but there is also a certain flatness to it, as if Burke were purposely distancing himself from any emotional resonance and keeping his eye on exterior details, the horizonal overview of what things look like without measuring the interior of the heart. Yet at the same time he displays a crisp muscular style when he creates scenes of action and sudden violence. Then the prose comes to life, as it does in the often elaborate set pieces and descriptions and in the twisted, fate-driven plot itself. We can also glimpse an early lyricism that will come to dominate much of his later and best writing: "The day was bright and the sun reflected off the tin roofs of the barracks in a white glare, and the air was very still and heavy with the smell of the pines and dust and heat" (*Half* 135). In these lines the details and descriptions gather momentum, and the long unwinding rhythm of the words in their slower hypnotic movement roots the images in the humidity and blistering blaze of the Southern afternoon.

Whatever good occurs in the lives of Broussard, Winfield, and Boudreaux, each is inevitably destroyed. Broussard, paroled at last from prison, is arrested for drunken driving, after a lyrical and sensual reprieve in New Orleans with an old girlfriend, and is returned to the penal camp: "Nothing seemed real to him except the jail and returning to the work camp. He listened to the men arguing in the dark" (*Half* 279). Winfield turns to drugs, seduced by the crooked talent scout, Virde Hunnicutt, and his would-be singer, April Brien; takes Nashville by storm but writes his only song for a segregationist politician's roadshow; and awakens dazed and shattered by the railroad tracks, dying of the inevitable heart attack in the hospital: "J. P. died alone in the room shortly after midnight, and when the nurse found he was dead she called the intern and the body was removed, because the space was needed for others" (263). Boudreaux survives the sadistic guards and spell-casting Brother Samuel, a redbone preacher, in the penal camp, but when he escapes into the marsh, having withstood more than enough, he is finally cornered and shot: "His head sagged on his chest, and he fell backward in the leaves with his arms stretched out by his side" (201). The richness of the characters, the alliances forged between them, Burke's sharp eye for detail, and his barely quelled horror at what the system can do to the individual makes *Half of Paradise* a fine first novel. He has clearly laid claim to the territory he will occupy in his later work.

Successive novels deepen and extend Burke's dark domain. *To the Bright and Shining Sun* takes place in the hollows of the Cumberland Range in Kentucky in the early 1960s and explores the lives and landscape of coal miners, focusing an unsentimental eye on unions and mining companies, assassinations, social workers, family feuds, bootleggers, poverty and perpetual pollution, picket lines and scabs, murderers and broken families, revenge and betrayal. Through it all, the stubborn, single-minded, sixteen-year-old Perry Woodson Hatfield James manages not only to survive but to prevail, with help from the Job Corps in North Carolina, upholding his own wary sense of morality and legacy, underscored by his recognition of the kind of stubbornness and loyalties that perpetuates the terrible system of dependency, exploitation, and vengeance. James is a far more realized, a deeper character than any of the men in *Half of Paradise,* the kind of self-reliant, moral-wrestling, soul-searching male Burke will pursue and elaborate on in the characters of Hackberry Holland in *Lay Down My Sword and Shield* and the splendid Iry Paret in *The Lost Get-Back Boogie.*

The title of Burke's second novel comes from an old Bill Monroe bluegrass song, another example of Burke's use of and attachment to country music: "Run, ole Molley, run,/Tenbrooks is going to beat you/

To the bright and shining sun./Out in California where Molley done as she pleased" (*Bright* 26). His style is sharper, more resonant: "When he finished his cigarette he ripped the paper back along the seam and rubbed the tobacco between his palms into the waste basket, as though he were grinding some fierce energy out of his body" (*Bright* 23). He captures the dialect of the area: "A feller could work and save his money all his life and not be able to buy nothing like that, he thought. You don't get things like that for your sweat. They got it by stealing it from the Indians, and they held onto it by cheating other people out of their money and paying a man hardly nothing for planting and cutting their tobacco. A feller don't ever get anything worth keeping for the work he does" (135). Burke's sense of landscape also acquires a dark, more feral edge to it:

The quiet fear was always there in his stomach, and there was an unnatural feeling inside him that he could never describe. In some ways the mine had the smell of an opened grave, and something primeval in him rebelled against his entering the earth. The weight of the ground above seemed to crush upon his head, and the spiral cut of the corridor made him lose his sense of equilibrium, as though he were rushing straight downwards towards the center of the world. . . . As he shoveled the coal and slag into the empty cars, he felt the fear of the earth's interior begin to grow in him again. (165, 168)

Here vision and landscape, personal feeling and atmosphere merge, transcending the flatter details and more horizontal point of view of Burke's first novel. Plenty of details still remain, unadorned and often too systematic in their presentation—the mining operations, the rules and regulations of the Job Corps, the making of illegal whiskey—but they occupy less fictional space and slow down the narrative much less than before.

Hackberry Holland, thirty-five-year-old heir to a Texas ranch, natural gas wells, Southern history, and a political machine, strides through *Lay Down My Sword and Shield* like a wounded colossus, drunk, confused, desperate, vaguely out of sorts, paralyzed by memories of Chinese prisons and frozen boxcars in the Korean War and his father's suicide. He moves easily if unsteadily through cheap motels and cheaper whores, ostentatious cocktail soirees and drunk tanks, encounters rich and ruthless oil cutthroats, slippery politicians, and local rednecks, and is saddled with a ruthless alcoholic wife and his own massive sense of guilt. "I wanted power itself, the tribal recognition that went with it," although Holland is plagued by "that old problem of time and loss and the failure of history to atone in its own sequence" (*Lay* 35, 226). In "my torn concept of self" and the feeling "that the land breathed with the presence of those dead men who had struggled on it long before we were born" (*Lay* 69, 129-30) and in his Southern belief "that through conditioning and experience you could accept with some measure of tranquility any of the flaws in the human situation" (116), Hack Holland emerges fullblown as Burke's first existential hero, a predecessor to Dave Robicheaux. He despises "the rigid social attitudes of the new rich . . . [the] bigotry, [the] illiterate confidence in the reasons for [their] success, and [their] simplistic and sometimes brutal solutions for the world's problems" (106), and in launching himself into the circumstances that surround the arrest and subsequent murder of Arturo Gomez, a Mexican friend involved in the organization of the United Farm Workers in Pueblo Verde, he rediscovers his sense of justice, moral vision, and love.

Burke relies on his own Southern and family background here to enrich his fierce tale that pits the newly rich against the downtrodden and poor, Mexican fieldhands against the country yahoos and cops determined to crush them, Hack's rich self-righteous wife Verisa against the young and savvy social worker Rie, and Hack's own self-devouring guilt at having informed on his fellow prisoners about their plans to escape from the Chinese camp in Korea against his present state of liquor-ridden paralysis and coddled despair. Burke uses similar materials about the betrayal in Korea in his story, "We Build Churches, Inc.," in the collection, *The Convict and Other Stories*.

The Holland family, which is based on Burke's maternal ancestors, and Burke's fascination with them has spawned other novels and stories as well in an almost Faulknerian-inspired legacy of family violence and pain. Hack's grandfather hauled the noted criminal, John Wesley Hardin, into jail, a much-touted tale recounted in the short story "Hack" in terms of man's propensity for and the lasting legacy of violence despite what side of the law he was on; Son Holland, an earlier relation, participated in the Battle of San Jacinto (a tale told in comic and picaresque terms in the delightful yarn-spun *Two for Texas*); and his father, Sam Holland (Sam Holland is the actual name of Burke's maternal great-grandfather who appears more or less as his actual self in *Cimarron Rose* [1997]), a New Deal Congressman who committed suicide over a political bribe. Another younger Hack comes up against racism and the bigotry of self-righteous, fundamentalist preachers in the short story, "Uncle Sidney and the Mexicans." Clearly Burke is mining a valuable load of Holland lore here, which he returns to in *Cimarron Rose*.

Burke's sense of justice triumphs over and transcends the dark domain in *Lay Down My Sword and Shield,* though of course the overall environment and landscape he paints continue as before. Just as Perry

James finally manages to elude and escape from the crushing cycle of violence and vengeance of his coal-mining existence in Kentucky, so Hack Holland joins the union organizers in Pueblo Verde, uses his connections to help the cause, divorces the voracious Verisa and marries the socially active and morally committed Rie, refuses to participate in the on-going politically corrupt deals and swindles of Senator Allen B. Dowling and the Texas Democratic Party, and puts to rest his own demons: "Since then I've come to believe that one's crimes and private guilt, those obsessions that we hide like that ugly black diamond in the soft tissue of the mind, are really not very important to other people" (*Lay* 223). Clearly his sense of moral outrage, his obsessive guilt and existential angst, his alcoholic stupors and dazed sense of self-worth pave the way for Dave Robicheaux's similar flaws and furies and attest to Burke's own.

Burke's earlier work culminates in the short story collection, *The Convict and Other Stories* and in *The Lost Get-Back Boogie*. In both we see him wrestling with similar themes but with different fictional structures and perspectives—the first-person narrator, the driving sense of guilt and moral choice, and the labyrinthine layers of the psychological and moral complexities of his characters. And in Iry Paret he creates his most complex character yet, the ultimate forerunner to Dave Robicheaux's own querulous quandries.

The first-person narration seems to have freed Burke from his often too intensely focused vision on mechanical details and explanations. It is probably the break-through decision in his art. In this more confessional mode, the narrator easily attaches both his own mood and the world around him more closely to one another; the physically visible reflects much more clearly the spiritual malaise and uncertainty of the narrator. In "The Pilot," for instance, Marcel tells his own tale, describing himself as "a Louisiana coonass . . . short and thick-bodied, overweight from too much beer and crawfish . . . restless and lonely whenever I leave the Bayou Teche country; I think slow; maybe I'm dumb" (*Convict* 35). In "Losses" Claude, a fifth-grader at St. Peter's Catholic School in 1944, who has heard tales of Nazi submarines torpedoing oil tankers off the coast of Louisiana, broods on his own compulsive sense of guilt and his recognition of the dark domain that surrounds him: "I believed that a great evil was at work in the world. . . . Sometimes I would dream of an infinite, roiling green ocean, its black horizon trembling with lightning, and I'd be afraid to see what dark shapes lay below its turbulent surface" (*Convict* 19, 31). His confrontation with Sister Uberta and her own demons, feeds his sense of inadequacy: "I was afraid of her, afraid of what her words about sin could do to me" (21).

In the morally complex tale, "The Convict," Avery Broussard, the young narrator (a younger version of the character in *Half of Paradise*), has to face up to his father's helping a convict escape, then realizing that the convict is, in fact, a murderer and must be stopped. In effect "the same man who turned him in also helped him escape" (*Convict* 144). He also experiences one of those epiphanies that finds its way into Burke's best fiction and remains at the heart of his moral vision within and yet triumphant over the dark domain: "Many years would pass before I would learn that it is our collective helplessness, the frailty and imperfection of our vision, that ennobles us and saves us from ourselves" (*Convict* 144). The same recognition surfaces in the most ambitious story in the collection, "Lower Me Down with a Golden Chain": "He knew that courage and faith are their own justification and that heaven's prisoners [a phrase that recurs as the title of the second book in the Robicheaux series] don't worry about historical place" (*Convict* 129).

The moral complexities and juxtapositions of "Lower Me Down with a Golden Chain" reveal the apogee of Burke's art of fiction in its short form before their further development in *The Last Get-Back Boogie* and the best of the Dave Robicheaux mysteries. As a journalist, a Catholic, and an observer in creative writing from Wichita State University, the first-person narrator finds himself interviewing several participants in the civil war in Guatemala. He first talks with Father Larry, an American priest who runs a mission in San Luis and is determined to help anyone who needs him. Captain Ramos, whom the narrator meets next, leads the Guatemalan death squads against the Marxist fanatics he is convinced are leading the rebellious guerrillas: "A man must serve his prince," Ramos insists, "and an unfortunate man must sometime serve a bad prince" (*Convict* 121); thus he maintains the typical moral—or amoral—position of being only a functionary in a larger cause. The narrator then talks with Francisco, the guerrilla leader, who upbraids him: "I saw you through field glasses when Captain Ramos killed all those in the ditch" (125). The narrator had watched as Ramos stripped several cane cutters down to their purple and orange undershorts and then slaughtered them. Francisco has asked Father Larry for bandages and medicine and thus provides Ramos with the excuse he needs to attack the priest's mission and the priest, after his men have killed sixteen Indians: "They stabbed him to death with a bayonet" (128).

Amid the slaughter, trapped in the violent web of civil war, the narrator begins to assess his own tenuous position: "I feel like a voyeur in search of misery with camera and pen" (*Convict* 122). Dave Robicheaux will discover a similar fatal attraction in himself. As Ramos tells him, "You can afford to be a moralist because you are not a participant"

(121). The narrator remembers seeing American survivors of two freighters torpedoed by the Nazis in 1942: "I felt as though I were looking into hell itself. I couldn't accept that the war, the Nazis, had reached into my world. . . . I was drowning in the thought that truly wicked men could do whatever they wished to us" (127). He also remembers segregation in his native New Orleans: "Mr. Faulkner was wrong about this one. There were southerners who questioned the laws of segregation" (122). And he remembers an elderly black man in the Baton Rouge jail singing, "Lower me down with a golden chain / And see that my grave is kept clean" (123). He also recalls Daniel Berrigan's protesting against the eighteen Titan missiles that lie "out there under those frozen, snowy wheat fields" back in Wichita (128).

Burke carefully juxtaposes all these incidents within the first-person narrator's memory and narration. Present events parallel past ones. Moral issues take on different attributes, yet remain naggingly similar whether they arise from civil war, nuclear missles, segregation, or the narrator's own uncertain position. He acknowledges, as Dave Robicheaux will as well, his attraction to violence and horror, at the same time insisting on his need to make the right moral choice in relation to them. Historical context vies with absolute moral positions in a shifting landscape that leaves him confused and frustrated, though he finally acknowledges that the morally good and justified of this world, the Father Larrys and the old black man in his cell, teargassed during a protest against segregation, shouldn't as "heaven's prisoners . . . worry about historical place" (*Convict* 129). Such an absolutist vision is both celebrated and questioned by the layering of the narrator's stream-of-consciousness narration in the story, though it remains a necessary and all too human choice. Extremes in the tale exclude any middle ground for compromise and reveal a polarized macho landscape of cruelty and violence, a mythic pattern of ritualized aggression. This is a landscape Burke both viscerally conjures up and morally condemns in his Robicheaux mysteries, torn as he seems to be between the high drama of blood and brutality and the moral necessity to choose the right side. In "Lower Me Down with a Golden Chain," we get all the moral complexities of the best of Burke's fiction and a splendid forerunner to the Robicheaux confrontation with mesmerizing violence and moral vision. Here is the heart of Burke's heartbreakingly visible dark domain of the human spirit.

In Iry Paret, Burke creates a richly complex character who is probably the true heir to Dave Robicheaux, himself a descendent of Hack Holland and, to a lesser extent, Avery Broussard. In *The Lost Get-Back Boogie* Burke launches swiftly into the fiercely self-scrutinizing, confessional mode of the first-person narrator. This gambit, as in the best of his short stories, remarkably energizes his style and deepens the psychological and moral complexities of his vision. The main character's compulsions and rationalizations take center stage, gradually emerging as Paret himself begins to acknowledge his own limitations and self-delusions.

Burke carefully lays out his usual landscape of prisons, dreary bars, holding cells, pickup trucks and gun racks, oil rigs and sleazy roadhouses, in which the ex-con, Iry Paret, tells the tale of his parole, released after having stabbed a man in a bar, and his journey from Louisiana to Montana (which parallels Burke's own) to work on the ranch of his prison-buddy's father, Frank Riordan. In the course of the novel, Paret literally replaces Buddy Riordan, his friend from prison, by succeeding on the ranch, befriending his father and helping him with local environmental battles. In doing so he unintentionally turns the populace against Buddy and finally ends up by marrying Buddy's ex-wife Beth. In effect the story of this redneck's redemption is a complicated psychological process, for Iry's survival seems to depend ultimately upon Buddy's death, which finally occurs in an almost suicidal manner. Such Oedipal-insinuating conflicts between killer brothers provide the novel with its terrible economy of vision that personal triumph necessarily begets personal betrayal. Such a dark psychological subtext pervades all of Burke's subsequent novels.

In such a world nature affirms and abides: "Montana . . . reached out with its enormous sky and mountains and blue and green land and hit you like a fist in the heart. You simply became lost in it" (*Lost* 121). Within it stagger, strut, drink, and stab the ex-cons, cowboys, lumberjacks, and mill workers whose marginal lives suggest an instinctual, chaotic, adolescently swaggering and solipsistic grappling with existence. Gruff, lewd, and threatening they also display an aching yearning and longing for country music, women, impossible dreams, one another, and escape, with their tortured memories "of bleeding hangovers, whorehouses, and beer-glass brawls" (*Lost* 145). Life becomes a perpetual war: "In Korea I believed truly for the first time that I was all right, because I realized that insanity was not a matter of individual illness; it was abroad in all men, and its definition was a very relative matter" (202). Muses Paret, "I can't get over the number of people around here who always have a fire storm inside themselves," including himself, he comes to discover (177). Within the firestorms of existence, Paret recalls the memories of his childhood in southern Louisiana, seen through his Southern- nostalgic haze (he "parrots" his own culture's sensibilities and values), trying to re-capture it in his guitar-strumming country tunes: "It was twilight, and I was alone in the cabin, slightly drunk on a half-pint of Jim Beam and my own music and its memory of the rural South" (165). He tries to write a song about it, "The Last Get-Back Boogie," but "when you try to catch all of something, particularly something very good, it must always elude you in part so that it retains its original magic and mystery" (220).

In Paret we again come upon the guilt and shocks of recognition we found in Hack Holland and will find in Dave Robicheaux, coupled with the self-justifications that in any first-person narrative try to make the narrator look as good as possible. He loves his music, trying "to contain all those private, inviolate things that a young boy saw and knew about while growing up . . . in a more uncomplicated time" (*Lost* 95). In fact he stabbed a man who interrupted his singing, which led to his prison sentence. At first he decides that "I was just a juke-joint country musician who had acted by chance or accident in a beer and marijuana fog without thinking," but then he comes to realize "that I killed that man because I wanted to" (113). He believes that "rural southern music is an attitude, a withdrawal into myths and an early agrarian dream about the promise of a new republic," but then he recognizes that it really generates "a false sense of romance," that it is "the most cynical kind of exploitation of poverty, social decay, ignorance of medicine, cultural paranoia, racial hatred, and finally, hick stupidity" (166, 184). He begins to also recognize his own betrayals, his sexual hunger for his buddy's estranged wife, his need to score and get even, "constantly scraping through the junk pile of my past," his drunkenness, his evasiveness, and his darker truths: "You go in one direction or the other, or just stand still, for the same reason—you're too scared to do anything else. It doesn't have anything to do with what you are" (184, 152). "I was betraying a friend, living among people who were as foreign to me as if I had been born in another dimension . . . justifying what I did in a romantic abstraction about the music of the rural South" (184).

Even Paret's relationship with Buddy Riordan comes down to the fact that they served time together in prison, "the only thing we shared: an abnormal period in our lives, since neither of us was a criminal by nature, that contained nothing but degradation, hopelessness, mindless cruelty . . . or the unbearable sexual heat that made your life misery" (*Lost* 188). When Iry joins Buddy on Buddy's father's ranch near Missoula, Montana, the two of them drink, ride, hit bars, and dig fenceposts together, but while Paret begins to heal and right himself, Riordan sinks deeper into alcohol and drugs. It is as if Buddy's descent must coincide with Iry's ascent; personal victory demands its personal victim. Slowly, inevitably Iry replaces him—in Buddy's tough father's eyes, in his estranged wife's bed, in his own self-redemption. As Iry acts—attacking the attackers who oppose Frank Riordan's environmental stands, rescuing a horse from the Riordans' barn after it has been set on fire by his enemies—Buddy remains paralyzed, and in a final rash action dies in a fiery car crash in pursuit of the villain. Beth, Buddy's ex-wife, and Iry settle down on twenty acres, and Iry scores with a hit song on the radio. He can, however, always "see Buddy's cabin faintly in the gathering dark," and he continues feeling as though he betrayed their friendship in some way, a sense that remains with him as omnipresent as "the beating of my own heart" (*Lost* 241). Paret has survived and prevailed, but in Burke's dark domain there is always a terrible price to pay, and in this case it turns out to be Buddy's incinerated corpse. In a way the Iry-Buddy relationship foreshadows that between Dave Robicheaux, the honest cop, and his violent, impulsive colleague, Clete Purcell.

When Burke turned to writing mysteries, he obviously had to rely on the tried-and-true mystery formula: the crime(s), the investigation and interviews, and the solution.[1] To do so something had to give; something had to be sacrificed. For one thing his plots, however elaborate, had to become more systematic, more linear. The formula demands a simpler, more programmatic view of the world. Other mysteries—human motive, moral complexities, psychological compulsions, the fascination with and repulsion toward violence and crime, the contradictory quirks of character and circumstance—had to be "shoe-horned" into the narrative. Clearer targets emerged: evil resides in the mob in New Orleans, complicated CIA and DEA scams and deals, Central American civil wars, and the like. Whatever compromises and connections Burke made, the good guys had to triumph over the bad guys. In the earlier novels sometimes his characters triumphed, and sometimes they failed. In both cases the plots remain unpredictable until the very end: characters can go either way, Avery Broussard back to prison or Hack Holland's return to his basic sense of justice and law, Perry James's self-willed escape from his coal-mining background (thus breaking the violent eye-for-an-eye cycle of revenge and retribution) or Wesley Buford's death in the battle for Atlanta in 1864 in "When It's Decoration Day." In a mystery the resolution has to be much clearer. Whatever tensions and ambiguities arise, the ending or solution has to defuse them, resolve them, and in some way dismantle them.

At first glance James Lee Burke continues the hard-boiled school of American mystery writing. Such mysteries reveal a violent world of corruption, personal treachery, and infinite betrayals. Such writers create almost Dickensian characters who speak tough, crude, naturalistic dialogue. Their vision of the world remains cruel, often heartless, and instinctively chaotic. And the detective or main character's moral point of view begins to look like an anomaly in such a dark domain.

Burke's characters and his southern Louisiana landscape fit all of the above. His characters inhabit a Darwinian combat zone of existence at the edge or margin of conventional society. His Vietnam vets, psychopathic killers, redneck racists, and corrupt cops lead a crude and violent life, driven by their own testosterone tactics in a raunchy moral wasteland of compulsive predators. Burke's knack for raunchy dialogue skewers his characters in their own disturbing realm between sadism and sentiment, terror and tenderness. And his elaborate plots, served up in an intricate labyrinth of betrayals, double-crossings and double-dealings, frame-ups, and set-ups, embody this often nihilistic domain, even when the mystery formula is constantly at work, assuring us (barely) that beneath the murky mayhem lies some kind of rational order and moral victory, albeit shifting and often elusive.

In the first Dave Robicheaux mystery, *The Neon Rain,* which Burke described as "a story of hope and recovery," the villains include Julio Segura, a Nicaraguan, who has a black hooker drowned, deals drugs, and sends money to General Abshire, who uses it to supply the Contras in the Nicaraguan civil war; Bobby Joe Starkweather, Erik the Israeli, and addict Philip Murphy who are hit men tied in with arms dealers and Abshire; and Didoni "Didi" Giacano, a local mob boss, who has Robicheaux's brother killed because he will be used as a witness against him in a Grand Jury indictment. The good guys, however compromised, include Robicheaux; Sam Fitzgerald, a Treasury agent, who is killed by Starkweather; Annie Ballard, a social worker, whom Robicheaux meets and with whom he falls in love; and Clete Purcell, Robicheaux's ertswhile partner who, nevertheless, kills Segura and Starkweather, has been paid $10,000 by Murphy for Starkweather's death, and flees to Guatemala to escape the consequences. Robicheaux, shattered in Vietnam and an alcoholic, upholds an old-fashioned, Puritanical sense of honor: "I suspected that John Calvin was much more the inventor of our Southern homeland than Sir Walter Scott. . . . I simply had to set some things right. . . . I was never good at complexities . . . as a virtue [honor] had little to do with being reasonable" (*Neon* 71, 263). His brother tells him, "You just believe in the world that should be, rather than the one that exists. That's why you'll always be the driven guy you are" (198). And Robicheaux acknowledges his own limitations: "I don't like the world the way it is, and I miss the past. It's a foolish way to be" (238). Despite the fact that General Abshire survives the collapse of his schemes, the viscerally evil hitmen are killed, Giacano is checkmated, and Robicheaux, reinstated in the police department after his questionable tactics, emerges with his love for Annie Ballard intact.

Burke, however, does manage to rattle the cage of the usual mystery plot and in doing so deepens, extends, and in part subverts it. First of all he "front-loads" his mysteries with a plethora of disreputable characters, so many in fact that their very presence and number color the way we see the world. Such a dark domain emerges as a thriving nightmarish world, claustrophobic, interconnected, rotten to the core, and is so overwhelming that no matter whom Robicheaux manages to nail, there will always be higher-ups, more corrupt contenders, and loose ends that will forever escape his net. No matter how the mystery itself is solved, so many tangents have been introduced that they cannot possibly be accounted for nor systematically overwhelmed. No matter what solutions Robicheaux manages to uncover, how many puzzles and connections he is able to put together, the dark domain remains intact, continuously dense, and omnipresent. The complexities of the text itself produce a dark labyrinth whose very nature thwarts the formula's reliance upon cause-and-effect, or as Richard Poirier has suggested, "Literature . . . exists in and through the act by which it questions what at the same time it proposes. . . . its words tend to destabilize one another and to fall into conflicted relationships" (147). As Burke has decribed this more complex state of affairs in *Burning Angel:*

I've often subscribed to the notion that perhaps history is not sequential; that all people, from all of history, live out their lives simultaneously, in different dimensions perhaps, occupying the same pieces of geography, unseen by one another, as if we are all part of one spiritual conception. (38)

There is obviously more to Burke's fictions than hard-boiled realism encapsulated within the mystery formula. His grimmer realm suggests what F. R. Jameson has written about Chandler's: "Raymond Chandler's novels have not one form, but two, an objective form and a subjective one, the rigid external structure of the detective story on the one hand, and a more personal distinctive rhythm of events on the other . . . peopled with recurrent phantoms, obsessive character types, [and] actors in some forgotten psychic drama through whom the social world continues to be interpreted" (142). In Burke's books as in Chandler's we are aware "of some incomparable larger solid . . . created being, of a shadow projecting three-dimensionality out from itself" (Jameson 143). Once the detective becomes implicated, his very involvement propels the story in different directions. His investigation creates new and violent results, "a reaction which nothing can stop . . . as though they existed already in a latent state . . . waiting for a single element to be withdrawn or added" (144), as if Dave Robicheaux's own sense of guilt and complicity can only add to that around him, a reflection of the dark domain he himself inhabits, and increase his own apprehension of waste, despair, and spiritual expiation.

In addition to Burke's spreading and irretrievable stain of a finally unfathomable and frightening realm that is ever present and which no rational investigation can ever adequately "solve" or "de-code" (since it is Burke's vision of the dark night of the human soul), Dave Robicheaux does appear to fulfill at first the traditional role of the outsider-detective as merely an observer of the characters and the seedy landscape they inhabit. "Dave is what I admire most in people," Burke has explained. "He represents courage. He's ethical. . . . He understands the world of blue-collar people, people who are inarticulate but with profound feelings. And he's able to give voice to them. At the same time he's flawed, like the tragic hero—sometimes with pride, sometimes with anger. I guess he's my attempt at Everyman" (*Recipe*). However, he becomes more and more personally involved with the issues at hand. The murder of his brother in *The Neon Rain* leads him to Didi Giacano. Drugged and set up in a car accident, Robicheaux is suspended from the police force and launches his own personal investigation. His own alcoholic nightmares, his experiences in Vietnam, the failure of his first marriage, and his relentless and consistently confessional self-scrutiny transform his anxieties into a major focus of Burke's novel as opposed to a mere addendum to his policeman's morality, loyalty, and sense of justice. In fact his first-person testimony often suggests the spiritual autobiography of an anguished Puritan in its Louisiana Catholic incarnation, desperate to discover the salvation that he cannot possibly fathom in such a nightmarish world from which the deity is obviously absent. Robicheaux's cases are complicated by his own psychic battlefield, his often perilous identity with the very psychopaths he pursues.

Glenn W. Most has defined the kind of complicity Robicheaux experiences with his investigations and the people he tracks down as one of the particular attributes of the American as opposed to the English tradition in mystery novels. In the English tradition the detective remains the outsider, aloof, remote, kept free from any acts of sex or violence. One thinks of Wimsey, Poirot, and Dalgleish, despite Dalgleish's more complex psychological makeup. On the other hand in the American tradition, "the detective is not only the solution, he is also part of the problem, the catalyst who . . . both provokes murders and solves them" (347). Robicheaux thinks that the hitmen, Starkweather or Murphy, must have killed his brother, as yet unaware of his brother's connections with Didi Giacano, and so he pursues them, which results in Starkweather and his crew kidnapping both Robicheaux and Sam Fitzgerald, the Treasury agent, killing Fitzgerald, and setting Robicheaux up as the drugged, drunk driver.

But Most also goes on to suggest that "the difference between the English and the American traditions resides [also] in the way in which they conceptualize the activity of reading," the detective more or less standing in for the reader within the text (Most 349). The more insulated English detective "is designed to create one privileged discourse within the text. . . . The American tradition focuses upon the pain of the process of interpretation . . . caught up in the uncertainties of the activity of interpretation itself" (349, 350). That uncertain act of interpretation underscores the main narrative tradition in American romance from Poe and Hawthorne to one of Burke's more obvious antecedents, William Faulkner, and Toni Morrison. Poe, especially, foreshadows Burke's fiction with his Southern background, fascination with nightmares and prophetic dreams, focus on relentless self-doubt, the *frisson* of possible madness, and descriptions of gothic landscapes and architecture, haunted by the curse of a damning past. In Burke's hands, as a result this approach helps to undermine the binary restrictions—good guy versus bad guy—of the mystery formula, subverting it from within, as Burke's sense of sin, cruelty, heartlessness, and moral dilemmas spreads like a visionary stain throughout his entire texts, tainting both the good guys and the obvious villains.

Along with Robicheaux's own psychologically complex and spiritually anguished soul, Burke deepens and extends the mystery formula by his reliance on mythic dimensions and religious references. For instance when Robicheaux confronts General Abshire at the end of *The Neon Rain,* he remarks, "I'll go now. Read Saint John of the Cross. It's a long night, General. Don't try to get through it with apologies. They're all right between gentlemen, but they don't have much value for the dead" (277). He also raises questions about the nature of evil: were such men like Giacano "genetically defective, or evil by choice?" (207). At one point after he has been suspended, Robicheaux explains, "It's the nature of ritual. We deal with the problem symbolically, but somebody has to take the fall" (128). In this way Burke deepens and widens the popular mystery formula and makes it irrevocably his own. Even some of the titles in his Robicheaux series indicate this perspective, such as *Heaven's Prisoners, A Stained White Radiance*—from Shelley's lines in "Adonais": "Life like a many colored glass/Stains the white radiance of eternity"—and *Burning Angel.* In *Burning Angel,* for instance, Robicheaux remarks, "St. Paul said there might be angels living among us, so we should be careful how we treat one another" (324).

Perhaps Burke would agree with Richard Alewyn that the true roots of the mystery lie not merely in rationalism and Enlightenment thought but in their contradictory cousin, romanticism: "For romanticism, mystery is the condition of the world and all external appearance is merely the hieroglyph of a concealed meaning. . . . Romanticism saw reality as the detective novel does: an everyday and peaceful and deceptive surface, with abysses of mystery and danger underneath" (74, 76). Danger in Burke's world is up front and "in your face," but he also manages to convey those "abysses of mystery," which will not go away and will not scare.

There are many aspects of Burke's vision that we could examine: his Catholicism, the influences perhaps of Tennessee Williams, and the differences between the urban world of New Orleans and the rural world of the bayous. Each may contribute to his fiction that deepens and enlarges the necessary polarizations of the mystery genre. In his mysteries he sets up a basic confrontation between the abiding beauties of the natural world and the stark, cruel, marginal existence of many of his characters. These characters pollute the world they inhabit like the stain of guilt and murder—the wave of decapitations, eviscerations, and dismemberments—which taints and destroys most of them. When Burke writes about the world of the Texas-Louisiana gulf coast with its swamps and bayous or of the blue mountains of Montana, he produces a lyrical prose, a pastoral vision, filled with affirmation and awe, that pointedly contrasts his naturalistic dialogue and savage contests. But in its descriptive clarity and imagistic evocations of weather, light, aromas, and colors, it is as sharp in its own way as is the other: "The rain was falling through shafts of sunlight in the west, and the rain looked like tunnels of spun glass and smoke rising into the sky" (*Burning* 35).

Burke writes with a Thoreauvian attention to detail and often a Whitmanic delight in the sheer boundlessness and variety of nature and the America that has strangely peopled it. Such a romantic sense of oneness and transcendence parallels his characters' thwarted desires for escape in sex, country music, violence, and nostalgia—another trait of a Southern writer—but it also emerges intact in its own right as a legitimate visceral celebration. As Iry Paret comments, "The sky was so clear and deeply blue that I thought I would become lost in it" (*Lost* 204). One could draw up long lists of images that never become repetitive or stale, but one such peroration stands out in *Dixie City Jam*:

. . . we . . . stumbled out into the wet light, into the glistening kiss of a new dawn . . . gulls gliding over the copper-colored roll of the bay. . . . But the scene needed no songwriter or poet to make it real. It was a poem by itself, a softly muted, jaded, heartbreakingly beautiful piece of the country that was forever America and that you knew you could never be without. (224, 225)

Burke interweaves in this extended passage man's contemporary world as well:

. . . we . . . stumbled . . . into an industrial-rural landscape of fish-packing houses, junkyards, shrimp boats rocking in their berths . . . stacks of criss-crossed ties, a red-painted Salvation Army transient shelter among a clump of blue-green pine trees . . . oil-blackened sandpit . . . the smells of diesel and salt-water, creosote, fish blood on a dock, nets stiff with kelp and dead Portuguese men-of-war, flares burning on offshore rigs, freshly poured tar on natural gas pipes, the hot, clean stench of electrical sparks fountaining from an arc welder's torch.
     And in the distance, glowing like a chemical flame in the fog, was Morgan City, filled with palm-dotted skid-row streets, sawdust bars, hot pillow joints, roustabouts, hookers, rounders, bouree gamblers, and midnight ramblers. (*Dixie* 224, 225)

Burke doesn't leave out the human pollution, but the rhythms of his prose sweep it all up into one long Whitmanic burst. You can see the range, the energy, the scope of the American landscape. Other descriptions are usually shorter and imagistic, but the power in them remains the same. It's a Southern pastoral vision, updated to include the polluted present, with its natural wonders that delight as much as they instruct, and it is one more contradictory or contrapuntal piece in the overall depth and breadth of Burke's prose and mysteries.
     Once the Robicheaux character and Burke's use of the mystery formula had been sufficiently established, Burke clearly decided to develop both more fully. Most mystery writers establish a life and history for their main detectives, but Burke amplifies Robicheaux's anguish in a substantially darkened manner. The alcoholism and the Vietnam nightmares expand to include memories of his father's death in an explosion on an oil rig, his mother's sexual exploits and degradation, and the horror of his wife's Annie's murder. Burke also develops a more gothic and mythic approach to his tales, stengthening his nightmarish and haunted atmosphere and ruminating on the forces of evil in the world, which is further heightened by often strange and inexplicable circumstances. And in the later mysteries, though it has always been there, he broadens those themes that reveal his strong social conscience, especially when dealing with issues of race and the politics of racial confrontation.

"Sometimes I recall a passage from the Book of Psalms," Robicheaux admits in *Heaven's Prisoners*. "I have no theological insight, my religious ethos is a battered one; but those lines seem to suggest an answer that my reason cannot, namely, that the innocent who suffer for the rest of us become anointed and loved by God in a special way; the votive candle of their lives had made them heaven's prisoners" (187). In this second Robicheaux mystery, the innocents would include his wife Annie, who is murdered by thugs working for Bubba Rocque; Father Melancon and two women, who have escaped from the civil war in El Salvador but been blown up in a plane; Alafair, the Hispanic girl Robicheaux manages to rescue from the plane (her name also happens to be that of Burke's maternal grandmother and his own daughter), who becomes his adopted daughter; and the people of Alafair's Indian village and in Vietnam who have been slaughtered in war. The villains wind up dead, but Robicheaux is devastated by the death of his wife.

Dave Robicheaux, the self-proclaimed, "one-eyed existentialist" (*Heaven's* 252), has been a New Orleans policeman for fourteen years, killed three people (including a Federal witness), resigned from the force, was wounded twice in Vietnam, is divorced from his first wife Nicole, and adores Annie. He is also an alcoholic, undergoing self-destructive firestorms of guilt, self-recrimination, and despair: "There were times when you are very alone in the world and your own thoughts flay your skin an inch at a time" (60). Despite the fact that a friend describes him as "want[ing] to be a moral man in an amoral business" (261), he is only aware of "the alcoholic succubus that seemed to live within me, its claws hooked into my soul. . . . I burn inside to drink . . . [knowing that] that self-destructive passion, that genetic or environmental wound festered every day at the center of my life" (33, 115, 117). He also recognizes other dark facets of his being: "I was not simply a drunk; I was drawn to a violent and aberrant world the way a vampire bat seeks a black recess within the earth" (66).

Annie was dead because I couldn't leave things alone . . . the bourbon-scented knight errant . . . but the truth was I enjoyed it, that I got high on my knowledge of man's iniquity, that I disdained the boredom and predictability of the normal world as much as my strange alcoholic metabolism loved the adrenaline rush of danger and my feeling of power over an evil world that in many ways was mirrored in microcosm in my own soul. (139)

"Like the hunter, you feel an adrenaline surge of pleasure at having usurped the province of God" (240). He recognizes "the fact that my own mind always became my worst enemy during any period of passivity or inactivity in life. . . . Old grievances, fears, and unrelieved feelings of guilt and black depression would surface . . . and nibble on the soul's edges . . . like a dark electrical current" (230, 231). He sees conspiracy and the dark domain everywhere—in others, in the world at large, and in himself. And if one constituency isn't acting up, the other surely will. This strikes me as Burke's own recognition of the charge of writing such fiction, the dark delight in conjuring up such an obsessive vision.

Robicheaux's self-lacerations pursue him in his nightmares; "the nocturnal landscape is haunted by creatures forged in a devil's furnace" (124), especially of the innocent dead, Vietnam, his own father, Annie. He becomes a man possessed, as if demons are literally rooted in his tortured soul: "But I feel the same way when I relive Annie's death, or remember Alafair's story about her Indian village, or review that tired old film strip from Vietnam. I commit myself once again to that black box that I cannot think myself out of" (187). His father's body was never found, "and sometimes in my dreams I would see him far below the waves" (258). And he cannot predict when the black box will rise from his soul and imprison him: "I never had an explanation for these moments that would come upon me. A psychologist would probably call it depression. A nihilist might call it philosophical insight" (186). It is as if Burke's plots have to be that way in order to accommodate or at least try to match the tortuous vision that lies in Robicheaux's damaged consciousness. And he constantly asks himself, "Why did Dave Robicheaux have to impose all this order and form on his life?" (135), as if questioning the very order and form the mystery formula itself finds it necessary to enact. Burke's existential angst never overwhelms the mystery, as it threatens to do, but he is able to create a plot and realm that reflect and encompass it, thus deepening the anguished cries of his main character.

At times feeling trapped both in his own nightmares and the world that surrounds them, Robicheaux often wonders about the nature of evil and the soul: "How do you explain evil to a child?" (48). He takes Alafair to church, believing "that ritual and metaphor exist for a reason. Words have no governance over either birth or death, and they never make the latter more acceptable" (29), strange insights of an ex-cop stranded in the ritual and metaphor of a mystery. He describes his alcoholism to a priest in the confessional and worries "about the origins of the personality and the mysteries of the soul" (118). And despite his lost Cajun world, the nostalgic New Iberia of his childhood, and his personal knowledge of evil in the world, "I marveled at the innocence of the era in which I had grown up" (125), thus suggesting that he, too, is one of heaven's prisoners.

At times Burke's vision of the dark domain borders on the Manichean notion of a world trapped and imprisoning, constructed by a virulent and savage Old Testament God who never could have created an Eden at the beginning of time. Beneath the more orthodox Christian morality play of the struggle between good and evil lies this bleaker region within which good and evil know one another all too well and are mysteriously interdependent. Only a glimpse of gnosis, of wisdom and knowledge on Robicheaux's part, allows for his insights into this murkier territory, a spiritual quest which alone can help him survive, not as the orthodox good guy but as the superior consciousness in a swamp of barely conscious cretins. As such he knows that "we never go for just one guy. . . . We throw a net over a whole bunch of these shitheads at once" (*Heaven's* 111). But of course only Robicheaux is wise enough to realize that he wears "guilt . . . over [his] head" (245).

Robicheaux's anxieties will continue to plague him throughout the series. When a perilous order is restored in *Black Cherry Blues,* he feels violence receding "like the shadows of the heart that one fine morning have gone with the season," knowing full well that sanctuary is only momentary, that strange moments and the black box will re-emerge to claim him (310). In *A Morning for Flamingos* he rediscovers Bootsie, his first love and now the widow of a mob boss, and marries her, but still he cannot escape from "bone-grinding periods of depression and guilt that seemed to have no legitimate cause or origin" (77). And in the end, "I had grown weary of federal agents and wiseguys, narcs and stings and brain-fried lowlifes . . . in the province of moral invalids" (314). Even though he is happily married to Bootsie, although she has lupus, and adores their adopted Alafair in *A Stained White Radiance,* he still feels "wrapped so tight that my skin felt like a prison. I could hear the tiger pacing his cage. . . . Sometime I imagined him prowling through trees in William Blake's dark moral forest, his striped body electrified with a hungry light"; and he knows "that I was one drink away from their fate—despair, murder of the soul, insanity" (75, 228). "What might be considered irrational, abnormal, aberrant, ludicrous, illogical, bizarre, schizoid, or schizophrenic to earth people . . . is usually considered fairly normal by AA members," he concedes in *In the Electric Mist with Confederate Dead,* and seeing "the fatal light in their eyes," the eyes of murderers, he realizes yet again "that the contest is never quite over, the field never quite ours" (344). Throughout the series Burke intends to "wound us once more with a dark knowledge about ourselves" (*Dixie* 175), and in *Burning Angel,* Robicheaux seeks absolution from a priest, at the same time wondering "if our most redeeming quality, our willingness to forgive, was not also the instrument most often used to lay bare and destroy the heart" (*Burning* 247). In Robicheaux's dark domain such complex psychological and metaphysical visions continue to coincide and reflect a "moral moonscape" in which people too often "lived by the rules that govern piranha fish" and stared through "the keyhole to the abyss" (*Burning* 235, 38, 236).

The Southern tradition in fiction has also produced gothic writers such as Poe, Faulkner, and Carson McCullers (in *Reflections in a Golden Eye*), as well as the playwright, Tennessee Williams, among several others, the atmosphere of their novels and plays haunted by ghosts, curses, doomed plantations, and that sense of inevitable defeat and damnation. Burke also employs this dimension, the violent chaotic society he creates akin to the nightmarish world of gothic novels.[2] Both mysteries and gothic thrillers are clearly close cousins in the world of popular formulaic fiction. Both domains threaten all possible frameworks of law and order and plunge readers and characters into an unendingly visceral and treacherous "new world order." Things may remain unresolvable, because they cannot be adequately comprehended, or they may suggest that stranger powers and forces are at work beyond man's rational consciousness. We have, therefore, entered newer, uncharted territories of both the individual psyche and of society. For example in both *In the Electric Mist with Confederate Dead* and *Burning Angel,* ghosts haunt the tale, the ghost of General John Bell Hood in the former, who becomes somewhat of an adviser to Robicheaux, conjured up within his own hallucinations and nightmares but at the same time seemingly separate from them, and the ghost of the murdered mobster-mercenary, Sonny Boy Marsallus, in the latter. Rumors persist about Marsallus: "The rebels started calling him the red angel. They said he couldn't die" (*Burning* 37). And even when we find out that he had worn a flak jacket into the ambush that started the rumors, once he is finally murdered, he is still mysteriously seen or heard by four other characters, two of whom are Robicheaux's wife and adopted daughter. Remarks Bootsie, Dave's wife: "'But I know that voice, Dave. My God. . . .' But she didn't finish" (*Burning* 334).

As the Robicheaux series builds, so does Burke's interest in taking on racism and Southern politics, thereby extending his social consciousness into the realm of the mystery. For instance, in *A Stained White Radiance* he celebrates as usual the Southern landscape, those "haunted places . . . deep into the green light of the marsh [where] the morning air was moist and among the flooded trees, and in the shadows and mist rising off the water you could hear big-mouth bass flopping on the edge of the lily pads, hear a heron lift and flap his wings as he flew down a canal through a long corridor of trees and disappeared like a black cipher in a cone of sunlight at the end" (278). But at the same time he recognizes the darker aspects of being "down into the redneck, coonass, peckerwood South [with its] boys who went nigger-knocking . . . who shot people of color . . . had burr haircuts, jug-ears. . . . Each morning they got up with their loss, their knowledge of who they were, and went to war with the rest of the world, [a] permanent underclass, the ones who tried to hold on daily to their shrinking bit of redneck geography with a pickup truck and a gun rack. . . . They were never sure of who they were unless someone was afraid of them" (145, 65, 291). Robicheaux himself despises Bobby Earl, the "Robert Redford of Racism," a slick David Duke who embodies the redneck rage and religion, but also hopes that Earl's "contract of mutual deceit" with his people will eventually result in his erecting his own gallows (302, 303). Robicheaux is decidedly disappointed when he finally discovers that Earl is not involved in the gunrunning, drug-dealing activities of the CIA, as if hoping that his racism alone should be enough to convict him.

In *Burning Angel* Burke explores the doomed interracial love affair between a rich white man, who inhabits a world of air-conditioned mansions and country clubs, and a poor black woman who lives on the remnants of his plantation. In the course of yet another intricate plot, Moleen Bertrand, the white man, has become involved with mobsters and mercenaries to destroy the remains of his plantation for some kind of pollution-spawning corporate gambit, operating ironically enough under the name of the Blue Sky Electric Company. In doing so he must evict his long-time lover, Ruthie Jean Fontenot, the black woman, from the place. In the course of events she becomes pregnant, undergoes an illegal and brutal abortion and becomes permanently crippled. Bertrand has also killed a black boy in a hit-and-run accident which is covered up by his white wife Julia (a revelation that holds the embittered marriage together) and the local (white) police. The upshot leads to a mutual suicide pact in a New Orleans motel between him and Ruthie Jean.

But what disturbs Burke are the betrayals and secret deals that have been made to keep the interracial affair secret. Ruthie's brother murders the man who has been blackmailing Bertrand about Bertrand's relationship with her, and Bertrand is able to save him from the electric chair. At the same time bulldozing Bertrand's plantation involves uprooting an ancient slave graveyard on it, an evisceration of the past that Robicheaux cannot stomach. All of this "had reenacted that old Southern black-white confession of need and dependence that, in its peculiar way, was a recognition of the simple biological fact of our brotherhood" (*Burning* 339). The graveyard becomes "our original sin, except we had found no baptismal rite to expunge it from our lives. That green-purple field of new cane was rooted in rib cage and eye socket" (215-16). Robicheaux would like to believe that one day "all those nameless people who may have lain buried in the field—African and West Indian slaves, convicts released from the penitentiary, Negro laborers whose lives were used up for someone else's profit—would rise with the smoke and force us to acknowledge their humanity and its inextricable involvement and kinship with our own" (172). This doesn't happen, of course, since despite everything "we seldom know each other and can only guess at the lives that wait to be lived in every human being" (339). Still at the end of the novel Burke leaves us with the image of columns marching in the mist "four abreast out of the trees, barefoot, emaciated as scarecrows [and with] just a careless wink of the eye, just that quick . . . you're among them, wending your way with liege lord and serf and angel, in step with the great armies of the dead" (339, 340).

The Dave Robicheaux of *Cadillac Jukebox,* which appeared for several weeks on the New York Times best-seller list (*Dixie City Jam* was Burke's first book to make it there in 1994), shows signs of healing and emerging from his self-loathing past and self-inflicted angst:

But time has its way with all of us, and today I didn't brood upon water as the conduit into the world of the dead. The spirits of villagers, their mouths wide with the concussion of airbursts, no longer whispered to me from under the brown currents of the Mekong, either, nor did the specter of my murdered wife Annie, who used to call me up long-distance from her home under the sea and speak to me through the rain.

Now water was simply a wide, alluvial flood plain in the Atchafalaya Basin of south Louisiana that smelled of humus and wood smoke, where mallards rose in squadrons above the willows and trailed in long black lines across a sun that was as yellow as egg yoke. (8)

This in part accounts for the swift, stream-lined sleekness of *Cadillac Jukebox,* the well-honed speed of its labyrinthine plot and host of odd-ball, fiery-eyed, doomed characters. Robicheaux hasn't lost his edge, however, for he becomes obsessed with Buford LaRose, the man running for governor, and his wife Karyn, who had been Robicheaux's lover years before either of them had married. LaRose represents money, power, and position, a perfect foil for the blue-collar, Cajun-speaking Robicheaux. The dialogue between them is perfectly pitched as Robicheaux pursues and LaRose evades, the former in his hard-edged declarative way, the latter seeking solace behind the Southern graciousness of good manners. Buford has Dave's number: "You're a classic passive-aggressive, Dave, no offense meant. You feign the role of liberal and humanist, but Bubba and Joe Bob own your heart" (56). But Robicheaux has his as well, stripping the racist past of any nostalgia and patina provided by the Knights of the White Camellia, which the LaRoses rode with. Buford says he wants to atone for that past, but he prides himself on the Southern, aristocratic manners that it maintained: "Shakespeare says it in *King Lear,*" Robicheaux tells him. "The Prince of Darkness is a gentleman. They terrorized and murdered people of color. Cut the bullshit, Buford" (96). All roads seem to lead to the LaRoses' plantation. "You serve a perversity of some kind," Robicheaux tells him. "I just don't know what it is" (159). Neither do the readers for a while, wondering if perhaps Robicheaux is just exercising his own prejudices: "The presence of power and celebrity gave it a glittering mask. The LaRoses were what other people wanted to be . . ." (129). Can this be true of the mellower Robicheaux, too?

Marilyn Stasio has described *Cadillac Jukebox* as "the most incoherent of the crime stories that James Lee Burke has [written]. . . . Nobody reads these sprawling, sweaty novels for narrative sense anyhow" (*New York Times* Book Review 18 Aug. 1996: 28). It is labyrinthine and sprawling, but it is not incoherent, and the idea that narrative sense does not matter seems grossly exaggerated. As usual Burke front-loads his novel with several seemingly unrelated characters. By page thirty-four we have met or been introduced to Aaron Crown, a wonderfully mad redneck who claims he did not murder the NAACP leader, Ely Dixon, and wants Robicheaux to clear his name; Buford LaRose, who is running for governor and has written a book on Crown proclaiming Crown's guilt and using him as an example of what to run against in a campaign; his wife Karyn LaRose, who still smolders visibly in Robicheaux's presence; Sabelle Crown, Aaron's slatternly daughter, who works as a prostitute and is somehow involved with the LaRoses; and several others. Buford LaRose's campaign, it becomes clear, is involved with a slew of wild characters. He has made a Faustian pact with prostitutes, the Giacano family, blackmailers, drug dealers, Sixties' gurus and the like, and they now seem to be in control of him and his campaign.

Burke's world remains viscerally intact from a harrowing description of gang rape and murder in prison—"*I'm gonna take your eyes out with a spoon*" (*Cadillac* 50)—to the description of Aaron Crown's eyes: "They flared with a wary light for no reason, looked back at you with a reptilian, lidless hunger that made you feel a sense of sexual ill ease, regardless of your gender" (2). Crown, one of Burke's best characters, escapes from prison and is on the prowl with a certain agenda in mind:

Even before he had been a hunted man, Aaron was one of those who sought out woods and bogs not only as a refuge of shadow and invisibility but as a place where no concrete slab would separate the whirrings in his chest from the power that he instinctively knew lay inside rotted logs and layers of moldy leaves and caves that were as dark as a womb. (146)

This is that domain of "unnecessary cruelty, the kind that was not even recognized as such, that hung in the mind like an unhealed lesion" (242). And the characters who fester and kill in this nightmare zone become strangely familiar and eerily close at hand:

So the job becomes easier if you think of them in either clinical or jailhouse language that effectively separates them from the rest of us: sociopaths, pukes, colostomy bags, lowlifes, miscreants, buckets of shit, street mutts, recidivists, greaseballs, meltdowns, maggots, gorillas in the mist. Any term will do as long as it indicates that the adversary is pathologically different from yourself.

Then your own single-minded view of the human family is disturbed by a chance occurrence that leads you back into the province of the theologian. (251-52)

The brutal economy of the social and moral tragedy that plays itself out in this latest mystery, in which "much madness is divinest sense" and justice of a kind wreaks its vengeance on everyone, shimmers with Burke's penchant for religious and mythic allusions. "You should have sat at the elbow of St. Augustine," Buford LaRose tells Robicheaux in one of their perfectly controlled but overheated confrontations. "You were born for the confessional" (133). He and his wife Karyn are described as Orpheus and Eurydice—"Orpheus went down into the Underworld to free his dead wife. But he couldn't pull it off. Hades got both of them" (CJ 70)—and in a final scene in the fiery inferno that has become their mansion, Burke fulfills the mystic imperative:

Then we saw them, just for a moment, like two featureless black silhouettes caught inside a furnace, joined at the hip, their hands stretched outward, as though they were offering a silent testimony about the meaning of their own lives before they stepped backward into the burning lake that had become their new province. (294)

Is it any wonder that a character named Persephone is in many ways responsible for the LaRoses' blazing demise? Or that Robicheaux, ruminating on the latest horrors he's lived through, concludes this mystery with the following?

The air was suddenly cool and thick with the sulfurous smell of ozone, the wind blowing dust out of the new cane, the wisteria on our garage flattening against the board walls while shadows and protean shapes formed and reformed themselves, like Greek players on an outdoor stage beckoning to us, luring us from pastoral chores into an amphitheater by the sea, where we would witness once again the unfinished stories of ourselves. (297)

The tragic inevitability, the smooth sensuous flow of language, the intimation of mythic patterns, the pastoral reincarnation of southern Louisiana, the worldly sense of satiation and a perilous wisdom with its hint of gothic atmosphere, a dark domain momentarily relieved of its legacies of cruelty and vengeance: this is the true territory of James Lee Burke's art.

James Lee Burke's mysteries clearly continue and elaborate upon the hard-boiled school of crime and detective fiction, but they do so in his own manner and with a deeper, darker vision. His own lyrical descriptions of the natural world, his meticulously raunchy dialogue, the patter of "swinging-dick talk" (*Duke* 237), his metaphysically mysterious and labyrinthine plots, the psychological depths of guilt, obsession, and self-loathing that affect many of his characters and certainly his detective hero, the lasting shadow of the Vietnam War, his own deeply affected and affecting social conscience and proletarian perspective, his religious imagery and speculations: all of these carve out a literary landscape that is his own. Within the traditional mystery formula of calculated revelation, he works elaborate literary wonders, born of the Southern tradition in American fiction, and consistently exposes the darker, more frightening side of contemporary American life. And though the legally guilty may be captured and/or killed, and justice works its havoc and its savage economies, that violent landscape, beautifully and heart-breakingly rendered, remains ominously and luminously intact.

Epilogue: Cimarron Rose

Cimarron Rose, Burke's latest novel that does not feature Dave Robicheaux[3] and which Marilyn Stasio praised as "fertile territory for Burke" with its "richly detailed . . . crack-of-dawn freshness" (*New York Times* Book Review 10 Aug. 1997: 18), combines the Texas roots and the interest in social justice of his earlier work—*Lay Down My Sword and Shield* (1971), *Two for Texas* (1982), and the stories, "Hack" and "Uncle Sidney and the Mexicans" from *The Convict and Other Stories* (1985)—with the swift bold scenes and complex, tightly woven mystery plots of the Dave Robicheaux series. The plot pits the poorer and racially mixed families of the West End in the little town of Deaf Smith, Texas, against the richer white ones who belong to the Post Oaks Country Club in the East End, as well as Vernon Smothers' honest and law-abiding son

Lucas against Jack and Emma Vanzandt's cruel and deranged son Darl, who likes to think of himself as invulnerable, like "Greeks who lived above the clouds" (*Cimarron* 277). Darl displays "a strange solipsistic attitude toward others. . . . [His] insensitivity was almost a form of innocence" (81). Lucas is accused of raping and killing Roseanne Hazlitt one night outside a local hangout, a crime which leads his defense lawyer, Billy Bob Holland, into a maelstrom of mayhem, drugs, corruption, and murder, all of which lead to Jack Vanzandt's business dealings and a renegade Mexican drug agent.

In the first six chapters, as swiftly paced and set up as a Robicheaux mystery, we find out about Billy Bob's family background, that he is Lucas's real father, that evidence on the night of Roseanne's death has been tampered with, and that Jack Vanzandt wants Billy Bob to defend Darl for beating up a Mexican. In jail Lucas Smothers overhears the sociopath Gerald T. Moon telling another cellmate, Jimmy Cole, about Moon's murdering a family in California (it will later be discovered that Moon murdered Billy Bob's father when Holland fired him for having mutilated a black girl). Harley Sweet, the deputy, abuses some Mexican prisoners, Cole escapes and strangles Sweet, and Cole kills the only witness who can identify Moon, thus insuring Moon's freedom. Moon proceeds to hound Billy Bob, Lucas despises Billy Bob, Billy Bob is haunted by his family's violent past, and Moon may be out to get Lucas who overheard his confession.

Burke deepens Billy Bob's sense of his own guilt. Not only has Billy Bob's great-grandfather been an alcoholic gunfighter, but his grandfather was a violent Texas Ranger who managed to capture the notorious outlaw, John Wesley Hardin, and chase Pancho Villa into Mexico, and his father was blown up in a welding accident years ago. Violence relentlessly pursues him: "I knew the old enemy had once more had its way and something terrible was happening in me that I couldn't stop" (224). As Gerald Moon snarls, "A man got that much hate in him is a whole lot more like me than he thinks" (178). And Billy Bob recognizes as much: "The day you understood a man like Moon was the day you crossed a line and became like him" (207). Billy Bob has been a Houston cop, a Texas Ranger, an assistant United States attorney, and is now a defense attorney, haunted by the ghost of his legendary partner, L. Q. Navarro, whom he shot by accident during an unauthorized and illegal raid on drug runners across the border in Coahuila, Mexico. Navarro appears in dreams as a kind of conscientious advisor and prophet of things to come, the type of phantom counsellor who appears in several earlier novels, especially *In the Electric Mist with Confederate Dead*. His death is why Holland gave up the federal prosecutor's job. As in all Burke's fiction, the past casts a long shadow: "So every new day of your life you're condemned to revisiting what you can't change" (226).

As in much of Burke's fiction, redemption is possible. Billy Bob discovers his great-grandfather's journal and reads it throughout the novel. In 1891 Sam Morgan Holland fell in love with Jennie, a woman connected with the Dalton-Doolin gang. She is the rose of Cimarron of the title, he rescues her from them, and the two of them escape across the Pecos River. Sam becomes a preacher and "put aside his violent ways" (*Cimarron* 271). Past and present have become reconciled, and the apotheosis of the Hollands is complete.

In *Lay Down My Sword and Shield* and *Two for Texas* Burke created one incarnation of the Holland family. These included Son Holland, who was involved in the Battle of San Jacinto; his son who jailed John Wesley Hardin; his son, Sam Holland, who committed suicide over a political bribe; and his son, Hackberry Holland, the novel's main character and eventual hero. As noted above Sam Morgan Holland was Burke's actual maternal great-grandfather, and the tale of arresting John Wesley Hardin is true. The colonial past in Texas is much closer to the present, since it is so recent, Burke has insisted,[4] and therefore he is very much still attached to his own family's legacy of violence, alcoholism, and religion as if it were a kind of curse. His great-great-grandfather, William Burke, part of the "Irish Brigade" during the Goliad Massacre in Texas on Palm Sunday in 1836, fled to New Iberia in southern Louisiana where the Robicheaux series takes place, and William's sons, Burke's great-grandfather and great-uncles, fought on the Confederate side during the Civil War. In fact Deaf Smith, the name of the county seat in *Cimarron Rose,* is the actual name of the man who cut Vincent's Bridge for Sam Houston and allowed Houston to cut off Santa Anna in *Two for Texas.* Burke's connections with this Texas past are abundantly clear and have provided him yet again with the family history for his latest fiction.

One other strand from Burke's earlier work appears in *Cimarron Rose.* This is his attack on what he calls "the emissaries of Empire" (286) and "the forces of Empire that no government ever acknowledged" (269). These assassins and virtual outlaws have been trained at the School of the Americas at Fort Benning: "Their graduates have a way of murdering liberation theologians and union organizers or anybody they don't approve of" (78). Felix Ringo, drug runner, double agent, and murderous criminal, is such a graduate, and his involvement with Jack Vanzandt leads to Vanzandt's downfall.

As usual Burke's eye for detail is at once lyrical and sharp: "The typical isolation unit in a prison is a surreal place of silence, bare stone, solid iron doors, and loss of all distinction between night and day. Its intention is to lock up the prisoner with the worst company possible, namely, his own thoughts" (103). After Billy Bob has accidentally killed Navarro, he returns to the scene of his guilt:

I went back across the river, without a badge . . . then down into the interior, across dry lake beds and miles of twisted moonscape that looked like heaps of cinders and slag raked out of an ironworks, into mountains strung with clouds and finally a green valley that was glazed with rain and whose reddish brown soil was lined with rows of avocado trees. (109)

In *Cimarron Rose* Burke is writing at the top of his form. This latest novel combines and improves upon all that has gone before and foreshadows more to come. As noted in the *Los Angeles Times* Book Review, "James Lee Burke has emerged as one of the very best American crime writers. The pleasure of reading Burke's prose is immense, and his evocations of place [and] atmosphere are not to be dismissed as mere genre writing. . . . [His is] an uncommon mixture of taut realism and poetic eloquence."[5] At the end of the novel Billy Bob "thought of Comanche Indians and saddle preachers and trail drovers and outlaws and was sure that somewhere beyond the rim of the world Great-grandpa Sam and the Rose of Cimarron turned briefly in their saddles and held up their hands in farewell" (*Cimarron* 288).

INTERVIEW WITH JAMES LEE BURKE
JUNE 1996 AND AUGUST 1997

Sam Coale: You seem to know a lot about prisons, penal colonies and barracks and Korea and the Job Corp, Vietnam. I was wondering if you had any personal relationship to those institutions or whether you research these things?

James Lee Burke: I never do research. You know once in a while I call the Reference Library and get something straight, but in one way or another, most of the things I write about will come out of my experiences and experience of people I've been around. Vietnam, for instance, is just part of Dave Robicheaux's fictional background.

SC: You focus on the unrelenting confrontation between the individual self and the system.

JLB: Well, if a protagonist has a moral vision, he is going to be in contention with the world. That's inevitable both in fiction and in ordinary life.

SC: Many of your characters are social underdogs, such as Marcel in the short story "The Pilot." He's a Louisiana coonass who is restless and lonely, and you could go down the list with Hack and the Mexicans and J.P. Winfield and Iry Paret. Is that part of your own personal background, or is it a political vision?

JLB: Well, for instance, I went to high school in Houston and experienced the very wide social abyss between the very, very rich and the very, very poor. Again it also goes back to the earlier premise that we just discussed. The moral protagonists or anyone who has any clarity of moral vision eventually is going to find himself not welcome in one way or another with people who are usually running things. It's the nature of the world. I don't think there's been a society in the history of the earth that champions the altruist. We do it retroactively. We revise ourselves every day by taking up the cause of those who are already martyred. The martyr himself is seldom applauded in his lifetime. George Bernard Shaw said that we do not learn from the reasonable man. The reasonable man adapts himself to the world, whereas the unreasonable man changes the world.

SC: In your earlier novels, you can follow the journeys of your characters from the Cumberland Mountains in Kentucky to Texas and Louisiana. For instance, Son Holland came to Texas in 1835. In *Two for Texas* and *To the Bright and Shining Sun* many of your characters live in present day Yoakum, Texas. Does this parallel your family background in some way?

JLB: Well, I've lived in a whole bunch of places. My mother's family is from Kentucky. I've lived all over. Sam Holland, the great-grandfather in *Cimarron Rose,* is my own great-grandfather on my mother's side. He really did capture the outlaw, John Wesley Hardin. Holland's daughter, my grandmother, was named Alafair, the same name as my own daughter and Robicheaux's adopted daughter.

My great-great-grandfather on my father's side was William Burke. His sons rode with Lee on the Confederate side in the Civil War. After the Goliad Massacre in Texas on Palm Sunday in 1836, where the Mexicans rounded up about 350 American soldiers, had them kneel and then clubbed or shot them to death—the "Angel of Goliad" was a prostitute who begged for mercy for some of those soldiers and saved their lives— William fled to New Iberia in southern Louisiana. So I'm dealing with a real family history in its true context and culture.

SC: You've also done so many different things, such as being a truck driver, a social worker in South-Central Los Angeles on Skid Row and on the Mexican East Side, and been a reporter, a worker in the oil fields . . .

JLB: Yeah, it comes down to a very bad employment record!

SC: Even though you were born in Houston, would you consider yourself a Cajun?

JLB: Our family is Irish that came from Ireland originally. I grew up on the Louisiana Texas coast. My father was an engineer and worked for a pipeline company there.

SC: Do you think there is also that sense in your books that in some way geography contributes to a person's fate, that there's a kind of relationship between the psychological state of a character and the landscape that he or she occupies?

JLB: Well, I was heavily influenced as a young writer by the naturalists, certainly Stephen Crane, John Steinbeck and I would say John Dos Passos. To my mind John Dos Passos is one of the greatest writers that our country ever produced. And he's not read today. Dos Passos is a great writer.

SC: You have a very real and visceral sense of a moral vision, and that moral vision has a hell of a time in the world where it is. In one short story, "Losses," you wrote about a boy named Claude at St. Peter's School in 1944, and he experiences a very deep sense of guilt, as strong as that found in stories by Hawthorne and Faulkner, which infiltrates and penetrates his consciousness. Other characters confess to ratting on their fellow prisoners of war in Korea. There's Robicheaux's participation in the Vietnam War. Do you personally feel this? Is this part of your own Catholic background? Is it something that you also mine to make your characters more emotionally complex?

JLB: Well, each of those characters whom you mention is different in some way. Dave Robicheaux doesn't bring guilt back from Vietnam. And the positive situations are all different, but the books, all of them, deal with the search for redemption. It becomes convenient very often for people to look for the origins of guilt which is often called "Catholic guilt." People who use the term usually don't look into the psychoanalytical origins of an obsession with guilt within themselves. A person earns his way out of it through a passage that is very difficult. This is oftentimes in psychoanalysis the Gethsemane experience, a kind of going to hell without dying. It's the Dark Night of the Soul that St. John of the Cross describes, and its origins are myriad and difficult to explain. There's probably no one origin, but it goes back in all probability to the family.

SC: Do you look at your books, therefore, as a kind of exorcism, whether for you, the writer, or for Robicheaux?

JLB: No. Art as therapy is something that someone who has never written thinks about. It's not worth talking about.

SC: In the Robicheaux novels, where the plots are so incredibly complex, it's almost as if you're setting up these complications so that the characters can work through them toward a kind of personal redemption. But the world in which they find themselves is a very Manichean world. It is a prison, a living hell. Do you see in your own work a kind of perilous balance between characters' seeking some kind of personal redemption and a world which you once described as a place of moral psychosis?

JLB: You're absolutely correct. That's the heart of it and the oldest thing in world literature. It's not new, it's not singular in any way, it's the oldest thing, but it is one which in my view is seldom treated today. In part because we live in an era in which responsibility is collectively described. I think it has to do with some problems of conscience which we have as a nation. We have involved ourselves in some behavior collectively, that which is contrary to all of our best traditions. And I grew up in the South where every intelligent Southerner knew that our worst members were allowed to function only because men and women of conscience looked askance. We gave them sanction by not acting on the problem regionally. Northerners see very quickly the problems. But that's simply a microcosm for the macrocosm.

Both Faulkner and Hawthorne took Young Goodman Brown's journey, which all people take whether they're aware of it or not. I think, for instance, that Hawthorne, with his fascination with the workings of the mind, is the real forerunner to film noir and both detective and gothic tales: the notion of pride, a historical Christian attitude, the fall from grace.

A Franciscan theologian, a friend of mine, once said that the difficulty in dealing with evil is that it's in a fashion that is seldom detestable and that it's always innocuous, and it insinuates its way into our lives. That's the nature of evil. If it were horrendous and physically repellent, we wouldn't have any problem with it.

SC: Is there something in violence and evil and betrayal that Robicheaux and some of these other characters find immensely attractive? In the short story "Hack" the old man recognizes that a fascination with and for cruelty lurks in himself. Is that part of the nightmarish landscapes you create, because even though they're evil and horrible, there is something about them like the dark forest that Goodman Brown goes into that's incredibly attractive?

JLB: It's in all police officers. And most who are honest will tell you. They're out on the edge, the rush, and also I think that most police officers would tell you that they can speak more readily with people who inhabit their nether world, even though those people might be their antagonists, than they can speak with ordinary people. Were you ever a journalist? You work in a news room, you realize very quickly how a city operates and how opposed it is to the way that operation is reported. That's why most newspaper people are cynics. You know who's on a pad, you know how stories are influenced by the advertisers, you know the publisher in all probability is a conservative, a Republican. For years, Sam, I gave interviews about the early books and the Dave Robicheaux series. I mean, for years I talked about one of the most prevalent things, namely, the American involvement with the death squads and the Contras, the bloodshed going on in Central America, the drugs, the drug-dealing ties between the Contras and our intelligence people. I mean this absolutely. I think with one exception every reporter's hand stopped; it never made print for years. I think one reporter, Kate Reagan at the *San Francisco Examiner,* used the material in her column, but it would never make print during the Reagan/Bush era. Not once.

SC: Maybe this was because Reagan referred to the Contras as just like our founding fathers.

JLB: Oh, yeah, sure. I knew that this was material that no one was going to feel comfortable with. You got some guys saying, you know, that priests and nuns are being murdered there with M16 rifles made in Connecticut, made by the Colt Arms company. They didn't want to hear that, but that was common knowledge. *The Neon Rain* was written before the Iran-Contra story broke. It was published just after the story broke, but it was already in print, in galleys, before that story became commonplace. Well, the truth is that story was available back in the early Eighties. It wasn't any secret. I was in Amnesty International, and we heard about what was going on between the Israelis and the Iranians, that we were funneling arms from Israel into Iran. It was a secret deal between Reagan and the Ayatollah. But if I could hear this at an Amnesty International meeting in Wichita, Kansas, I don't think that it was a very well kept secret. And when the story about the illegal arms to the Contras broke—I think that was on a CNN report about 1983—it was ignored.

SC: In *The Lost Get-Back Boogie,* you write about country music and the agrarian dream and the wonderful relationship between and expression of each of them, how one reflects the other. And then about twenty pages later Iry Paret says, "But that's bullshit. I mean . . . the reality is incredibly different." One of your strategies or part of the vision is the way you compare or contrast that kind of self-image or the mythic image with exactly what's going on, so there's always a kind of jolt when you come face to face with such powerful discrepancies.

JLB: Iry is reflecting upon the finality that's always involved with the commercial sale of anything that's dear, the music that Iry lost. But that's the nature of the world, that once the cash register starts ringing . . .

SC: What about *The Lost Get-Back Boogie*?

JLB: That book was rejected over a hundred times. One agent had it for nine years. It was rejected by over a hundred New York editors. My agent, Philip Spitzer, kept it out there nine years, and Louisiana State University Press finally published it in 1986, and it was nominated for a Pulitzer prize. *To the Bright and Shining Sun* came out in 1970. Then *Lay Down My Sword and Shield* came out in 1971. And it was thirteen years before I published in hardback again.

Louisiana State University Press put me back into print with *The Convict* in 1985. I was totally out of print, and then the following year they published *The Lost Get-Back Boogie,* so I'll always owe those people for the rest of my life. Michael Kingston passed away. He was a marketing person who did so much for my career. He died last year. But I can never repay the debt I owe LSU Press.

SC: I saw an interview in the newspaper about the alcoholism and all that . . .

JLB: Yeah. I am in the twelve-step group today and have been for quite a while. Those thirteen years were spent writing books that I couldn't sell.

SC: You never knew that would happen.

JLB: No. I couldn't believe it. I'd been able within thirteen years to publish one paperback. Of course I published short stories in magazines. And in 1985 I was totally out of print, and then four years later I won an Edgar and a Guggenheim Fellowship. I also want to mention my editor, Patricia Mulcahey. She and I have been together on eight books, and I call her "Saint Pat." She really took enormous risks. I told her, "Pat, if this goes belly-up, you and I are both going to be looking for work." She'll rip the butt out of an elephant for one of her books.

SC: Looking back, do you know why?

JLB: They wouldn't buy 'em. Let me tell you the story. There's no mystery to it, that I was a young writer and I had an enormous amount of success. I published *Half of Paradise* in 1965. Finished it in 1960. I never published easily. It was always hard for me, but I wrote that book when I was only twenty-two years old, and then Houghton Mifflin bought it four years after I completed it, and then it came out the following year and got great reviews. I also was the Breadloaf Fellow [at Middlebury College].

Those were all what were called midlist books, and in publishing a writer has a better chance with no track record, than say two or three books that are midlist. Also during that period it became, I think, more and more difficult to sell male-oriented writing. The market slipped quite a bit. Now I am not making excuses, but I couldn't sell anything, and I wrote during that time I don't know how many novels and short stories. Actually I published quite a few stories in some nice places like the *Atlantic Monthly,* and *Southern Review,* but I just could not sell in hardback. My agent sold *Two for Texas* in 1982 as an original paperback. But the novels I wrote during that period—one dealt with the search for the Holy Grail in modern times, and one dealt with John Bell Hood, the Confederate cavalry officer. I wrote about a young Cajun prize fighter, a Marine corps veteran who was named Robicheaux, and the title of the book was *Heaven's Prisoners,* and I could never sell it.

SC: Do you ever consider bringing these back now?

JLB: No, no, because, you see, eventually those failed books that I could not sell were incorporated into the Dave Robicheaux series. All the characters would later reappear, but you see I had to relearn an old lesson, Sam, namely, that in one way or another what a writer writes as well as he can will eventually find a home. It may not find a home in the form that he currently envisions, but eventually his purpose will be realized.

SC: How did you decide to write *The Neon Rain* and as a mystery? Mysteries do sell, particularly because people expect a particular formula. Do you write differently or approach it differently? Does the mystery formula cramp your original style?

JLB: I was influenced to write *The Neon Rain* by Rick DeMarinis, who was fishing with me one day, and he said, "Jim, you've written every other kind of book except a crime novel," and I said I'd give it a try. But *The Neon Rain* was different from earlier work only in one respect: the narrator, Dave Robicheaux, was this sometime police officer. But the story, the locale, the themes, the people, are all the same. They are no different from the people, the themes, that we meet in the earlier work. I've always found that if an author finds himself doing something that someone else has done or doing anything that is predictable even unto himself, he should abandon it. I never know how a story is going to end. I never see more than two scenes away. Going into the last chapter, I do not know how the book is going to end.

SC: I've already mentioned your labyrinthine plots, the different levels and layers, the many characters, and the elaborately intricate maze of cause and effect. Why are your plots so labyrinthine? Is it because you just keep upping the ante, so it will be harder for you to work your way out of what you've gotten into?

JLB: I often plan the books, and I've always believed the stories are already written in the unconscious. *Burning Angel,* for example—in one way or another all of the characters are biographical, so are the events. What I've never quite understood is that often those who write about the book, the critics, often miss the clear biographical replications that are there. For example in the series, the story of the underground railway, the smuggling into the country of El Salvadoran and Guatemalan refugees, the murder of the Maryknoll priest, Father Stan Rother—all are real stories, and no one to this date has ever made mention of that fact that I use the name of Father Stan Rother and the massacre at the Maryknoll mission there in Guatemala. Again and again, all of those things happened. A friend of mine was there, and the Indians were massacred and put on a US Army helicopter and thrown out at high altitudes across the countryside to warn the other people. The priest was bayoneted to death, he was from Oklahoma, and this material is always overlooked. It's a peculiarity as if I made it up. The story is right there. It's always at the end of people's fingertips. It's not in creation. It's in recognition.

Our record in Latin America is not a good one. The School of the Americas appears in the series repeatedly. I've yet to see a mention of it in a critical review, never, not on one occasion. The School of the Americas at Fort Benning. It's as though it doesn't exist on the page. Or if it exists on the page, it doesn't exist in reality. The School of the Americas is a school of assassins. These are the people who murdered Archbishop Romero, who ran the death squads, who killed the Jesuits in El Salvador. It's disgusting stuff.

SC: Is that the place where Noriega and people like that went?

JLB: That's correct.

SC: In the short story, "The Golden Chain," not only does the first-person narrator, the reporter-journalist, talk with both the guerrillas and Captain Ramos, fierce opponents in the war he's covering, but he's always reassessing his moral stance. He feels troubled about it to begin with, and it begins to erode and crumble. He begins looking at things in different ways. Does "The Golden Chain" foreshadow the concerns of the Robicheaux plots?

JLB: That's correct.

SC: When you write in the first person, so that it's like reading a confession, it seems to loosen up your style.

JLB: The first-person point of view is the most difficult to use, because physically, of course, or epistemologically the narrator is limited as to what he can realistically describe. But also the advantage lies in the immediacy that is established between reader and narrator. Washington Irving writes about that relationship in his travel books, I think. The difficulty in using the first-person point of view has to do with humility. The first-person pronoun is the most intrusive entity.

Go through a critic's column with a red pencil and circle the words, "my," "my," "my," "myself," and see what the arithmetic is. But the first-person narrator has to accomplish confidence in and establish an affinity with his reader. And it has to be a humility that extends itself naturally out of the author. Humility and survival in an artist are absolutely imperative. Humility isn't a virtue as much as a necessity in a person.

SC: Students trust the first-person narrator, whether it's Joan Didion or Henry James, implicitly. It's difficult to make them stand back and look at what the person is saying or how she's justifying her actions. Once a student asked me, "You mean, we have to be suspicious?!"

JLB: Well, the voice has to be one that we accept, in effect a gentle voice, one that reminds us what is best in people. There might be exceptions, but I can't think of one. When we think of great first-person narrators, we remember lines like, "Call me Ishmael." We think of Frederick Henry, and we think of Huck Finn.

I was listening to this guy, the creator of the idea of that western television series, "Bonanza," and he was asked, "How did you create a soap opera on horseback that lasted for so many years?" He said that they created people whom an American family felt comfortable inviting into their livingroom. It's a very good line. In other words, he's saying that he respected the viewers of his medium, which is not true of most producers today. They have absolute contempt for how they feel. You know that great statement from that wonderful sociologist, P. T. Barnum: "No one ever lost money by underestimating the intelligence of the American public."

SC: Do you see yourself developing in the several Robicheaux books? The later books focus on much more emotionally and socially involving issues. The drugs and the gangsters have always been there, but then you bring in a fundamentalist preacher, a "Robert Redford racist."

JLB: It's in all of us. It was there. I didn't make it up. All of it. An artist is a person who sees meanings and dramas in their narratives, in the ordinary events that surround us all. We're always in the vortex of history, but it's seldom that we realize it or recognize it as such. It's the world we all live in. The two biggest problems that have beset our nation since World War Two are race and the vestiges of the vigilante movement since colonial times, McCarthyism. We've never dealt with them, and they are pervasive in our culture. If we're talking about Pat Buchanan, we're talking about Joseph McCarthy. We're talking about the America First Committee. And the problems of race are pervasive in the culture, and we've never dealt with it. I don't know what the answer is, but I think it has to do with the recognition of our past sins. You can only atone for sins by recognizing the transgression, but we've never done it. We've dealt with the problem obliquely. We've dealt with

McCarthyism, which in effect is a rebirth of that vigilante movement that is characteristic of the frontier. But it's based on the passions of the mob and groups of people who cannot accept pluralism. That's the nature of the problem. It's in every city, it's in every rural area, it's in every all-white suburb. It is the logos.

SC: In the later Robicheaux books, you've added gothic touches like General Hood's ghost and the Red Angel in *Electric Mist with Confederate Dead.*

JLB: It's a literary device. *Electric Mist with Confederate Dead* was my attempt to incorporate the "Morte D'Artur" into a modern novel. Also the story's antecedent lies in Ibsen's "Enemy of the People." It was meant to be my attempt at taking a classical story, the knight errant who promises upon his death to return to his country in a time of need. It's Arthurian. To what degree of success I'll leave it up to another's judgment. The novel, *Burning Angel,* is based on St. Paul's admonition, that there may indeed be angels living among us. Hence we need to be very careful as to how we treat one another. Actually his admonition was about the necessity of charity. That's what the story was about.

SC: You create such wonderful descriptions of weather and landscapes. You can be extraordinarily lyrical. In *Burning Angel,* for instance, there's that description of the Louisiana Gulf evoked in very long sentences that are very Whitmanesque. It didn't deny the ugly things that were there, the oil rigs and all, but it included all of them. So there's this sense of a poetic, a sensual landscape. At the same time the dialogue you write is really brisk, brusque, tough, raunchy, to the point. Do these evoke different facets of your own personality?

JLB: Well, thanks. It comes from the process of learning how to write. It takes years and years, probably one of the hardest art forms to accomplish. Ernest Hemingway put it much better than I, when he said, "First you have to learn the craft, then you have to learn the subject," namely the nature of the human family. Then he added, "Every writer who writes about the country knows that that country is in his heart, and his writing becomes the artist's greatest vice as well as his greatest pleasure. Only death can separate him from it."

SC: Do you do anything in terms of listening to dialogue, in terms of what people call "having a good ear"?

JLB: Every writer does that. 10% of a conversation a writer will hear will be meaningful. 90% of what people say is by way of protocol and politeness, but there's that 10% of what you hear that makes a story. It goes back to Wordsworth's statement about where the true poetry of language is always found, and he says it's in the lives and the mouths of humble and rustic people.

SC: The stories you write and the kind of dark domain that you write about is so different from the environment of teaching, which you once lived in.

JLB: I've hung it up six years ago. The stories never change. It doesn't matter the place where you live or where you work. The stories always say that what some people may call the dark side of life is in our living room. It's not to be found on Skid Row. The most insidious, oftentimes the most injurious human behavior I've seen, and I've known very bad people, I've found oftentimes in a university faculty. I've known of no place, and I mean in my experience—I've known mainline recidivists and sociopaths—but I've known no place where I've seen people who would collectively conspire to do physical, financial, professional, and emotional injury to someone with such forthright deliberation than on the university campus. Do you know of any community in the American enterprise that treats its people as badly? These are the liberals that pay TAs and, what do they call them, the Teacher Adjunct Faculty? No benefits, and salaries that are below minimum wage. Give them 7:00 a.m. and 7:00 p.m. classes, work them in a way you wouldn't work an animal, and then cut them loose and hire someone else. Keep the turnstyle moving, so that these guys can't lay claim to tenure. That sounds like a jaded view, but it's not. I guess the California University system is very upfront about it. They use, what is it, 60% or 40% adjunct faculty? No corporation would do something like that to its membership.

So in other words, the dark side of the world is in every human being. Its potential is there. And when is the last time you heard faculty anywhere say they didn't want their pension funds invested in the Boeing Company? You hear all of the hollering about tenure in order to insure the right of free speech on campus. Great, I just don't hear the free speech producing anything other than, well, where's my lifetime tenure card, so I can teach less hours and put the burden on some poor guy who's trying to get his Ph.D. and live on $6,000 a year? You've lived in the academic world. My point is that the exploitation and use of people is not confined to any one area. It's always there.

It's like the fact that Judas Iscariot in historical art is always portrayed as ugly. We make him ugly and different from ourselves. We don't like to feel that he's simply one of the gang. He's us, and so I worked on Skid Row with all kinds of people, every kind of person in the world. These people are those who live at the very bottom of our society. They're harmless people. They're in and out of jail, detox centers; they're harmless people. They're also the people upon whose labor we all depend to harvest our crops.

One theme in my work—it's that the message of Joe Hill and Woody Guthrie, and the Catholic Worker Movement for me is the only reasonable point of view that I see as a way out of our problems. I honestly believe that the great heroes of our culture, the real Jeffersonian radical egalitarians, are the people about whom we seldom write. And I'm talking about Joe Hill, you know, murdered, shot to death. And I'm a big supporter, or I try to be a supporter of the Catholic Worker Movement. I try to be a bigger financial supporter probably than I am. They're great guys. They live it. They walk the walk.

SC: What's the name of the new book?

JLB: *Cadillac Jukebox.* And I have another book finished that's in the editorial process, *Cimarron Rose.* The book is about the Holland family again. And it's going to be the best book I've ever written. This is a home run. But I'm really proud. I'm proud of them all, but this one is an extraordinary book. It's the story of Billy Bob Holland, an ex-Texas Ranger who becomes a defense attorney. And it will be out in '97. *Cadillac Jukebox* makes use of Greek mythology. It goes back into myth, like *Electric Mist.* It is based on the story of Orpheus and Eurydice and the journey into the underworld, Hades and Persephone.

SC: Do you really feel, too, that you're at the top of your form and that things have come together? Is this redemption writ large?

JLB: I had to learn lessons many years ago, and I wrote under difficult circumstances. It was hard for thirteen years to have everything rejected that I wrote, that I submitted to New York, and I've learned again the lesson that I learned as a young writer when I wrote in the oil fields—I used to work offshore, oil exploration—that you do it a day at a time. You never worry about the fate of it. Remember only one admonition and hear it in your heart. You write to make the world a better place, and if you do it with that spirit, God will never let you down. I had to learn that lesson over and over again. But a time comes, Sam, when you don't hear either the applause or that. That time comes, and you learn that success is a very fickle companion. I had it when I was younger, and it went away. It can go away again. But, I always admired what Raymond Carver said right before he died: "If it all ends tomorrow, if I died tomorrow, I'd be the happiest man on earth." It's a very brave statement, because he'd lost one lung already.

SC: Did you know as a child you wanted to write? Was it there?

JLB: Yes. My first cousin is Andre Dubus. We're four months apart. We've been each other's base support all our lives, and he's finally getting the recognition that was denied him. He's doing really well. He's one of the great short story writers of our time.

SC: Do you follow any particular schedule when you write?

JLB: I write about a thousand words a day, usually in the morning. Then I go to the health club, do chores, business. Sometimes I do some long-hand writing at night. I usually start a scene—a man walking in the rain, for instance—and go with it. It's letting the unconscious unfold. It is scary sometimes. And it's all real, however metamorphosized it becomes.

5

RACE, REGION, AND RITES IN WALTER MOSLEY'S MYSTERIES

Traditionally the mystery formula has been a white man's and woman's territory, aligned with the rational values and solutions of the Enlightenment as preached, if not practiced, in the United States, England, and elsewhere. Such notions of personal liberty and pursuits of happiness, spawned by that overarching creed, have historically bypassed and marginalized people of color. Since the mystery formula is supposed to appear to be more or less mimetic, despite its highly conceptualized shape and structure, what happens when its subject is seemingly at odds with its form? Can that form empower the powerless? The mystery is also notoriously based on otherness, the confrontation of the hero with the villain. What happens when it tries to incorporate difference, which has no exact opposite against which to define itself? Can a black detective operate in a generally white world? And if he can, how much will that world and the language out of which it is created change the mystery formula itself?

"I was surprised to see a white man walk into Joppy's bar" (*Devil* 1). With that opening line, the new voice of Easy Rawlins, Walter Mosley's main character, entered the mystery realm in 1990. Mosley is the son of a black maintenance supervisor and a Jewish woman, who grew up in the Watts section of Los Angeles, who worked for awhile as a computer programmer, and who in the course of about eight years managed to write five mysteries, one "straight" novel, and one gothic tale of growing up black in the deep South. It is the voice and the language of that voice that seems to have made the writer. He who has "created a world of almost Faulknerian density" (Lewis), who "displays a pitch-perfect gift for capturing the cadences of black speech" (White), and who made the best-seller list with his fourth mystery, *Black Betty,* in 1994, once told D. J. R. Bruckner of the *New York Times:* "I wrote out a sentence about people on a back porch in Louisiana. I don't know where it came from. I liked it. It spoke to me."[1]

In her book, *The Curse of Cain: The Violent Legacy of Monotheism,* Regina M. Schwartz explores the contradictory problems of identity in the Bible and relates them to the vision of a single God who could incorporate or obliterate all others. In such identity formation she investigates the origins of violence implicit in monotheism and decides that in the Bible "identity is a question rather than an answer" (142). For our purposes her ideas about monotheism can also be used in a discussion of monologue in looking at a first-person narrator as richly formed and constructed as Easy Rawlins in Mosley's first mystery. As a monotheist, the monologist excludes as much as he includes; his creating and forming a self in many ways is an act of violence against the other, the people he is set against or finds himself in opposition to. That act of identity formation remains in many ways provisional and arbitrary, except when defined by the color of one's skin, as Mosley's America relentlessly defines it. Such an identity is constructed in a world of scarcity, in a Darwinian realm of winners and losers, or as Schwartz sees it, as a realm based on "the assumption that one can only prosper when someone else does not" (83). Such an assumption "proliferates brothers and murderous peoples. . . . We are the heirs of Cain, because we murder our brothers" (83, 2).

Easy Rawlins' sense of exclusion is visceral: "I was surprised to see a white man walk into Joppy's bar." Conflict erupts immediately on the basis of race. Faced with the white man's "off-white linen suit and shirt with a Panama straw hat and bone shoes over flashing white silk socks," with his strangely "pale eyes; not a color I'd ever seen in a man's eye," when this apotheosis of whiteness stares at him, he "felt a thrill of fear, but that went away quickly because I was used to white people by 1948" (*Devil* 1). Rawlins establishes his sense of self and the surrounding territory, including his own, very differently, for instance, from the way James Lee Burke does in *The Neon Rain:*

. . . . a light rain started to fall when I came to the end of the blacktop road that cut through twenty miles of thick, almost impenetrable scrub oak and pine and stopped at the front gate of Angola penitentiary. The anti-capital punishment crowd—priests, nuns in lay clothes, kids from LSU with burning candles . . . were praying outside the fence. But another group was there too—a strange combination of frat boys and rednecks—drinking beer from Styrofoam coolers . . .

. . . "I'm Lieutenant Dave Robicheaux, New Orleans police department," I said to one of the guards on the gate. I opened my badge for him.

"Oh yeah, Lieutenant. I got your name on my clipboard. I'll ride with you up to the Block." (1)

Notice the differences in authority. Robicheaux has penetrated the "impenetrable scrub oak and pine" to get to the penitentiary. He is a cop with a mission. He announces his name and his title. He is in charge here. The "I" knows exactly what he is up to. There is no sense of restrictions on him, nor does he seem to feel any. Rawlins is far more circumspect. He, too, announces his territory—we know that he's non-white in that very first sentence—but his realm is far more circumscribed. The very white white man observes him. Rawlins is very much on the receiving end of a penetrating look from the man who was filling the doorway "with his large frame." The mood suggests immediate wariness, tension, and uncertainty, as Rawlins quickly zeroes in on the time period. The "I" finds it necessary to explain right away why and how he has become "used to white people," as if coming upon a strange breed or cult: "I had spent five years with white men, and women, from Africa to Italy, through Paris, and into the Fatherland itself. I ate with them and slept with them, and I killed enough blue-eyed young men to know that they were just as afraid to die as I was" (*Devil* 2). He knows them because in many ways they share his essential fears. The race issue is something else, a matter of violence and exclusion based not upon one's common humanity but upon the far more prevalent vision in 1948 of separation and distinction, of winners and losers, of superiors and inferiors in a social if not a really personal sense.

Easy Rawlins' place is far different from Dave Robicheaux's. He has transplanted himself from his native Houston, Texas, to Los Angeles to find work in the post-World-War-Two economic boom, but he soon realizes that "life was still hard in L.A., and if you worked every day you still found yourself on the bottom" (*Devil* 27). He has had a job at Champion Aircraft but been let go when he refuses to work an extra hour, because he is exhausted, and the boss "tells me that my people have to learn to give a little extra if we wanna advance" (28). Thus, he needs the money to pay his mortgage, and DeWitt Albright, the white man who "produced a white card and a white enameled fountain pen" (6), tells him about a Daphne Monet who "has a predilection for the company of Negroes. . . . But, you see, I can't go in those places looking for her because I'm not the right persuasion" (19). It is Joppy, whom Easy realizes that Albright is making nervous, who introduces Easy to "Mr. Albright," who then asks him to "call me DeWitt, Easy" and offers him a strong handshake "like a snake coiling around my hand" (2). Unlike Dave Robicheaux Easy Rawlins is very much on his own, a position demarcated by the color of one's skin: "It was a habit I developed in Texas when I was a boy. Sometimes, when a white man of authority would catch me off guard, I'd empty my head of everything so I was unable to say anything. . . . I hated myself for it but I also hated white people, and colored people too, for making me that way" (13).

Clearly Walter Mosley's Easy Rawlins is very conscious about his perilous position in a white society. But exactly what does that voice do?

Does Mosley create a particularly black perspective? If it is too clearly bounded by its own vision, can it possibly be developed or deepened in any way? What does such a voice bring to the mystery formula? And if, as Mosley suggests here, race is socially constructed and erected in many ways as an artificial barrier between people, are there ways through or beyond this position that he can exploit in terms of creating his narrative voice?

Like Jim Chee and to a lesser extent Kate Fansler, Mosley's Easy Rawlins occupies a middle ground between both white and black societies. He participates in each, as best he can, and in fact is often employed by white men to investigate black men in that black urban world that white men cannot penetrate. At the same time Mosley chronologically creates historical periods in each of his mysteries, so that he can comment on the changes he sees from one era to the next, much like August Wilson has done in his continuing series of plays that focus on one decade of black experience at a time. That historical development helps to broaden and deepen Rawlins' own sense of his experiences and background, suggests some progress in American race relations, and in doing so involves the reader in the continuing struggle. The barriers of race may be artificial, but they remain ineradicable in most instances, however, a constant in Mosley's world that sharpens the landscape of his fiction.

White men often employ Easy Rawlins to penetrate the black world and culture in a way they cannot. DeWitt Albright sets him up in *Devil in a Blue Dress*. In *A Red Death* (1991) an FBI agent asks Easy to shadow a suspicious Communist and Jew, Chaim Wenzler, who works charity runs at the First African Baptist Church. "You can go where the police can't go," a governor's aide tells Rawlins in *White Butterfly* (1992) (49). "You can ask questions of people who aren't willing to talk to the law." To be a black man throughout the series is forever to be an immediate suspect, subjected to sudden arrests, imprisonment, "legal" violence, and police harassment. "Any Negro who dared to believe in his own freedom in America had to be mad" (*White* 145), Rawlins exclaims. "I wondered at how it would be to be a white man; a man who felt that he belonged" (WB 45). Even whites who think that they are bridging the racial gap come in for Easy's clear-eyed scorn: "They often take the kindest white people to colonize the colored community" (54). Rawlins is always aware of "the rattle of chains. . . . The first thing a black man and a poor man learns is that trouble is all he's got so that's what he has to work with" (*Black* 268, 137). "The air we breathed is racist" (50). "Even in my dreams I was persecuted by race" (133). And when he is approached by a friendly white woman, Barbara Moskowitz, from Des Moines one evening, her white male sidekicks immediately taunt him: "Hey you! Black boy! . . . Nigger's trying to pick up Barbara" (*Devil* 53, 54).

The effects of Rawlins' inferior position continually surface, as his own black consciousness develops and becomes more explicit: "A black man or woman in America, with American parents, knew that innocence was a term for white people. We were born in sin" (*Yellow* 198). Secrecy and self-possession mark his approach toward the rest of the white world: "Where I came from you kept everything a secret—survival depended on keeping the people around you in the dark" (197). "I came from a place where to show your fear was like asking for death. It was suicide; a sin" (*Black* 255). He must keep his essential self hidden, self-protected, an "invisible man," at the same time he often wonders exactly what that self is. Easy's rage often consumes him: "Because if you insist on makin' me out a nigger I ain't got no choice but to be one. No choice at all" (233).

When Bruno died I realized that I'd always be surrounded by violence and insanity. I saw it everywhere; in Fitt's innocent face, in Dickhead's diseased gaze. It was even in me. That feeling of anger wrapped tight under my skin, in my hands.
And it was getting worse. (*Black* 72)

He also recognizes that from his position the colonizers and colonized, the police and the criminals, often seem to be as amoral and as crooked as one another: "They're both the same and interchangeable. Criminals were just a bunch of thugs living off what honest people and rich people made. The cops were thugs too; paid by the owners of property to keep the other thugs down" (*Black* 265); "I had played the game of 'cops and nigger' before" (*Devil* 69). "I was poor and black and a likely candidate for the penitentiary" (121).

The effects of being black on Easy's professional and personal life are equally appalling. In *Devil in a Blue Dress* he more or less has to accept DeWitt Albright's offer of a job, since he has just been fired, and the perilous situations he finds himself in automatically complicate the issues of his innocence and guilt. Working within the margins of American society, he is not just automatically perceived as being up to something, but in order to survive and succeed, the very nature of his new job spins its web of complicity and betrayal which snares him. In the army he had been "trained to kill men but white men weren't anxious to see a gun in my hands. . . . If a black man wanted to fight he had to volunteer" (98). When he buys three buildings in 1953 in *A Red Death* with the tainted money he received from his involvement in his first mystery, he is pursued by a tax agent. He covers his tracks, knowing that he will be suspected of worse deeds: "Everybody thought I was the handyman and that Mofass collected the rent for some white lady downtown. . . . On top of real estate I was in the business of favors. . . . I wasn't on anybody's payroll" (4-5). At the same time he has adopted Jesus, the sexually abused and silent boy from *Devil,* who had been kept by the obese homosexual mayoral candidate in that mystery.

By *White Butterfly,* in 1956, Easy Rawlins is thirty-six, has been married for two years to Regina Riles, a nurses' aid at a local hospital, and together they have a daughter named Edna. However, he refuses to let Regina in on the darker side of his various jobs: "There were so many secrets I carried and so many broken lives I'd shared. Regina and Edna had no part of that, and I swore to myself that they never would. . . . I had lived a life of hiding before I met Regina. Nobody knew about me. . . . I felt safe in my secrets" (*White* 28, 31). He learns how best to use his enforced invisibility in his detective work, while at the same time it impairs and destroys his personal life: "I was working to find something. Nobody knew what I was up to and that made me sort of invisible; people thought that they saw me but what they really saw was an illusion of me, something that wasn't real" (*Devil* 128). It is that very necessity to keep certain things secret that destroys his marriage, and Regina, left out of Easy's secret life, runs off with Dupree Bouchard and takes Edna with her. At the end of the mystery Easy buys Feather, the little girl who is the daughter of the murdered stripper, Cyndi Starr (who is also a UCLA coed named Robin Garnett), for $500. He has a family—"son" Jesus and "daughter" Feather—but these are the victims of the murderous chaos of his mean streets. By the time we reach 1961 in *Black Betty,* Easy has adopted Jesus and Feather, divorced Regina, and become involved in a new mystery that mixes black and white in a devastating family tragedy. And by 1963 in *A Little Yellow Dog,* Easy has become the supervising custodian at the Sojourner Truth Junior High School in Watts; Jesus, who has remained mute, has begun to speak, and he is a long-distance runner and a freshman in high school; Feather is seven, and Easy becomes involved with another woman.

Of course this urban landscape with its violence, cheap sex, and battered morality is very much a product of the hard-boiled tradition in American mysteries. Mosley recognizes and exploits the Darwinian power of money in such a dark domain: "When you owe out then you're in debt and when you're in debt then you can't be your own man. That's capitalism. . . . Money was why Coretta was dead and why DeWitt Albright was going to kill me" (*Devil* 101, 121). Such a world is as grim and as realistically drawn with its multiple murders, blunt and often brutal dialogue, and belligerent betrayals as Burke's world, but Mosley adds the ruthless racism and steamy sex of his often ghettoized landscape. As in the hard-boiled school of mystery fiction, all of this threatens to upend and destroy whatever fragile morality exists. Survival often transcends moral judgment—as it must—in the bitter world of whorehouses, grungy bars, pool rooms, and wasted marginal lives. As Easy realizes,

If a man wore gold chains, somebody was going to hit him on the head. If he looked prosperous, women would pull him by his dick into the bed and then hit him with a paternity suit nine months later. If a woman had money, the man would just beat her until she got up off of it. (*Black* 140-41)

But there are some significant differences in Mosley's world. First of all, as Stephen F. Soitos has pointed out, a strong sense of black community prevails. In fact black writers of mysteries have often used the popular formula to examine racism and social injustice in American society, using "a Euro-American popular culture form to express African American cultural identity" (51). They have "used detective conventions as a vehicle in which to express social critique of mainstream attitudes towards race, class, and gender" (Soitos 52) at the same time that they rely on the conventions of the tradition: the emphasis on the solitary detective figure, on plot over characters, the individual over the group, the urban landscape, the on-going conflict with the official police, the first-person narrative, the use of women as sexual objects, and the overall psychic outlook of disillusionment, fatalism, and ennui (23-24). Within the confines of the traditional formula, Mosley creates his labyrinthine and loyalty-bound black community.

Easy Rawlins' best friend, an engaging sociopath, the id to his ego, is Raymond Alexander or the Mouse as he is nicknamed. He reminds the reader of Dave Robicheaux's similarly sociopathic sidekick, the irrepressible and violent Clete Purcell. In *Gone Fishin'* Mosley returns us to the violent and dark roots of the relationship between Rawlins and Mouse, which we will consider below, but in *Devil in a Blue Dress* he is very much Easy's reliable, if murderous, sidekick. We know, for instance, that Mouse has killed his stepfather and blamed it on someone else, also killed his stepfather's son, who had come to hunt him down, and that Easy, appalled by these acts of violence, has fled from both the Fifth Ward in Houston and from him. He has also loved Mouse's future wife, EttaMae Harris, an uneasy and fiery relationship that will continue to plague both Easy and Mouse in future novels. But Mouse follows Easy to L. A. and rescues him, as he will do in later years, and discovers that Easy has changed and developed, that he has become less frightened and more self-assertive in his new-found role as a detective. The tight knit and often very funny relationship between Easy and Mouse complicates every mystery. Theirs is a brotherhood of violence and mutual guilts, but in its own cohesive and initimate way, it remains very much a close and necessary community.

Easy's relationship to Mouse is not the only long-lasting one, however. In *Black Betty* Easy acknowledges his debt to Odell Jones and Martin Smith: "If it hadn't been for Martin and Odell I would have died when I was a boy. They had taken me into their homes and fed me when there was nothing but cold and hunger outside" (62). Easy's parents have fled and died—his mother died when he was eight, and "in Houston I was a wild boy riding the rails" (13)—he was raised on a sharecropper's farm in Texas, and if it weren't for such friends, he never would have survived his childhood. He is very much aware of "my native black community, a community that had been transplanted from southern Texas and Louisiana" (39); "California was like heaven for the southern Negro" (*Devil* 27).

Black men often congregate in bars and barbershops, in pool rooms and on the streets. However marginal their way of life in contrast to the mainstream white culture, it has its own rules, cues, customs, and conceits: "The barbershop was like a social club. And any social club had to have order to run smoothly" (*Devil* 133). In *White Butterfly* Bone Street is a grim urban neighborhood, "broken and desolate to look at by day, with its two-story tenementlike apartment buildings and its mangy hotels. But by night Bones, as it was called, was a center for late-night blues [where a man] was going to lose himself in the music and the booze and the women down there" (61). Bone Street is an urban wasteland, but it also clings to its own battered sense of community. Watts displays all of its poverty and desperation, its gyms and boxers and bookies, its seedy apartments and seedier watering holes, but Easy manages to achieve a more or less steady and middle-class life style there by the time he becomes the supervising custodian in 1963:

Southeast L. A. was palm trees and poverty; neat little lawns tended by the descendants of ex-slaves and massacred Indians . . . a place that was almost a nation, populated by lost peoples that were never talked about in the newspapers or seen on the TV. . . . You might have heard about a botched liquor store robbery (if a white man was injured)—but you never heard about Tommy Jones growing the biggest roses in the world or how Fiona Roberts saved her neighbor by facing off three armed men with only the spirit of her God to guide her. (*Little* 32)

In 1963 Easy even has Mouse and EttaMae working for him. The wasteland still prevails, but so do the fragile and tenuous strands of community and fellow feeling:

Men like John and me didn't have lives like the white men on TV had. We didn't roll out of bed for an eight-hour job and then come home in the evening for The Honeymooners and a beer.

We didn't do one thing at a time.

We were men who came from poor stock. We had to be cooks and tailors and plumbers and electricians. We had to be our own cops and our own counsel because there wasn't anything for us down at City Hall. (*Black* 252)

Mosley also allows Easy to make connections between his own oppressed role in life and that of others. For instance when Easy hears the story of the brothers-in-law, Abe and Johnny, who have come from Auschwitz—and he remembers the concentration camps he helped evacuate at the end of the war—he recognizes their immediate kinship: "That was why so many Jews back then understood the American Negro; in Europe the Jew had been a Negro for more than a thousand years" (*Devil* 138). Mosley's own background helps underscore this shock of recognition. At the same time Easy also realizes that his Mexican friend Primo shares in their sense of kinship: "A Mexican and a Negro considered themselves the same" (177). Both blacks and Jews became suspected minorities during the post-war anti-Communist witchhunts of the 1950s and in *A Red Death* team up in order to try and outwit the real villains. Easy also realizes when racism may be applied for the wrong reasons:

I'd picked up Huckleberry Finn. . . . A few liberal libraries and the school system had wanted to ban the book because of the racist content. Liberal-minded whites and blacks wanted to erase racism from the world. I applauded the idea but my memory of Huckleberry wasn't one of racism. I remembered Jim and Huck as friends out on the river. I could have been either one of them. (*Black* 13)

Within a racist world there are moments of genuine community, however isolated and delicate.

Sex is often quick and easy, sexual alliances created as swiftly as they disintegrate, as if this in many ways is the closest people can come to family situations, the fragile and evanescent grasp of a conventional life: "And you know Jackson stick his business in a meat grinder if it winked at him" (*Black* 132). Easy rescues both Jesus and Feather who become his children, a family literally wrenched from the mean streets of Rawlins' life. They are obviously not blood kin, but they are a family, and Easy works hard to maintain them as such, despite or because of the failure of his marriage and disappearance of his daughter. Regina and Edna have returned to Mississippi, but Easy cannot leave the lure and the violent labyrinth of the L.A. he has come to know and inhabit.

Within the racist system there is some progress as Mosley makes clear. Easy grows and thrives in terms of his own self-awareness and financial success. He is able to work within and at times almost transcend the injustice of the post-war era with its unions and red scares, its segregated society and brutal divisions. He does create a very real family, however patchwork and incomplete it first appears, and he does manage to prosper, despite the personal scars and dark violent world he inhabits. Like August Wilson in his series of plays, Mosley follows a clear cultural trajectory, describing the improvements and the horrors that seem to arise simultaneously within and alongside it. As Digby Diehl explained, "The insightful scenes of black life . . . provide a sort of social history that doesn't exist in other detective fiction" (312).

By *A Little Yellow Dog,* although the novel ends with John Kennedy's assassination in 1963, Easy seems to be not only surviving but beginning to prevail. Of course this is always seen in a fragile and tenuous light, and it can evaporate at any moment when America's racist society takes a turn for the worst. Even in 1963 prisoners inhabit the cages of police stations: "Just thirty or so men living in cages underground. Like livestock waiting for some further shame to be laid on them. Like sharecroppers or slaves living in shanty shacks on the edge of the plantation. There was evil in that room, and on that plantation too. Because, as I knew too well, if you're punished long enough you become guilty of all charges brought against you" (147). The abyss is never very far away.

The oral tradition has always been particularly strong in the American South. One thinks of William Faulkner's novels and tales, as well as James Lee Burke's first-person narrators. But in the black tradition, language—the dialects, the jazz rhythms, the images, the signifying— carries at least a double burden. In some cases it establishes and restores the black culture and sense of continuity, which cannot be taken for granted in any other context. Walter Mosley is clearly aware of this, as is Easy Rawlins: "I always tried to speak proper English in my life, the kind of English they taught in school, but I found over the years that I could only truly express myself in the natural, 'uneducated' dialect of my upbringing" (*Devil* 10). That dialect becomes part of Rawlins' developing sense of self, both in terms of his communal connections within his own group and also in terms of his separation and alienation from the mainstream white culture. Of Mrs. Stella Keaton, the white librarian in *White Butterfly,* Rawlins comments: "To her Shakespeare was a god. I didn't mind that, but what did she know about the folk tales and riddles and stories colored folks had been telling for centuries? What did she know about the language we spoke?" (54). Easy goes on to recognize that black children had "come to believe that they would have to abandon their own language and stories to become part of her educated world" (54). Rawlins' awareness of his language is part of his blackness, that "blackground" that white police and felons rely upon to get into the black community where they cannot go. Such a vernacular literally creates both Rawlins' self and world as well as Mosley's literary landscape. There is no way that anyone could mistake Easy's ruminations with a character out of a P. D. James, Amanda Cross, or Tony Hillerman mystery. And this way of speaking is clearly "posited against the negative, closed, oppressive system of white-dominated worldviews in the typical detective novel" (Soitos 49).

Black literature, asserts Henry Louis Gates, Jr., clearly exists within and against a white tradition, thereby creating a kind of double voice, a voice that is perfect for the self-effacing and calculated ploys the black detective must rely upon to ferret out the information he is seeking (Gates, *Loose* 39, 26, 75). And such a vernacular clearly reveals its culturally identifiable oral roots (33), so much so, according to Gates, that blackness becomes not an absolute essence or metaphysical condition but a biological fiction based in part on the uses of language "that are shared, repeated, critiqued, and revised" (*Signifying* 54). To DeWitt Albright, at the very beginning of *Devil in a Blue Dress,* Easy Rawlins offers up a question: "And what kind of work is it that you do?" (5). When Albright has left, and Easy is alone with his friend Joppy, he considers the fact that Albright reminds him of his violent friend, Mouse: "But he always got his business in the front'a his mind, and if you get in the way you might come to no good" (10). To which Joppy replies, "'Might come to no good' is a bitch, Easy, but sleepin' in the street ain't got no 'might' to it" (10). The conversation continues:

"Yeah, man. I'm just feelin' kinda careful."

"Careful don't hurt, Easy. Careful keep your hands up, careful makes ya strong. . . . They gotta sayin' for his line'a work, Ease."

"What's that?"

"Whatever the market can bear." He smiled, looking like a hungry bear himself. "Whatever the market can bear." (10)

The play with language, however modest and low-keyed here—"no good" is a "bitch," the market and Joppy can bear anything they have to, and Joppy himself is described as a bear: three "bears" in three sentences—suggests the kind of language games and forms of figuration that Gates refers to in black language as signifying: "One does not signify something . . . one signifies in some way" (*Signifying* 54). And that signifying becomes a code which the black characters can understand and within which they operate as opposed to and separate from the white language and diction that surround and oppress them. Mosley will expand on all of this in his major non-mystery novel, *RL's Dream* (1995).

What Mosley has achieved is combining the mystery form with black dialect as have other black writers before him:

Ghetto Pedagogy

"Dad?"
"Yes?"
"Why do black men always kill each other?"
(long pause)
"Practicing." (*Black* epigraph)

That language extends and subverts the form itself, but on the face of it, Mosley has succeeded in reaching "a new and wider audience as the novels comment on a tradition of mainstream detective writing in America while continuing aspects of the black detective tradition" (Soitos 179). Mosley's mysteries are an excellent example of a pluralistic culture, the kind that Gates and Toni Morrison describe that is both dynamic and porous and not at all narrowly ethnocentric, not grounded only in a kind of disciplinary essentialism. Mosley's world becomes polycentric; the central and marginal cultures in a way mutually constitute one another in terms of form and often experience—"Of course, I always knew that there was no real difference between the races" (*Devil* 47)— even as they rend each other apart in terms of racist antagonisms, murderous family plots, and differences in language. As Easy remembers, "The way he called me *son* instead of my name returned me to southern Texas in the days before World War Two; days when the slightest error in words could hold dire consequences for a black man" (*Devil* 32). It may sound like a decidedly uneasy and perilous alliance, but it works.

Soitos quotes W. E. B. DuBois in terms of this inherent doubleness, these contradictions that both constitute and rupture the goal of a more pluralistic society, "this sense of always looking at one's self through the eyes of others. . . . One ever feels his twoness—an American, a Negro: two souls, two thoughts, two unreconciled strivings" (*Blues* 33). Easy is always aware of looking and being looked at, of assessing and being assessed more readily than if he could just blend in with the mainstream white culture. Again in the opening pages of *Devil in a Blue Dress,* Mosley makes this very apparent, and we feel and see the gazer gazing on the other who is gazing back at him, relegating him, at least from DeWitt Albright's perspective, to the subservient and inferior position of just another down-and-out black in need of ready cash. The *fabula* of the narrative, the events as they happen, is often at war with the *discourse,* the way these events are described or mediated. The events are obviously seen differently from a black character's perspective than a white's. We are, therefore, made doubly aware of "something which is put into language" by someone like Easy Rawlins than we are if a white character were "speaking" (Bonnycastle 156).

All these contradictions, crossed signals, dialectical dynamics and shifts in language create a veritable site of conflict that does not merely lie in the mystery form itself. We experience a kind of on-going deconstruction as cultural diversity is targeted within the typical mystery formula. We find ourselves trying to penetrate even more perceptively or carefully the discourse and the *fabula* of the tale. Assimilation becomes both possible and impossible. Easy Rawlins becomes himself a victim, the victim of a racist country and language in the way that they alienate, imprison, mold, shape, and define him. But as the main detective he is also on the move, searching for suspects or clues, initiating the very kind of rational pursuit and analysis that at times seem engineered to exclude him. Rawlins stands for unearthing the truth, but he also has to survive in a world that is rigged against him. His access to easy money and his often troubling concerns and doubts about his moral position only help to exaggerate and confirm his marginal status. He is both a part and not of the culture he operates in, a position no white detective, however isolated or solitary, can ever experience or appreciate.

Part of that marginality appears in Mosley's style as well. Gates, for instance, explores in depth the subtleties and rhetorical strategies of every black text which he sees prefigured in Esu, the Yoruba trickster figure, in the various uncertainties of explication, the open-endedness of the texts themselves, and the dialectical dynamic or process that often remains indeterminate. Interpretations shift and shimmer, as black writers, employing their own "black double-voicedness," set out "to disrupt the signifier by displacing its signified in an intentional act of will" (Gates, *Signifying* 51). In effect such signifying must clearly disrupt the mystery formula itself, which may be the reason Mosley delights in seeking out other fictional forms as in *RL's Dream* and *Gone Fishin'*. The trickster figure resides not merely within the black detective or the villain(s) in the mystery but also in the black writer himself.

Mosley's plots are as notoriously baroque and labyrinthine as Burke's in many ways. This may be his way of subverting and expanding the very mystery formula he works with. He is his own Esu. He creates so many masks, disguises, mistaken identities, and geneological mazes because he is not only elaborately using the mystery trope but is also undermining and exposing it for what it is: a false and too clearly analytical and rational formula that cannot explain the deep structure of race, race relations, black and white antagonisms and frustrations, and the extravagant trouble his characters must experience to try and disguise and evade all of this. As Gates suggests about black literature in general, Mosley's mysteries repeat the form but with a difference; they signify the many wounds and effects of racism that such a white formula by its very nature usually avoids.

Racism scars and distorts the intricate family relationships in Mosley's mysteries, even in the case of Daphne Monet, the woman DeWitt Albright has sent Easy Rawlins to find: "Daphne has a predilection for the company of Negroes. She likes jazz and pigs' feet and dark meat, if you know what I mean," Albright tells Rawlins (*Devil* 19). This complicates her already complex role as a victim and a victimizer, a murderer, a victim of incest, a sexual predator and sexual prey. She is also part black. As she herself acknowledges, "I'm her *and* I'm me" (*Devil* 203). The racial mix in many ways accounts for her rootless, schizophrenic life: "She wanna be white. All them years people be tellin' her how she light-skinned and beautiful but all the time she knows that she can't have what white people have. So she pretend and then she lose it all" (205). Her marginality in so polarized a culture practically generates her dangerous life-style, and if it weren't for Easy's lying to the police about her role in the violent events that surround her, she never would have survived. Mosley adds insult to injury by revealing that Frank Green, a terrifying psychopath, killed her father because her father had consistently molested her—and Frank Green turns out to also be her half-brother.

The Gasteau twins, Roman and Holland, in *A Little Yellow Dog* and the white stripper, Cyndi Starr, who also happens to be the UCLA coed Robin Garnett in *White Butterfly,* complicate the plots considerably, but it is in the search for Betty Eady in *Black Betty* that Mosley so far has created his most complex family scandal involving race, money, and murder. Albert Cain, a wealthy white man, in his efforts to force Betty Eady, a woman who works for him, to sleep with him, sets up Marlon

Eady, her brother, on a robbery charge in his mansion in 1939 and then tells Betty that in order to insure her brother's freedom, she must obey his wishes. As a result of their sexual liason, Betty has twins, Terry Tyler, who becomes a boxer, and Gwendolyn Barnes, who becomes Cain's white daughter's Sarah's maid. When Cain dies he leaves all of his $50-million fortune to "Black Betty" who flees for her life on the night of Cain's death. Marlon turns up dead, Terry turns up dead, and Rawlins is stabbed from behind with an ice pick, on the run because he has come upon the bodies. In all of this, racism calls the shots, forcing the black characters into a subservient position whether it comes to sex or social status and affecting the motives of their white masters. And Albert Cain, the rich white man, has been pulling all the strings.

The pursuit of several murderers at once, which helps to deepen and complicate the mystery at hand, often remains open-ended, as if so many characters are capable of such violence and vengeance in Mosley's bitter underworld that it ultimately doesn't matter exactly who killed whom. For instance, who killed Roland Gasteau in *Dog*? Was it his twin brother Holland? Was it the thug, Joey Beam, and the mobster, Sallie Monroe? And was it because of drugs, because of the scam in the school system, because of entangled love affairs, because of rivalry in divvying up illegal profits? And who did kill Albert Cain? Could it have been Marlon Eady? Or his nephew, Terry Tyler? Or the two of them in league with one another? Or Ronald Hawkes, the Cains' gardener, whom Sarah Cain, his daughter, runs off with? And exactly how is their sickly and anemic son Arthur involved in all of this? In a world more or less polarized between black victims and white scams, does it matter? Is the racist-infected nightmare itself responsible, since so many people exist within it and act accordingly?

Walter Mosley has said that the moral crises that Easy Rawlins becomes involved in are what really interest him:

Mysteries, stories about crime, about detectives, are the ones that really ask the existentialist questions such as "How do I act in an imperfect world when I want to be perfect?" I'm not really into clues and that sort of thing, although I do put them in my stories. I like the moral questions.[1]

His mysteries acquire this deeper and broader sense of complicity and guilt, the complex issue of personal morality and survival as a brooding subtext in a dark world of conspiracy and racist disdain, because Easy is usually incredibly involved in the action. For instance the $30,000 that Daphne has stolen in *Devil in a Blue Dress* is split between her, Easy, and Mouse. As Easy makes clear, "A lot of people died . . . and we came away from it with ten thousand dollars apiece. The money was stolen, but nobody was looking for it and I had convinced myself that I was safe" (12). He uses it to buy real estate in *A Red Death,* which leads to complications with his taxes and the tax man—"I didn't pay taxes on the stolen money because it was still hot in 1948 and after that it was already undeclared" (41)—which leads to another mystery. In *White Butterfly* he ruthlessly outbids DeCampo Associates to keep the land he already owns near a major road where a major development is planned by sending Mouse to convince and persuade them to back down. Easy gets Calvin Hodge, the Cains' family lawyer, to help his employee—and "pretend" boss—Mofass to close down Mofass' real-estate partner.

Perhaps Easy's best deal to date surfaces in *A Little Yellow Dog.* In that book he manages to acquire the supervising custodian's job by getting rid of the man who already had the job, Bill Bartlett. It seems that Bartlett took his boss, Bartrand Stowe, to one of Sallie Monroe's, the mobster's, notorious parties. Monroe needs Stowe in a compromised position, so that he can blackmail him to get him to help him methodically empty several Board of Education warehouses. So Monroe pays Grace Phillips, a woman at the party who's strung out on heroin, to "do" Stowe. Unfortunately Stowe falls in love with her, but Monroe gets photographs of the two of them and uses them for his blackmail scheme. Easy volunteers to get the photos for Stowe from Monroe, if Stowe will give Bill Bartlett's job to him. The deal works and reveals how brilliantly Easy can work the system, even though we find out later that Bill Bartlett and Sallie Monroe are into wider conspiracies and more violent plots.

Raymond Alexander, whose nickname is "Mouse," accompanies Easy on his assignments and is very much Easy's dark twin, a violent and wonderfully vulnerable and funny psychopathic buddy, whom he uses on occasion or who shows up just in time to rescue Rawlins from certain death. Mouse's assistance suggests Clete Purcell's as well, the violent and near-psychopathic buddy to James Lee Burke's Dave Robicheaux. Easy like Robicheaux is often pressed to employ his friend's destructive and savage fury to eliminate or at the very least maim the most frenzied of his opponents. And Easy knows it: "When Bruno died I realized that I'd always be surrounded by violence and insanity. I saw it everywhere. . . . It was even in me. That feeling of anger wrapped tight under my skin, in my hands. And it was getting worse" (*Black* 72). This violence is very much a part of the marginalized racist culture he's forced to live in. "I could have gone home then—I should have," he acknowledges in *Little Yellow Dog,* "But the street had been calling me all day long. I had been seduced, hoodwinked, and blamed for a thief; I'd been bullied and looked at like a crook instead of an honest man. I could have gone home but I knew that I wouldn't be able to sleep" (51). Even at the risk of losing his job, he cannot resist the lure of the mean streets. "Somewhere on the lineup I had become invisible again. I'd taken on the shadows that kept me camouflaged, and dangerous. . . . For a moment the violence that we both wanted seemed okay, like it was just an expression between men—rough humor, healthy competition, survival of the fittest" (*Little* 154, 272). And in that same book he kills a gangster and falls in love with a murderer.

Easy recognizes Mouse's good qualities and his limitations: "Mouse was the truest friend I ever had. And if there is such a thing as true evil, he was that too" (*Red* 57). His association with him may, in fact, suggest a Faustian pact with the devil, to whom dues must be paid: "I never tried to explain. How could I? In the hard life of the streets you needed somebody like Mouse at your back. I didn't have a mother or father, or close family or church. All I had was my friends. And among them Mouse packed the largest caliber and the hardest of rock-hard wills" (*Little* 29). In *Devil in a Blue Dress* Mouse manages to kill three men. In *A Red Death* he kills the villain. In *Black Betty* Easy sets him up to kill his boyhood pal and cancer-ridden friend, Martin Smith.

Easy also prides himself on his looks and his sexual prowess. He has sex with Daphne, with Isabel Turner in *A Little Yellow Dog,* with EttaMae, Mouse's wife, whom he has had sex with before and after her troubled marriage; with Marla the whore in *White Butterfly;* and longs for Black Betty: "Men communicated to Betty with their bodies and sex. She didn't care about our words or our hearts" (*Black* 274). He admires Lips McGee, the jazz trumpeter, whom he has known since he was a child in Houston: "Lips was what every black man wanted to be. He was dapper and self-assured, articulate, and had money in his pocket. He was always surrounded by beautiful women, but what really made me jealous was the way he looked when he played his horn" (*White* 104). "I cleaned up and put on my good brown woolen suit. My shirt was buff silk and the cufflinks were yellow gold and onyx. My shoes were a soft, light brown leather, and the socks matched my shirt in fabric and in color. I looked at myself in the mirror and smiled. Then I thought about the Gasteau brothers; they were dressed fine too. It hadn't helped them" (*Little* 123).

Easy can never be straight with the police, even if on occasion he does share information with certain individuals. He will always be their victim, the black man as criminal, the shadow in the wings. When he discovers bodies, which automatically implicates him in their murders, he has to try and sidestep the fact, dodge the police, rig it so that he won't be immediately, if ever, implicated. In fact at the end of *Devil in a Blue Dress* he devises an entirely fictitious story in league with others to tell the authorities and in doing so leaves Daphne entirely out of the picture. She has killed, she has her reasons, and she is free. None of this comes easily to Easy whose complicity in his nightmare world, exacerbated and generated by racism and all that goes with it, cannot be helped if he is to survive at all. But such involvement brings with it Mosley's fascination with moral crises and amplifies the consequences of the personal dilemmas that Easy must resolve. Such dilemmas enlarge and profoundly broaden the range of Mosley's fiction.

In 1997 Mosley published an earlier novel that he had written, *Gone Fishin',* in which the earlier relationship and involvement between Easy Rawlins and Raymond Alexander, "Mouse," are clearly revealed. Jack E. White declared it "in some respects, the best of Mosley's novels. . . . Mosley displays a pitch-perfect gift for capturing the cadences of black speech that rivals the dialogue in Ralph Ellison's *Invisible Man*" (*Early*). Mouse, on the verge of marrying EttaMae Harris, is convinced that his step-father, Reese Corn, abused and killed his mother, and he wants his mother's dowry that he feels should now be returned to him. He asks Easy to drive him to the grim town of Pariah, Texas (the name reveals its social status), near the bayou to meet with Corn: "It was a crooked town, not more than two blocks of unpaved red clay street" (*Gone* 126). On the way they pick up a young man and woman, seventeen-year-old Clifton, who is fleeing from having beaten a boy to death in a bar for looking at Ernestina, the young woman who is with him. Mouse feels that he can use Clifton in his plan against Corn. He sets up Ernestine with Domaque, a sweet retarded hunchback, who is the son of Josephine Harker, "Momma Jo," a kind of swamp witch and huge voracious woman who in a hilarious and lubricious scene seduces Easy. Easy comes down with a fever, Mouse takes him to Miss Dixon's, an old white lady who lives in a big house crammed with furniture and owns everything around her, and then takes him to Miss Alexander's (Mouse's aunt's) general store and music bar to recover.

Mouse's plan slowly reveals itself. He decides to use Clifton to frighten Corn into surrendering his money. Clifton easily agrees, since if he can get some of that money, he can escape. At the same time Mouse tells the local deputy about Clifton's plight but not where he is. Thus, Clifton is frightened by the fact that a local deputy is after him, and it is then that Mouse tells him about Corn's money, having told Corn that there's a vicious killer named Clifton in the neighborhood. It is this chilling scenario that Easy finally figures out, when he emerges from his fever, and hopes to stop.

The novel is in fact a memoir. Easy is writing it in Paris after World War Two, having volunteered to fight in Patton's final push to prove that he isn't the coward the white men accuse him of being, and "I thought I could make up for my failure in Pariah" (*Gone* 242). He is concerned about his inability to prevent what finally happened back in Pariah and in a way is trying to atone for his complicity in Mouse's murdering his step-father and for Corn's murder of Clifton. The book thus becomes a rite of initiation into the violent world of mayhem and manhood which in Rawlins' life are practically one and the same.

As in most of Mosley's plots, the families in *Gone Fishin'* are broken and disrupted, and racism only adds to these distortions. Mouse not only hates the evil Reese Corn, his step-father, but kills him. Easy discovers that Sweet William, the musician at Miss Alexander's, is Mouse's real father, but Mouse doesn't know it. Momma Jo's father shot her lover, Domaque, the father of her son, Domaque. Clifton and Ernestina's love is cut short by Corn's bullet. Miss Dixon remains a spinster gloating genteelly over her position of white status and her furniture. Everybody hated her "because she owned everything, including the roads they walked on" (120). But for that reason she remains a sacred cow for the black community. Easy "knew that colored people are always in danger of doing the wrong thing when they have to deal with whites . . . because whites were always the boss. . . . It was fine in Fifth Ward down in Houston, or in little colored towns like Pariah, usually, because there weren't any white people around for the most part" (116, 117). And yet at the same time he recognizes that killing Miss Dixon "or even thinking of it, would be like killing the only dream we had. . . . she was white and being white was like another step to heaven" (120).

Easy's own father ran off years ago. He had to sell a horse to feed his family, but the white foreman at the slaughterhouse wouldn't pay him the $17.00 as promised: "'Niggah?' the white man exclaimed as he slapped the flat of the blade on his apron. 'You want sumpin'? 'Cause you know I'm just the man give it to ya'" (81). Mr. Rawlins decks him and then, of course, has to flee for his life. That's the last day Easy sees him: "You could see the fear in his face, and that fear is what I remembered most" (176). Shortly thereafter Rawlins' mother has a stroke, and Easy knows that he will have to make it, if he can, on his own. Will he run like his father had to? Or will he stay and stand up to his past? "I had risked my life to save Clifton only to fail. . . . I was following in my father's fleet footsteps . . . running to fight another day" (219). After the war he finally makes his decision "from this room in Paris. All I can do is follow my footsteps, not at all like my father, and go back home" (244).

Easy's friendship with Mouse continues to disturb him. He is appalled by and in awe of Mouse's violent ways. He knows that "his voice was the whisper of death, the slither of a snake over the nape of my neck" (218); "he created lead from gold. He created his revenge on Reese from his love of EttaMae or maybe he found that revenge in her love of him" (175). But he also admires Mouse's story-telling charisma: "It was like he was singing a song and the words were notes. . . . He'd turn phrases that I wanted to use myself but it seemed that I couldn't ever get the timing right" (24). Like the men of Pariah he can spin a good yarn: "It felt good to listen to them laugh and trade lies" (142).

Easy is horrified when to frighten Reese Corn, Mouse shoots one of his dogs: "Then he shot the other three: crack, crack, crack; like ducks in an arcade" (98-99). He can never forget it. Even after the tens of thousands of men who died in the war, Easy muses,

I never felt so close to death as when I saw those dogs die. . . . I was so upset that I couldn't sleep. I was afraid to sleep; afraid because I had seen death in a way where it was real for me. . . . I wanted my father again. . . . I wanted him to come back and protect me from death. (132-33)

Even at the conclusion of the novel, Easy can never forget that moment, the culmination for him of Mouse's violence, the certainty and proximity of death in his world, and his knowledge that he's on his own: "I thought of Reese's dogs and went cold somewhere; that one spot in my heart has never kindled again" (203).

Easy has always nourished a lyric sensibility within himself and his culture. He misses nothing and loves "a slow blues tune. I've always loved blues music; when you hear it there's something that happens in your body. Your heart and stomach and liver start to move to the music" (135). This love mingles with his love of story-telling, of that more lyrical side to Mouse's violence. Domaque reads the Bible so well that Easy realizes he, too, must learn to start reading, and as Dom suggests, "Remember to make it in yo' own words, Easy. That's how ya do it" (210). Fishing with Dom and Mouse becomes an Edenic experience. Early mornings suggest childhood: "Before the sun is out is like those magic times that you hid under the bed and in between the clothes hanging in your mother's closet. Times when any kind of miracle could come about just as normal as a spider making her web" (19). Mosley's own lengthy elegiac lines capture this lyrical perspective, as they do in his description of the bayou at night: "With those stars and lightning bugs I barely made out the path we walked on from the heavens. It was like walking in the black skies of night; my whole sense of up and down was gone" (71).

But such a childhood ease and grace are shattered, if not entirely lost, in Easy's failure to prevent Clifton's and Reese's deaths. At the same time Mouse pays him $300.00 which he desperately needs, money that has come from the dead step-father's cache. Such a payoff foreshadows the one in *Devil in a Blue Dress*. Moans Mouse, "You the on'y one know what happened. If you don't take that money then I know you against me" (218). The moral consequences outlive the fateful days in Pariah: "Even today, six years later, I feel guilt and fear. The same fear I had when I thought my father knew everything that I did wrong; every thought that I thought wrong" (221). Unable to live with or shoulder his guilt, he slips into a long dark night of the soul drinking himself to death in a room in Houston. It is EttaMae who rescues him, demanding that he accept Mouse's offer to be his best man at their wedding. Since Easy has slept with her a long time ago—another act of possible betrayal that will repeat itself in future years—he listens to her demands for him to stand up and be counted. If he doesn't, she tells him, he will die, and he recognizes the truth of her advice: "Reese was dead, Clifton was dead, but I was alive. There was nothing more I could do; I was just a man" (228). He also realizes that from that day on, he will be like most other people: "They all had secrets like mine but they kept on moving" (229). Pariah gets destroyed; Momma Jo, Domaque, and Ernestine disappear; Easy is off to Dallas on the train when he hears from an older couple that there exists the possibility of work in an airplane factory in California. He continues to dream about Reese and Clifton weekly—they will shadow him the rest of his life—but it is time to move on and make his own way alone. In such a fashion are his personality and priorities set before his work as a detective begins. The darkness that resides in the depths of his spirit will have to wrestle with the darkness—and racism—of the world he will encounter, and going fishing will hardly ever be a real option again.

Gone Fishin' clearly comes out of the gothic tradition of Southern yarns, but the moral choices that Mosley includes within it raise it above the merely gothic. The lyrical language also shapes its personal sensibilities and makes of it an initiation tale of boyhood into manhood. Mosley will never forsake the quirkier gothic aspect of his stories and plots in the future of Easy Rawlins' adventures. In fact this tradition both underscores and embellishes his mysteries. It is part and parcel of the voice itself, a lyricism turned dark, an observant eye that misses no sign of impending death and racist scorn. This gothic aspect and his continued fascination with moral questions enhances Mosley's "blackground," complete as it is with the haunted swamp and town of Pariah and Mouse's use of a voodoo effigy in his revenge on his step-father.

Clearly *RL's Dream* is not part of the Easy Rawlins' mystery series. It is, as Gary Giddins describes it, "a lyrical and original—if imperfect—leap beyond genre fiction, [with Mosley] working for the first time in the third person and substituting an omniscient probing of damaged lives for the modulated fastidiousness of Rawlins" (*New York Times* 13 Aug. 1995: 11). It is also Mosley's attempt to capture the rhythms and textures of his own black culture both in its content and in its form. Readers coming to the Rawlins mysteries for the first time might read it first to experience in greater detail the specific "blackground," the kind of Afro-American hoodoo (defined by Soitos as a syncretic religion, a distinctly American kind of voodoo) that Soitos describes in such detail in his book with its "recognition of a higher power or 'life force'; belief in ancestralism; belief in divination or prophecy; belief in animism; belief in a hierarchical chain of existence centered on the human being; and belief in the importance of full ontological being to happiness" (46).

Mosley moves easily between the present on the East Side of New York where old Atwater "Soupspoon" Wise is slowly dying of cancer and the past where Wise met the famous Delta blues singer, Robert Johnson, who died violently and young in 1938, and never forgot him. Wise hopes to spend his last days taping tales of old friends and acquaintances who can remember the days they played the blues. At the same time Mosley intersperses blues lyrics within his tale, dedicated to his father, Leroy Mosley (1916-1993). The recently dead father and the blues seem to fuse in Mosley's mind and narrative in a kind of prose ballad laced with images of futility and despair, often the blacks' lot in the culture of the white and the dominant. Perhaps this close identification accounts for some of the novel's more sentimental sections, such as the eighteen-year-old woman who makes love to Soupspoon. Instead of a swiftly paced first-person narration, we shift back and forth between present and past, an experience that reflects Wise's own state of mind, thus penetrating more perceptively the state of the black soul in both eras. And in each "we was the bottom of the barrel. We were the lowest kinda godless riffraff. Migrants and roustabouts. . . . They carried the whole world on their shoulders and when they sighed it came out the blues" (*RL* 140, 266). The blues exposes the battered black soul: "It wasn't so much freedom a poor black man wanted but release. That's a slave's freedom; a sharecropper's freedom. Release from his bonds and his bondage" (202-03). And when Wise at age eleven first hears the music, "a dark feeling came over him. . . . He didn't know that he had the blues" (74).

Clearly Soupspoon is infected by Johnson's music. It becomes his voice and the voice of his culture. He knows that Johnson sings "a hard song of disease and death," but his music is "so right that it's more like rain than notes" (196, 259). He may have been crazy, violent, a visionary of sorts, but "he took something of yours that you didn't even know you had. . . . And taking it away he left you with something missing—and that something was better than anything else that you ever had" (44). And this is what Soupspoon in his final dying days seeks to recapture, knowing that "black people's history is stories and words and music. Black people have built the culture of America with their play, and nobody knows it really because it's not written down in books" (220). Mosley's mission is to achieve precisely that.

Racism poisons the air of both past and present. After thirty years as the day janitor at the Calumet Building, Wise is let go and kicked out of his apartment, although almost miraculously he is taken in by Kiki Waters, a white woman (white trash from Arkansas) who that day has just been stabbed by a ten-year-old black boy and who is seeking a kind of personal redemption in her chosen role as a nurturer and friend. She works for Marshall and Pride Insurance, took care of her friend, Abby Greenspan, who also works there and was raped by the computer manager named Fez, and launches a clever embezzlement scheme that helps pay Wise's hospital bills. Yet racism colors everything. Kiki's boyfriend Randy pretends he is Egyptian, not black. "He's just a wannabe; wannabe white," Kiki quips (42). "He says he's South American and *Caucasian* North African, that means a light-skinned Arab." Yet Randy maintains that "black people . . . could never truly understand his world. Because of slavery and racism the world of blacks could never encompass the path that he intended to travel" (125). At the end when Kiki returns to Arkansas, she tells the tear-stained Randy, "Maybe in your mind you're John Wayne. But back here in America you're just another black man" (250). As for her, being white results in her marrying an old boyfriend. She "had four kids, and moved into an even bigger house surrounded by magnolia trees. She kept bees out behind the garage and gave up liquor" (264). Whiteness has its privileges.

Soupspoon Wise knows the score since he's seen and experienced it for so many years:

. . . nobody knows white people better than blacks. A black man knows the white man inside out. . . . Anything a white man did was okay because it was a white man doing it. But a black man was different. No matter how hard he studied or how righteous he was, a black man still had the mark of Cain on him. All you had to do was look.

But if your skin was light and your hair was good then you were treated better. Whites liked light-skinned Negroes more, and a light-skinned lover was the dream of many a dark heart. Light-skinned Negroes had better jobs. The lighter the better. And if you were light enough you might even slip through a crack and make it into heaven.

. . . . It was a hard life that made people want to pass . . . making it in the white man's world the way all colored people do: looking the man in the face and lying about what you feel and what you know—what you were inside. Everybody did that. Lying to the white man was both sport and survival. (128-29)

This is surely Easy Rawlins' testimony as well as Daphne Monet's and Albert Cain's and so many others. This is also a good example in which to point out the form of this testimony, its rhythms and repetitions, Mosley's use of "black" and "white," of "knowing" and "doing," of "light-skinned" and "lying" in such a repetitive manner that it builds up an almost hypnotic momentum, asserting and re-asserting the roots of the racist lie driven into one's consciousness like some universal truth. The religious overtones—the references to the "mark of Cain" and "mak[ing] it into heaven"—only add to the ideological and cultural power and traditional persuasion of such a perception. Such a description reveals its own blues roots in black consciousness or at least in the vernacular Mosley is so good at reproducing.

Soitos summarizes Houston Baker's argument that the blues are "the result of African American transformations of Euro-Americentric musical structure and [are] the primary metaphor for all African American expressive arts. The Blues then . . . becomes a matrix-establishing sign that stands for the ability of African Americans to re-create Euro-Americentric art forms for their own benefit" (*Blues* 9). Hence Mosley's use of the mystery form in terms of his ear for language, his labyrinthine plots (themselves a parodic, inversive spin on the typical white-rational and analytical formula), and his fascination with and use of the blues. This black difference for Henry Louis Gates, as suggested above, "manifests itself in specific *language* use . . . the black English vernacular tradition" (Soitos 10).

Soupspoon Wise, in effect, marries Mavis—"a barren marriage behind a bare blues life" (*RL* 197)—because she has slept with Robert Johnson. "Atwater married me, but it wasn't 'cause'a me," Mavis admits. "Even when he was lovin' me it was really Robert Johnson he was lovin'" (239). Johnson rescued her from a fire in a black club, the "Panther Barn," in the Mississippi Delta—she has a son from a violent man named Rafe who throws her against the wall during a night of wild dancing and breaks a kerosene lantern—and she slept with him that night, listening to his sad tale of his fifteen-year-old girl who died with his baby and the abuse he suffered at the hands of his step-father. After he leaves the next morning, Mavis flees to La Marque, Texas, where

Cort, her son, dies in a flash flood and where Wise finds her drinking herself to death. Wise had met Johnson during harvest time in Arcola, Mississippi, which was interrupted by white cops who carted them both off to jail. Experiencing spells and beaten in jail, Johnson is finally thrown out. "A few weeks after that," Wise tells Kiki, "I heard that Robert Johnson was dead. They said Satan come got him in a little place outside Greenwood, Mississippi. Satan or a jealous man" (143).

"Blues is the devil's music an' we his chirren. RL was Satan's favorite son," Soupspoon exclaims. "He made us all abandoned . . . the only way we could bear the weight of those days" (140). And in his present days, living with Kiki, playing at a local New York club, only momentarily experiencing relief from cancer, he recalls the Blues and Johnson as that which gave him voice and soul: "It's all about gettin' so close to pain that it's like a friend, like somebody you love" (182). He recognizes that his own music—he began by playing the spoons—is merely a "weak shadow" (143) of RL's, as indeed his entire life seems to be, but still he cannot live without it: "He saw the swaggering men who found the rhythm of their bluster in his songs. . . .When the music got good, and he closed his eyes to feel it right, he saw the backside of his life—the people who he'd walked with and left behind. . . . [It] would rip the skin off yo' back . . . a song of yelps and cries . . . it could make you cry" (209, 253). Music about pain and of pain: the art makes the suffering bearable.

Hence for Soupsoon Wise he realizes at the end of his life that all of it has seemed "*just a dream. The kinda dream that somebody like RL would have. A evil long-lastin' dream about all the bad things could happen here*" (266 sic). "It's like everything I did seems to be happen' all the time. Like things that was over start up again" (224). Wise is trapped in a racist nightmare, relieved by the blues but reflected in them as well. Violent and sudden death occur again and again—in the Delta of Wise's childhood and in present-day New York—as do personal betrayals, casual sex, abrupt eruptions of rage, and the sense of rootless disconnection and alienation. Nightmares repeat. Fez, the computer manager, attacks Kiki who shoots him. Kiki has nightmares of her father's raping her. A woman named Maretha kills a man named Shrimper in the black club of Wise's youth, the "Milky Way." Bannon Tripps tells tales of Afro-American culture as an excuse to rob whites, who finally capture him and set him on fire. Wise's parents and brother died of the flu. Mavis barricades herself in an all-white apartment. Wise visits Alfred Metsga, an old bass player, who can remember nothing. After finishing playing at Rudy's club at 2:00 A.M. one night, Wise, walking home, falls, and dies later in the hospital of a heart attack: "When the room was black he remembered who he was in a spiraling echo that played itself out" (267).

Mosley's careful cross-cutting between past and present and the exuberance of his use of black vernacular neither transcend nor transform the horrors and futility of *RL's Dream*—and we never do learn where the "RL" comes from or why—but they do create a buoyancy of tale and telling that lyrically transcends the tragedies. Racism is not defeated nor never is it circumvented, but what we remember are the sounds of the story, its rhythms and its music in much the same way that Easy Rawlins takes us through the sordid streets of his often marginal existence. Or the way we try and recall the labyrinthine and vertiginous plots Mosley spins, loading on subplots, personal escapades, family feuds, and the like. The sheer richness of the text and context promote the fullness and historical validity of the black experience. As with most mysteries the plots often dissolve in our minds once the culprits are caught, but Mosley's characters, atmosphere, and urban territories do not. These are his mean streets as conjured up in his distinctive voice, and Rawlins' sense of survival with its moral costs and choices in a belligerently racist world strengthens and transcends Mosley's treatment of the tried-and-true mystery formula.

Epilogue: Always Outnumbered, Always Outgunned

Sven Birkerts has described Mosley's newest novel, *Always Outnumbered, Always Outgunned,* an interconnected group of fourteen stories with fifty-eight-year-old murderer and ex-prisoner Socrates Fortlow at its center, as an exploration of "the implications of moral action in a society that has lost all purchase on the spirit of the law," a concept that could easily account for all of Mosley's work. Mosley himself has made this very clear: "Socrates . . . was *the* important philosopher. . . . His idea in life was that you had to discover knowledge, you had to go through life and you had to discover what was right and what was wrong" (*Guide*). What Mosley has succeeded in doing is grounding this moral view in a strong and complex character, desperately trying to carve out his decent deeds amid inner-city crime, drugs, murder, thieves, gangs, and con-artists.

Socrates Fortlow has spent twenty-seven years in prison for murdering a man and woman and raping her. In jail he also killed three convicts: "And then there was all the men I brutalized and molested, robbed and threatened. I either committed a crime or had a crime done to me every day I was in jail. Once you go to prison you belong there" (*Always* 122). In the novel he has moved to the Watts section of Los Angeles and struggles to survive by bagging and delivering groceries and helping those around him. He performs as a marriage counsellor; a mentor for Darryl, a street-wise but terrified boy who kills Socrates' rooster and has killed a retarded boy; and a moral guardian and teacher in various crises. He spends the night on the beach with a Vietnam veteran, leads the police to a firebug during the Watts riots, deals with a crack addict, secures morphine for his dying, cancer-ridden friend, and rescues a black dog from what nearly becomes a hit-and-run accident, assaulting the white man who wants to finish the job with a brick. Each of the stories sets up an encounter that Socrates must deal with, either with others or with himself. "I'm interested in . . . black people recognizing language and current history in the work," Mosley has stated, "white readers recognizing themselves in the decisions made by these people in a place that they may not have been in" (*Guide*).

Socrates has both his own destiny to fulfill because of his violent life and also the role of a black man to uphold, neither one being exclusive of the other: "He swore to try and do good if the chance came before him. That way he could ease the evil deeds that he had perpetuated in the long evil life that he'd lived" (*Always* 60). Other characters recognize his power: "You know I always felt bad when we'd be talkin' 'cause it seemed like you always thought'a everything already and was just testin' the rest'a us" (203). Socrates's blackness underscores his personal quest, for the biggest problem a black man has is in "bein' a man, that's what. Standin' up an' sayin' what it is we want an' what it is we ain't gonna take" (32). He recognizes the difficulty, "because any black man that ever did a thing for hisself broke the rules—he had to because the rules say that a black man cain't have nuthin'" (163). And he knows that the only thing a black man can do is to stand up for himself, despite or because of his knowledge that "you always outnumbered, you always outgunned" (131). In a dream he discovers a graveyard "for all the black people that had died from grief," and a man tells him, "Here! . . . We got to dig all'a them up now. It's time" (94).

The achievement of *Always Outnumbered, Always Outgunned* lies in Mosley's ability to ground such moral tales in the language and bleakness of inner-city streets. Socrates is no one-dimensional scold. His desire to do good springs solely from his will to recover himself and his past, knowing that the violence within him can strike out at any time—and does. At the same time he tries to achieve self-reliance in a world which barely recognizes him as a self or an individual at all, and that self-reliance rests squarely on his own willed self-restraint. He coaxes, threatens, cajoles, and points fingers, uncertain of exactly how things will turn out. He worries a situation relentlessly, determined to come through and make his point.

Mosley's language captures Socrates and his world exactly. He has been described as "a Wynton Marsalis of the printed page, his themes subtly, obliquely, quietly stated, almost imperceptibly bubbling up from the rhythms of ordinary life" (Bernstein). His is "the perfect ear for the vernacular of the street." His characters are also finely etched and sharply rendered, such as Darryl, "one of those lost souls who did wrong but didn't know it—or hardly did" (*Always* 80); Right Burke, the World-War-Two veteran and handicapped roomer who has prostate cancer, and Wilfred, the cocky, self-confessed thief.

Throughout the novel the sense of racial fate and the indifference of society hovers like a curse. At one point Socrates' aunt, Bellandra Beaufort, describes God not as black but as blue: "Blue like the ocean. Blue. Sad and cold and far away like the sky is far and blue. You got to go a long long way to get to God. And even if you get there he might not say a thing. Not a damn thing" (*Always* 114). Interestingly enough, Mosley's latest book, a philosophical work of science fiction, *Blue Light,* extends this same color scheme, as does a forthcoming essay, "This Blue Earth: Contemplating Our Chains at the End of the Millennium." Such a bleak and realistic outlook in Mosley's inner-city world permeates his fiction, but in *Always Outnumbered, Always Outgunned* he has presented it in his most spare and unrelenting, and often lyric, prose. Socrates is no saint. The world he inhabits, which Mosley meticulously creates, and the characters who suffer in it, are violent, uncertain, and brutal and remain the essential achievement of his art.

INTERVIEW WITH WALTER MOSLEY
JANUARY 1999

Sam Coale: You have said that you wrote a single sentence one day which spoke to you and that that got you started as a writer. Could you explain this in more detail?

Walter Mosley: I was working as a consulting programmer at Mobil Oil, not as an employee but working on my own. I was there on a weekend, so nobody else was there. And I was writing programs. I got tired of doing that, so I started writing this sentence: "On hot sticky days in southern Louisiana, the fire ants swarmed." And I thought, "That sounds like the first sentence in a novel." I'd read lots of novels, and that sounded good to me. So I decided to keep on writing. I was about thirty-four at the time.

SC: Had you always wanted to write?

WM: No, I hadn't. At various times in my life I'd taken a poetry workshop or something, but I'd never ever considered prose, before that day actually. It was a voice that I understood and that I could write in. I'm always a little leery of "it" speaking to me. When you say "it," it's like the id. If you want to go in that direction, okay. I wrote the sentence, started writing, and took a workshop again, but after several workshops, it wasn't working. So I went to City College and studied poetry with a man named Bill Matthews for about two or three years. I was working. I had left Mobil but came back, then I sold my first novel, *Devil in a Blue Dress,* and then I quit.

SC: Why did you pick the mystery form to write in?

WM: The first book I wrote was *Gone Fishin',* but nobody wanted to publish it, not because they were against the writing, but they couldn't figure out who would buy the book. Who would read this book? It's kind of an interesting notion. The publishing industry is incredibly Eurocentric and also white-thinking. The idea was that the people who bought books and read books were the people the publishers knew. Seeing that everybody in publishing is white, the idea that black people would buy books that were already being published was beyond them.

SC: So it is similar to Toni Morrison who worked at Random House and helped cultivate a black audience while she was writing the books that they would eventually buy.

WM: Yes.

SC: Did the publishers suggest to you the mystery form?

WM: No. Nobody suggested it to me. Everybody said that there was good writing in *Gone Fishin',* but it wasn't commercial, and come back when I had something else.

SC: But why the mystery form, which is essentially Eurocentric and white . . .

WM: I'm not sure it is. Let's get rid of your caveat. What happened was that I read a lot of mysteries, and the mysteries that influenced me were of three different kinds. Political, which I find Dashiell Hammett to be; funny, which Rex Stout is; and then that kind of exotic world, which, I think, Arthur Conan Doyle portrays, bringing people to the exotic realms of the British Empire in his work. I've always loved those three different kind of mysteries, where you're going into this new, exotic world or laughing at the voice that's telling you the story or becoming aware of the political nature of a narrative. I started writing definitely not knowing that I was beginning to write a mystery. It was only when I was about halfway through it, I said, "Well, it is kind of in that genre." And when I was finished with it, I realized, "Yeah, it is." So that was it.

Now of course there's also an economic issue involved. To begin with, when I wrote my first contract with Norton, it was for two books. The reason I wrote the next one is that they had already paid me for it.

SC: You had on to *Gone Fishin'* until later, until you were established.

WM: Yes, after *Black Betty*.

SC: Which was a great thing in the way you gave it to Black Classic Press to publish.

WM: Yes. It was a wonderful experience for all involved. We were all happy about it.

SC: When Hillerman writes about the Navajo, he has to fit them into the mystery formula. He makes Jim Chee caught in the middle of two distinctly different cultures. Did that same thing occur to you in terms of black culture?

WM: I have a notion in my head that novels are plots. There are other things that they are, but they're also plots. They're stories which are based on plot. I also think that the finer quality of story-telling is plot. People are sitting there listening to your story. They have to be excited to find out what happens next. Plot for me is the structure of revelation, how things are revealed on the pedestrian level but also for revelation on another level. For me the mystery is not alien to any other form of fiction. It's part of every form of fiction. For instance, *RL's Dream* has no mystery to it. That was a very hard book to write because of that. I'm interested in what happened and why it happened, though you still have the "what's-going-to-happen next" in that book.

SC: You also seem very interested in moral questions, in the choices your characters have to or are forced to make. The mystery formula can be relatively simplistic when it comes to morality, the good guys vs. the bad guys, but you conjure up a world which is much more complex than that.

WM: I'm less interested in the simple concepts of good and evil. It's not true, for one thing, so it's hard to believe in. In an important way it doesn't really satisfy a reader who has any sophistication whatsoever. When I was a kid, I'd read a book, and Winnie the Pooh was always good, and the good princess and the prince wearing light-colored clothes would make it. That's fine, but if there isn't any gray area, then the reader has no way to identify with and understand the characters and the world they're struggling with. Mysteries, especially nowadays, help people with their own struggles with right and wrong in the world.

SC: Do you see yourself as in some way subverting the traditional mystery form?

WM: Well, no. Dashiell Hammett did that. The Continental Op was a guy who was always involved in a world where good and evil blended. You couldn't destroy one without destroying the other. I don't think I'm subverting anything, at least not from that particular perspective. When you have a country that denies its genesis and denies its roots, you have a country that's based on successful genocide. You have a country that's built on the concept of slave labor. And it's still going on today. It denies the black blood in its veins, the black and the red and the brown and the impoverished labor that built it. Then if you make a hero like Easy Rawlins, to some degree and at some level, that's subversive. I feel like I'm telling the truth, and it's hard for me to call the truth subversive.

SC: Even though we figure out who did what to whom, there is still this whole question of racism and moral ambiguity in terms of Easy's role and the society he's in. Maybe subversive is the wrong word, but your complex plots open up or break down the simplistic idea of good and evil.

WM: It starts dealing with other issues outside the issues of dealing with the mystery. I think that I do do that. When you start talking about good and bad, you think, how bad can this guy be, if Mouse is standing on the other side of you? Mouse is evil. He's other things, too, but he's evil. He does some really bad things. And Easy has to deal with him. So how bad could anybody else be?

The issue isn't if somebody's good or bad. There are the problems that Easy's trying to solve. He's trying to live in a world where there is no law. He's trying to impose some sense of justice in a world that has no sense of justice.

SC: The very environment he's in practically denies his ability to make moral choices.

WM: Any choice that he makes is condemned on one level or another. And so is everything he does. Now this is not untrue in the rest of the genre. The thing is you have to remember that this is always the point. This is the point, for instance, of Philip Marlowe. He is always walking in that gray area, doing things that the law might think is wrong, but we think is right. Same thing with Ross Macdonald and Lew Archer. Archer often has to make decisions which don't necessarily go along with right and wrong and the law. Even Sherlock Holmes does that at times. Sometimes he lets people go, sees that they've done something but decides to do nothing about it.

It's how I'm using it specifically with this kind of racial-political bent to it that makes the mystery different, but it's not a new thing in the genre. As far back as you go, you'll see that the detective, especially the hard-boiled detective, is questioning the laws and the rules of the society that we live in.

SC: It is a balancing act, however, to both play within the formula and create an environment that is so nightmarish and hard-boiled and racist that whatever happens within that environment, opens up all kinds of different possibilities.

WM: Easy's job is different from the regular detective. When he's representing someone or trying to help someone, he's definitely going to be at odds with the police in ways that other detectives like Marlowe or Archer aren't. But the other thing that's amazing is that everybody's doing that all the time. Everybody in their lives is having to hide, having to lie, having to do things which makes him or her invisible or opaque to the law. You have to break the law in order to survive, because the law is against you.

SC: Do you buy DuBois' sense of double consciousness, both inside and outside the culture at the same time?

WM: Like Ralph Ellison in his *Invisible Man*. I've said before that Easy is a kind of concretized invisible man. And has to be because of the very nature of things.

SC: In the Rawlins' mysteries you cover the period of history, so far, from 1948 to 1963. August Wilson has done something similar in his plays. How did you decide to do that?

WM: That was my intention from the first when I wrote *Gone Fishin'* to follow that migration of black people to Los Angeles and to show what went on with them in L.A. as time went on, as people came from the deep South and moved up there.

SC: How much of Easy's history parallels or reflects your own family's history?

WM: My people, maybe; my family, not all that much. There are some aspects that cover my family. My father was a supervising custodian, and that's where Easy is right now. My father owned property and managed it, and Easy does that. It seems to be telling, but there's not much depth to it. All my father's side of the family came from Texas and Louisiana.

SC: It's similar then to the way James Lee Burke treats his family's history. Where does your mother figure into this?

WM: Partly because I'm writing it, my mother fits into it. As far as the Jewish side of my family, in the mysteries you have characters such as Chaim Wenzler and Saul Lynx who are major parts of books but not fifty percent of the books. Winsler was a Communist union organizer. Saul Lynx is a Jewish detective married to a black woman. I guess that's where that side of my family comes from.

SC: How do you feel about the many critics who refer to Easy Rawlins as a black consciousness?

WM: What does black consciousness mean? Easy is a black man, and he sees the world from the point of view of a black man. The world sees him as a black man. Because of this, a lot of people will see a world either that they never suspected existed or that they have experienced their whole lives but never seen in literature. In that, it is a black consciousness. Not *the* black conscience or consciousness, not the only way to see the world, but a way to see the world which comes from the other side.

SC: So blackness is very much a social construction from the historical world you're writing about?

WM: Yes.

SC: Do you see any progress from 1948 to 1963? I see progress with Easy in terms of getting his act together, becoming more stablilized.

WM: Do I see it in the books? I'm not sure. We'll have to see as it goes along. There's some progress and some backsliding. We'll see more in the next Easy mystery, *Bad Boy Brawley Brown.*

SC: Does your interest in music and the blues help to explain the qualities of voice in your fiction?

WM: I've always been good at dialogue. Period. I'm good at writing from particular points of view, not necessarily just black. The way that people phrase words, use words, leave words out—that kind of stuff. There's that. And I think that's a mark of any good novelist. When I was with Toni Morrison once, she got introduced as a novelist, and I got introduced as "the mystery writer." But I don't see myself just in that category at all. I'm really interested in black life in America.

SC: Your newest novel, *Blue Light* (New York: Little, Brown, 1998) is science fiction. Where did that come from?

WM: I've always wanted to write science fiction. I love it. My whole life I've read as much science fiction as I've read mysteries. The book on Socrates Fortlow [*Always Outnumbered, Always Outgunned*] came out of a very specific desire to make sure that people understand that they know what philosophy is and that it comes out of the black community. We have a way of thinking about and seeing the world.

A lot of people want to see American history as just European history with some exotic spices, some Native American spice, some African-American spirituals; they know how to hum to God. That kind of stuff. But really the understanding of the world comes from everywhere. I'm not trying to denigrate European history and the advances in science, but America is so crazy. If you were going to get an operation, they would rather give you medicines that might kill you, rather than use acupuncture, which works just as well. I have a friend whose father died from anesthesia. When he went to get the operation, the anesthesia killed him. But they'll say, "We're the most advanced in the world!" No. In this particular thing, acupuncture is more advanced. You should be using that. The thing is you have a culture that denies history, so writing about Socrates or writing something even like *Blue Light,* which is a very philosophical book itself. . . . I'm not only thinking about being black or about being the victim of the white world or whatever. There are all these other things. Some things fit inside of writing mysteries, which is why I like writing them, but in a mystery every few pages you've got to check back into the plot.

Writing science fiction frees you up to think about the world. Sometimes you start looking at so-called literary novels, and they're about the guy who's waiting at the busstop and got on the bus and saw the woman, and he remembered his father from long ago. And then he got off the bus, and he went to work. Sometimes it's brilliant, but when it sings for me—*Remembrance of Things Past, A Hundred Years of Solitude*—it goes way beyond things that you know or even believe. But you still believe them, even more, when you read them. I find it really exciting when you can ask, "What is the soul?"

I feel that there's an edict from the literary world, and that edict is that black people are best suited to address the nature of their own chains. But if indeed that's the only thing we ever do, then we'll never be free. You can't be free, looking at yourself as a victim or talking about the history of you being a victim. You have to be thinking about something else. So part of it was just writing a book that went way way out there, and started talking about, "What if we were not alone in the universe, and we were related to all other life? And what if we were equal to everything around us—mosquitoes and trees and jellyfish—that there's nothing really all that special that separates us from those around us? How would that compare to what we could be?" I thought about it and decided I'd put a black character in it, but it's not really a book about that. It's a book about race but more in a general sense.

SC: Does *Blue Light* relate at all to the American incarnation of voodoo, called hoodoo? The belief in a higher power or life force, the worship of the ancestors like Orde in your book, divination and prophecy, animism. Are you aware of that at all?

WM: I think it does, but it's not like I do some serious study of it. Right now when you called, I was reading this book on Plato. I'm interested in Plato. I read stuff like that. But I don't make copious notes on it. And I don't usually talk about it. It just usually becomes a part of you. I'm very involved in various organizations. I really got a lot out of being in Cuba [Mosley had just returned from a visit to Cuba with such luminaries as Danny Glover, the actor]. It kind of comes in, and it settles, and it simmers, and it comes out again. I'm not really trying to make an argument for any particular divination system. But they're there. And they're part of a dialogue. I see myself as the kind of person who opens dialogue. I think that's what novelists are. We open dialogue. If we do it right, the dialogues continue. People read about them, consider them, think about them. Either they talk about them or they write about them or they make music about them. But it goes on. The most successful person who does that in the English language is Shakespeare. I think that's wonderful.

SC: Is your writing part of a process of self-discovery?

WM: It is, but I wouldn't want to limit it to writing. Self-discovery goes on in a lot of things. It goes on in conversation. For instance, I was very fortunate when I was in Cuba with Trans-Africa. The last night Castro called us all to the presidential palace. We went to see him, and he kind of lectured us for two or three hours. It was wild, because a lot of stuff he was saying was completely new to me. And a lot of it was things that I have been thinking about. Which led me when I came back home to reading Plato. I thought about Plato's Republic and all of its good and bad aspects and how it has its reflection in Cuba.

And also as you start to think about it, when you're talking to the person next to you, ideas come up. I think it's very concentrated for a writer. If you sit there and say I'm going to write a mystery—the bad guy is this criminal who runs his empire without anybody knowing it; the victim is Little Nell; the hero is the detective, Charlie Proudfoot; this is what happens—the whole plot is worked out, and then you write it down. You'll probably sell a lot of books that way, but the thing is you're really not going to find out anything about yourself, because basically what you're doing is just structuring things. Some things don't fit when you first write it. That's what re-writing is. But it feels good.

SC: Were Chance's experiences at Berkeley in *Blue Light* like yours?

WM: Some, but not much. I used to hang out in Berkeley. I knew what it was like, and I like to talk about it. But it's very different from my own experience. I went to Vermont in 1971, and I was there. I went to Goddard College originally. I lived there for about four or five years, and then got into the state college finally. Then I moved down to Massachusetts, went to the University of Massachusetts for awhile, studied political theory. Didn't really like it. I liked political theory. I wasn't very interested in teaching. I was a cook, and cooks usually cook more than they talk about theory. Or Socrates for that matter.

SC: Do you feel that you are in a unique position because of your background, both inside and outside the culture?

WM: I don't know. One wants to be special with a unique view of the world, but the reality is that there are very few black people in America who are only black. Almost everybody has some Native American blood. There's Irish. Look at people's last names. They're not just made up things. Mc-Something or other. There's some Scottish in there somewhere. Somebody owned somebody, and there was some mixing. The languages we speak, the schools we go to. So the idea of me having a special view of the world—sure I do, but most other people do, too.

SC: Some recognize the multiplicity of identities, but our national politics seems to be moving in another direction. I find that scary.

WM: It is scary if you don't accept who you are. A lot of people probably are incapable of accepting it. One of the things I was amazed at in Cuba, when you talk to political leaders, they told us, "We all have black blood in our veins." You'd never see a so-called white leader in America saying that. So you have people who are denying their history, and, therefore, they're denying not just me but so many others.

I'm a writer. I write novels. I think the Easy Rawlins books are novels just as much as *RL's Dream* or *Blue Light*, and even my collection of short stories has that feel to it.

SC: Is *Black Genius* (New York: Norton, 1999), the new collection of essays, based on lectures that you and others, such as Spike Lee, Melvin Van Peebles, bell hooks, and Angela Davis, gave at New York University?

WM: Each of them wrote an essay. I put together the thing. I wrote the introduction. I gave one of the talks. I just finished a book for Random House for their series on ideas of contemporary thought. I wrote a piece for it, called "This Blue Earth: Contemplating Our Chains at the End of the Millennium."

It's not like I'm experimenting. It's like I'm a writer. If I've done something once, I've done it.

SC: Are you ever afraid of being typecast?

WM: I'm going to be writing about black characters mostly. Certainly in *RL's Dream* I have a major white character. In *Blue Light* there are many different characters of many different colors. You wouldn't come up to Bernard Malamud and ask, "What are you going to write about?" I'm not that interested in drifting that far away from my basic subject. I don't think that novels are purely entertainment. They are entertainment, but I'm also trying to do something. This is a way of crystalizing and holding the culture and also examining the culture and letting other people examine it while they read it.

SC: Where did *Gone Fishin'* come from, your first book?

WM: I was learning how to write then. Part of it was trying to write a novel in the worst way. I was taking a class with Edna O'Brien, and she said to me, "You have to write a novel." And I said, "Okay, Edna. I'll do that." And I wrote that book. It didn't take me long. It was about three months. I was very excited. It was the beginning. It was me working it out. It wasn't me coming back and trying to explain anything.

I get up every morning and write. I didn't write at all when I was in Cuba. I had a few hours every morning that I could have written, and I decided for the first time in ten years not to. When I write, everything points toward that writing. The whole world outside shuts down. And I didn't want to do that in Cuba. I wanted to see Cuba.

I'm writing a new detective series. I have a new detective named Archibald Lawless, Anarchist at Large. You're always looking for a new kind of twist. I figure that an anarchist is a perfect detective. But I'm writing this book, and I'm discovering that it's really about something else completely, which is shocking to me. I really thought I knew what I was writing about.

I'm going to come back to Easy. There's no problem with that.

I have all these books. I've written a book called *The Man in My Basement,* which is a literary novel. I've written the next collection of Socrates stories, called *Walkin' the Dog.* That'll come out next fall. I really love writing.

It's funny, because we live in this English system, and English is big, but it's not everything. The writers who really move me very much are the French—Zola, Balzac. Balzac wrote like a hundred and eight novels. Simenon wrote eighty Maigret novels, and then eighty other novels. If you write, that's what you do.

SC: Do you have a feeling that you're making up for lost time, since you came to writing relatively late in your life?

WM: It's not that, but the thing is that when you have a choice of what you're doing and where you're going and who you're doing it with, the real important thing I know is that I'm a writer. That's the thing I do that's important. I'm continually drifting in that direction. What would I like to do? First I'm going to get that three hours of writing in.

SC: Many mystery writers started out just writing mysteries. I have the feeling that if I were to interview you ten years from now, first of all there would be seventeen more books, but secondly the mystery would be only one part of the spectrum.

WM: It is a big problem for mystery writers, because they're defined by it. I saw a woman once in a mystery bookstore, and she'd walked to the door, opened it but didn't step across the threshold, and looked at the owner, and she said, "I have two questions. Is the new Parker a Spenser?" And the owner said, "No." And the other woman said, "Oh, well, there's only one question." And she left. She didn't even walk in. My God! Because the new Parker at that time was a crime novel. It wasn't a Spenser. But the woman wasn't even interested in him writing another crime novel. And it's true, because I'll sell many more Easy

Rawlins novels than I will *RL's Dream,* for instance, or Socrates. But if all that you were worried about was how much money you made and how many books you sold, you should go into real estate. That's where the money is. John Grisham makes a lot of money, but he doesn't make as much money as Donald Trump. Go into real estate! Buy buildings! People never get tired about buying real estate. They might get tired of your characters, but they never get tired about buying houses!

I really believe that my career is on an arc. If you're a real writer, you're writing words that are worth reading on their own account, not because of anything else but just because of the sentences. And the sentences help shape the structure of the story. Then you have a career, and that career has a long arc, forty years, fifty years.

SC: When you wanted to publish a book besides mysteries, did your publishers grumble?

WM: Grumble?! Oh, my God, grumble! Norton refused to publish *Blue Light.* It was what it was. They said we can't sell this book. And I asked, "Is there something wrong with it?" We don't sell science fiction. Which is not true. The other day I saw that Norton has an anthology of science fiction! I went to Little, Brown.

I just write. I feel that I've been pulled a little far afield, and I'd kind of like to get back to write the next Easy. I really do like the classic guys. I like Chandler, Hammett, and Ross Macdonald I think is a wonderful writer. But I also like Archie Goodwin's life. I don't care about the mystery; every plot is exactly the same. It doesn't matter really, because just reading his voice and his view of the world is more than enough. Archibald Lawless isn't exactly like that, because I always have a dark side to my work, but just to write a voice is fine. Lawless is not the narrator. He has hired a guy as his scribe, and the scribe is actually telling the stories.

Of course, writing in the first person is a very strong thing, especially for the hard-boiled detectives. I could write *RL's Dream* from a third-person point of view, and it was fine. I could never do that with one of the mysteries. With Easy you want to believe in him, and the first-person narrator helps make that possible.

6

RESOLUTIONS OF THE CRIME

Each of the four mystery writers we have looked at has brought many different things to that popular and conventional form, and because of this I have used somewhat different approaches in analyzing them. For instance in looking at the mysteries of Amanda Cross and Walter Mosley, I have relied upon feminist and black critical theories, as well as some postcolonial ones, such as those by Edward Said, Maureen Reddy, Stephen F. Soitos, and Henry Louis Gates, Jr. With Tony Hillerman's Navajos I have relied on a more historical approach and the general problem of representation in fiction, comparing and contrasting in broad terms the Navajo culture as it exists and as it appears in Hillerman's fiction. I have used a more mythic criticism in trying to show how James Lee Burke has relied upon and used the southern gothic traditions—the dark past, the family skeletons, the sense of doom and racial oppression—in his fiction. In all of them I have tried to deconstruct those polarities that are basic to every mystery—detective versus villain, good versus evil—to show how each of these authors has subverted and amplified them.

What this reveals is just how flexible the mystery form can be. Without ever surrendering the very necessary confrontation between good and evil that every mystery must endorse, Hillerman, for instance, has broadened that conflict to include the encounter between whites and Native Americans. Such a confrontation obviously influences and shapes the basic orientation of the other. Cross has done the same in terms of women and men and how our culture's socially constructed gender roles have determined how we relate to one another. And Mosley, by probing black culture, has also achieved this in terms of racism, poverty, moral choices, and the racial antagonisms that divide us.

As mentioned in the first chapter, the mystery must exclude certain things in order to function. In its popular form it remains basically mimetic, that is, it creates a recognizable world of cause and effect that seems realistic while we are reading it, despite the fact that it is really a highly patterned and often rigidly artificial structure. It, therefore, must more or less abandon all kinds of metaphysical and other issues, or at the very least suppress them, so that the plot can follow the prescribed narra-

211

tive. When the mystery formula becomes too self-reflexive and self-conscious, we get the more unconventional novels of Paul Auster, Joan Didion, and Tim O'Brien with their splintered narratives and fragmented epiphanies. Our four writers have managed to include the Navajo culture, feminist perspectives, the southern gothic curse and black culture with their appropriate styles and circumstances within the form and in doing so have managed to enlarge it.

These wider perspectives leave the reader with particular visions that manage to transcend the mystery plot itself. In Cross' fiction we read about the gender wars that are on-going despite the resolution of the specific mystery. The Navajo superstitions and fascination with witchcraft, survival in the black ghetto and the lasting racist scars, and the Manichean nightmarish realm of Burke's Louisiana at times threaten to overwhelm the plot but are held in check despite their ability to transcend it. These darker visions survive beyond the actual mystery, even as they affect it, since all four writers obviously have cultural, social, and racial concerns they wish to bring into focus for the reader.

How do these concerns affect the mystery form that they use? All the writers have said that they do not write a mystery backwards by figuring out the solution first and then working their way back from there. Each admits that the mystery is not clearly plotted out and outlined in advance and that they rely on the power of specific details to make the often fanciful plots appear to be more lifelike and plausible. And yet they insist that they use mysteries as skeletons, frameworks, and trajectories to get their specific view of their world across and into fiction.

Each writer subverts the mystery form in one way or another, without, of course, sacrificing the basic necessities of the mystery tale. Tony Hillerman suggests that the Navajo way of looking at the world can serve as a very real alternative to the Anglo-Saxon method of crime and punishment. Jim Chee's personal dilemma, trapped as he is between being a policeman and studying to become a shaman, results in some very different approaches to law enforcement and investigation. Amanda Cross' creation of female webs, her fascination with female bonding and finding new ways for women to express themselves and act, lead to mysteries which are much looser in form, less plotted, and more open-ended than the typical patriarchal ones. James Lee Burke and Walter Mosley create nightmare realms and a pervasive sense of evil that permeates all the actions of their characters, whether because of a gothic tradition and/or a racist one, and produce an atmosphere of extreme violence, elaborate betrayal, and labyrinthine relationships that often cannot be entirely explained or resolved by the solution of the mystery.

Each writer reveals a particular problem. In the case of the three male writers, their complex and complicated plots often embody the cultural and social divisions and antagonisms they have chosen to explore so completely that they transcend the framework of the mystery. At times they almost seem to overpower the very fabric of cause and effect that mysteries must rely upon, but their atmosphere and cultural confrontations leave the reader feeling that the world is a far more frightening and intricate place than any mystery solution can possibly resolve. At times these plots, particularly in the writers' later work, also threaten to engulf the atmosphere entirely, which results in a thinner and flatter text. Some of this can be seen in Hillerman's *The Fallen Man* (whereas his first novel, *The Blessing Way,* would be a good example of atmosphere at times immobilizing plot), Mosley's *A Little Yellow Dog* (which may be why he has branched out to write such books as *RL's Dream* and *Always Outnumbered, Always Outgunned*), and Burke's *Sunset Limited* with its quick cuts and fierce pacing.

In Amanda Cross' case, gender issues tend to override plots, so that the reader feels that she is overhearing political and cultural conversations in place of a mystery-driven linear narrative. This seems to be the case in such works as *The Theban Mysteries, An Imperfect Spy,* and *The Puzzled Heart.*

In each case each writer has had to make certain compromises with his or her subject in order to accommodate it to the mystery formula. Tony Hillerman frankly admits that he uses the outer skein of Navajo culture in his fiction, that his approach to it is far more descriptive than exploratory. In doing so there is a tendency to romanticize the Navajo mind with its faith in ceremony and ritual, in alliance with Hillerman's own rural background and his favoring the traditional Navajo over the city Navajo. Culture for Hillerman is a matter of place and landscape, not of blood, and this broader or at least less interior view of it fits well with his narrative methods. Of course he is the first to admit that no non-Navajo can ever really grasp or understand the consciousness and extent of the more secret details of their ceremonies and prides himself on revealing nothing that he should not. Still Hillerman's mysteries make for fascinating reading because of their concerns and support his intentions of bringing such perspectives to a wider American public. Whatever stereotypical views of Native Americans that we may have harbored before reading his mysteries cannot survive his insights.

Carolyn Heilbrun remains a fascinating character in her own right. Her views and fictions are filled with contradictions and cross currents. There is the "Chinese box" of Kate Fansler who is the created character of Amanda Cross who is the created character of Carolyn Heilbrun.

There is the Anglophile's delight in good manners and the afterglow of the Golden Age of British mysteries, at the same time there is the recognition that such things often hide horrendous attitudes and murderous antagonisms. There is the role of the female detective, a role that has been initially created by men, in such a way that women must use the male model to acquire their own self-possession and status at the same time they must transcend or transform it. Heilbrun's "pure feminism," which can somehow be disconnected from race, class, and ethnicity, may account for Kate Fansler's acedia in her latest incarnation but also points in the direction of a more essential self that for women—and men—can only be discovered through a feminist consciousness. If we are all basically androgynous in our innermost selves, then feminism is only one of several approaches to determine that. If the self has to be at odds with institutions, and if the two are radically different in what they seek, can the former ever really accomplish anything against the latter while being comfortably placed within them? And if, however facetiously suggested, to accept radical politics is to fail at syntactical accuracy, what does this do for a fiction that is trying to be both comfortably radical and more or less acceptably conventional?

I admit that these may suggest my own confusions more than Heilbrun's. I love the conversation in her mysteries, the literary allusions, the discussions of strategies, and the female machinations against male conspiracies. These things do produce a different kind of mystery, more flaccid for the reader who likes her mysteries tight, tough and swift, more accessible to others who enjoy the form taking on real social and cultural issues. Each reader must ultimately decide for herself, but at the very least Heilbrun has opened up the traditional mystery formula and taken it places where it has not gone before.

James Lee Burke's dark night of the Manichean soul is so powerful that it often theatrens to submerge the mechanics of the plot. His creation of a kind of subjective nightmare, laced with its southern roots in Puritan and/or Catholic guilt, racial tensions, family feuds, and the primal abiding curse of a dark and twisted past, always survives intact in a way that his plots sometimes do not. There always seem to be left-over threads, stray characters, and unresolved mysteries, although if you take the time to work it out, the plot does come together. It is Burke's search for a Christian kind of redemption in a dark domain, which reveals the contours of Manichean confrontation and the family obsessions of Greek tragedy, that powers his beautifully written novels. Dave Robicheaux's bonding with the violent and trigger-happy Clete Purcell, like Easy Rawlins' with Raymond Alexander, the Mouse, may reveal both writers' fascination with that midnight realm as they scramble in their complicated plots to find the ritual most likely to try and contain such horrors, but it also accounts for the seductive pull of such a vision. Burke's populist politics often collides with his bleaker perspective, but the battle between the two to win over the human soul is one that illuminates his mysteries and keeps them resonating in the mind long after the murderers have been dispatched.

Walter Mosley carefully creates and discloses the intricate network of debts, payoffs, betrayals, favors, and violence in the marginalized society of urban blacks in Los Angeles, complete with the racism, poverty, and strategies his characters need to survive. His is a very real world of ultimate survival in a place long ignored by mainstream society, and in his language and labyrinthine plots he captures the feel of the landscape, the depth of despair, and the day-to-day existence of his often reckless characters. In such a world justice must necessarily be tainted, and it barely emerges intact. But, of course, that is the dangerous beauty of his art, and his fascination with black speech and the blues has led him to write other fictions beyond the more conventional world of the mystery. Easy Rawlins' sidekick Mouse is both his truest friend and, from several perspectives, thoroughly evil, but the game of survival puts a different spin on Rawlins' necessary and violent choices and raises questions about our own moral choices and the society we live in. In a world where policemen are antagonists, where no one can be trusted, where even the landscape is circumscribed by race and Rawlins' own marriage collapses because of his own unyielding secretiveness, that any fragile order, moral or otherwise, can arise is a wonder. It is Mosley's art that creates, within the confines of the traditional mystery, such a perilous and luminous existence.

The music of Mosley's mysteries lingers on, as do the landscapes and lore of Hillerman's Navajos, the witty repartee and dialogue of Cross' characters, and the frightening but lush landscapes of Burke's Cajun world. Perhaps this is their greatest contribution to contemporary literature: a look into different cultural milieus and diverse places, by design and by cultivated differences, conjuring up at once stranger worlds that turn out finally to be far more familiar than we could have ever imagined. The mysteries offer wonderful puzzles and intricate plots, but it is the landscape of the soul as depicted within a particular culture and environment that stays with us. This is the true territory of these writers, the lingering panorama of their clever tales, and the legacy of their art.

Chapter 1

1. "No American literary genre is more commercially profitable than the mystery, of which millions of hard-cover novels are sold annually, and yet more millions in soft-cover, in flourishing sections in bookstores and in 180 independent 'mystery' stores." Joyce Carol Oates, "Inside the Locked Room," a review of *A Certain Justice* by P. D. James, *The New York Review of Books*, 2 Feb. 1998: 20.

2. In discussing "context control and domination" in his work on the postmodern condition, Jean-Francois Lyotard, in effect, explains what it is the mystery formula accomplishes: "it excludes in principle adherence to a metaphysical discourse. . . . it demands clear minds and cold wills; it replaces the definition of essences with the calculation of interactions; it makes the 'players' assume responsibility not only for the statements they propose, but also for the rules to which they submit those statements in order to render them acceptable. It brings the pragmatic functions of knowledge clearly to light, to the extent that they seem to relate to the criterion of efficiency: the pragmatics of argumentation [and] of the production of proof." Jean-Francois Lyotard, *The Postmodern Condition: A Report on Knowledge* (Minneapolis: University of Minnesota Press, 1984) 62.

3. Martin E. Marty, *The One and the Many: America's Struggle for the Common Good* (Cambridge: Harvard University Press, 1997) 10, 11. In Marty's terms, "*totalism* is the name assigned to the idea that a nation-state can and should be organized around a single and easily definiable ideology or creed," which in my use of the word suggests the ideology of the mystery formula in its totalistic formulaic patterns. *Tribalism*, Marty suggests, opposes totalism in that it assumes that "only the peoples and groups to which one naturally belongs, or chooses to belong, or even invents as new constructs, can provide coherence." Hillerman, Cross, Burke, and Mosley integrate their "tribalist" or cultural focus into the "totalizing" agenda and design of the mystery. In text as *One*.

4. This is discussed in more detail in the first chapter in terms of the detective novel as a religious ritual, in which the murder becomes the sin, the criminal is the high priest of this rite, and the detective suggests an even higher power who appears on behalf of the victim of such rites. The sin is exorcized, the criminal punished and expelled, guilt has yet again been assuaged, and normal Christian society is once again restored. Most mysteries work in a simi-

lar manner, but James' more visible link to such an exorcism suggests Amanda Cross' fiction in the third chapter.

5. Dennis Porter, "Detection and Ethics: The Case of P. D. James." *The Sleuth and the Scholar: Origins, Evolution, and Current Trends in Detective Fiction*, ed. Barbara A. Rader and Howard G. Zettler (New York: Greenwood Press, 1988) 16, 17. In text as *Sleuth*. For James "caritas" suggests a benevolent goodwill toward all of humanity, a kind of general public benevolence with its more lenient judgment of others. Love describes a more passionate attachment between individuals and can lead to murder in the way "caritas" usually does not.

6. Thomas Cranmer (1489-1556) was the archbishop of Canterbury (1533-1556) who revised the Book of Common Prayer in the Anglican Church in England.

7. "There nearly always is a 'place' first, and to an extent, that dictates what one is writing about. . . . Characters come very quickly afterwards" *(Interview* 27).

8. O'Brien is writing in the Hawthorne-Melville-Faulkner-Morrison tradition of American dark romance, a complex subject which deserves much more attention than I can give it here. For an in-depth discussion of this "mesmerized" fiction with its sense of ultimate mystery and haunted domain, I suggest my own *Mesmerism and Hawthorne: Mediums of American Romance* (Tuscaloosa: University of Alabama Press, 1998).

Chapter 2

1. Hillerman admires the plots and use of landscape in the novels of the Australian writer, Arthur Upfield, whose work he describes as the stories of "a half-breed Australian aborigine policeman who could solve crimes in the desert Outback because he knew the country and understood the culture" *(Mysteries* 27).

2. For all of these kind of definitions, I am relying on the *Dictionary of Native American Mythology,* ed. Sam D. Gill and Irene F. Sullivan (New York: Oxford University Press, 1992) 147. In text as *Dictionary*.

3. Children are initiated into their adult religious lives in the *kachina* cult initiation ceremony in which they learn "certain elements of esoteric knowledge, a ritualized whipping reminding them of the importance of secrecy, and the disenchanting revelation that the *kachinas* are actually the men of their own community—their male relatives—wearing masks" *(Dictionary* 148).

4. "Translation is always interpretation. Interpretation is always based on theory," Gill and Sullivan go on to explain, and "often stories and rites undergo extensive change from generation to generation, even from telling to telling . . . every story, every rite, is always on the verge of extinction" *(Dictionary* xii).

5. Edward W. Said, *Orientalism* (New York: Random House, 1978) and *Culture and Imperialism* (New York: Knopf, 1993).

6. One can compare Hillerman's use of landscape and weather with another mystery about the Navajo, *Blackening Song* (New York: Forge, 1995) by Aimee and David Thurlo. The Thurlos are excellent in creating adventure and suspense, filling their plot with skinwalkers' caves and plots, skeletal hands, fires, and strange occurrences. And they delve deeply into Navajo witchcraft. The plot involves the ritualistic murder of a Navajo convert to Christianity and the very real machinations of modern-day skinwalkers conjuring up ancient and evil powers to assist them in their takeover of the reservation. The fact that the villains are also tribal policemen adds to their powers. Religious rites permeate the text, including the Blackening Song, a ceremony to exorcise evil. Ella Clah, the Navajo FBI agent, is played off against her brother Clifford who has become a traditional *hataali*, a complex conflict that itself is played off against their father's Christianity and their mother's psychic history in the Navajo tradition of prophecy and second sight. Navajo manners and customs are carefully reported. But the Thurlos do not create Hillerman's atmosphere. His creation of landscape with its abiding and supernatural overtones embodies the Navajo sense of beauty and vision in a way that a "straight" mystery cannot.

Chapter 3

1. Carolyn Heilbrun, "Extended Family." *The Women's Review of Books*, XII.1 (Oct. 1994: 15). Heilbrun's "disagreeable chap" is J. M. Purcell: "Beneath a veneer of educated allusion, the Cross mysteries are fairly simpleminded, considered as mysteries. . . . the closed-society, upper-crust, comfortable-people style of book she and Sayers-Innes-Christie all write . . . never seriously attempting the more disturbing world of illusion and betrayal that we find in the structurally skilled mystery novel." "The 'Amanda Cross' Case: Sociologizing the U.S. Academic Mystery," *The Armchair Detective*, XIII.1 (Winter 1980: 36-40). *CLC* 255-56.

2. There are references strewn throughout the book to James Barrie, Wordsworth, Carlyle, James Bond, Norman Mailer, Oscar Wilde, Henry James, Edith Wharton, C. S. Lewis, Gerard Manley Hopkins, Keats, Jane Austen, Virginia Woolf, Shaw, et al.

3. "*Poetic Justice* could, both in mainstream and in mystery terms, have been her best book because she had the fascinating idea of attempting herein to turn her distinguished colleague and apparent friend, Lionel Trilling, into a mystery villain . . . [but] she also fails to invent for her fictional 'Trilling' a criminal act or moral offense that will articulate whatever serious criticism she is making of him." J. M. Purcell. *CLC* 255.

4. An interesting point Reddy makes is that for all of Kate's solidarity with other women, there are "no intense friendships with other women, and no

friendships of any kind that last beyond a single novel in the series. She seems able to connect most closely with dead or otherwise-absent women . . . and to make that connection through reading the woman's work." *Crime* 65-66.

5. What Kate realizes more explicitly, as has Heilbrun before her, surfaces in her May lecture at Agassiz House, where "she spoke on the new forms possible to women in making fictions of female destiny" (*Death* 157). This realization Heilbrun will develop in greater detail in the next two mysteries in the series, *Sweet Death, Kind Death* (1984) and *No Word from Winifred* (1986), in which she includes various characters' journals and discussions about the necessarily biased construction of biographies that open and expand the usual trajectory of the mystery formula.

6. Again Reddy has been very helpful here: "As Kate investigates Janet's death, we read Janet from Kate's perspective and Harvard from both Janet's and Kate's, remaining—like the dead woman professor and the living one—always on the outside of the community of male scholars, beyond the ivied walls. The novel forces us to read as the Other, the excluded one, and by doing so helps us to feel what killed Janet . . . that the whole society in which Janet lived, including Janet herself, is responsible for her death. We are left with disorder, not a restoration of order. . . . indeed, the novel suggests that the restoration of order is a false ideal, as the order to which Harvard would like to return is built upon the systematic exclusion of women. It is order, in fact, that killed Janet Mandelbaum. Cross's metaquestion is 'who kills women and why?' Her answer, in part, is 'the established order.'" *Crime* 13-14. In 1997 only 11% of the tenured professors at Harvard were women.

7. Edith Hamilton, *Mythology: Timeless Tales of Gods and Heroes* (New York: New American Library, 1942) 157. I have also relied upon explanations found in Thomas H. Carpenter and Robert J. Gula, *Mythology: Greek and Roman* (Wellesley Hills, MA: Independent School Press, 1977).

8. May Sarton, quoted by Heilbrun. *Gift* 75.

Chapter 4

1. As the only novelist in this book who enjoyed a prior career of writing fiction before writing mysteries, Burke has often wondered how this has affected the public response to his works. In his latest non-Robicheaux novel, *Cimarron Rose,* he has expressed his concern that he was once again reviewed as a crime and mystery writer, as if he were doomed to that category no matter what he chose to write. Walter Mosley, for example, has been able to transcend the mystery category, and his non-mysteries have been reviewed as "real" novels in such places as the *New York Times* Book Review.

2. Maureen Reddy has argued for a counter, a female tradition in the mystery genre, originating in the works of such female gothic writers as Ann Radcliffe. Perhaps the Poe-Holmes-Hammett line can be seen as just another

example of a patriarchal myth, misreading or suppressing actual historical circumstances. According to Reddy, the female tradition violates linear progress, undermines the authority of the single masculine isolated point of view, steers clear of male polarizations, and focuses on the web of relationships. It is a dialogic approach to writing more than the one-dimensional monologic method. It subverts the cerebral, disconnected, sacrosanct aura of the male detective— Poe's Dupin, Doyle's Holmes, Christie's Poirot—and opens up a wider, more three-dimensional "webbed" realm of human entanglements.

3. The newest Dave Robicheaux mystery is *Sunset Limited* (1998), a streamlined and splendid example of the series that involves labor agitators, the usual sociopaths, Chinese gangsters, and racist murderers. I wanted to conclude with *Cimarron Rose* here, since it returns Burke to earlier territory and displays those narrative skills and techniques he has acquired since creating the Robicheaux series. It is interesting that in this latest novel, the characters who are pro-labor and who seem closest to Burke's own political convictions are themselves as manipulative and deadly as the murderous rich.

Chapter 5

1. Walter Mosley to D. J. R. Bruckner of the *New York Times, Contemporary Authors,* XII: 312.

WORKS CITED

Primary Sources

Auster, Paul. *City of Glass*. New York: Penguin Books, 1985.

Burke, James Lee. *Black Cherry Blues*. New York: Avon, 1989.

——. *Burning Angel*. New York: Hyperion, 1995.

——. *Cadillac Jukebox*. New York: Hyperion, 1996.

——. *Cimarron Rose*. New York: Hyperion, 1997.

——. *The Convict and Other Stories*. New York: Hyperion, 1985/1995.

——. *Dixie City Jam*. New York: Hyperion, 1994.

——. *Half of Paradise*. New York: Hyperion, 1965/1995.

——. *Heaven's Prisoners*. New York: Pocket Books, 1988.

——. *In the Electric Mist with Confederate Dead*. New York: Hyperion, 1993.

——. Interview with Jocelyn McClurg. "James Lee Burke Finds That Crime Does Pay." From the *Hartford Courant* in the *Providence Journal* 6 Aug. 1995: E8.

——. *Lay Down My Sword and Shield*. New York: Hyperion, 1971/1995.

——. *The Lost Get-Back Boogie*. New York: Henry Holt, 1978/1986.

——. *A Morning for Flamingos*. New York: Avon, 1990.

——. *The Neon Rain*. New York: Pocket Books, 1987.

——. *A Stained White Radiance*. New York: Hyperion, 1992.

——. *Sunset Limited*. New York: Hyperion, 1998.

——. *To the Bright and Shining Sun*. New York: Hyperion, 1989/1995.

——. *Two for Texas*. New York: Hyperion, 1972/1995.

Cross, Amanda. *The Collected Stories*. New York: Ballantine Books, 1997.

——. *Death in a Tenured Position*. New York: Ballantine Books, 1981.

——. *An Imperfect Spy*. New York: Ballantine Books, 1995.

——. *In the Last Analysis*. New York: Avon Books, 1964.

——. *The James Joyce Murder*. New York: Ballantine Books, 1967.

——. *No Word from Winifred*. New York: Ballantine Books, 1986.

——. *The Players Come Again*. New York: Ballantine Books, 1990.

——. *Poetic Justice*. New York: Ballantine Books, 1970.

——. *The Puzzled Heart*. New York: Ballantine Books, 1998.

——. *The Question of Max*. New York: Ballantine Books, 1976.

——. *Sweet Death, Kind Death*. New York: Ballantine Books, 1984.

——. *The Theban Mysteries*. New York: Ballantine Books, 1972.

——. *A Trap for Fools*. New York: Ballantine Books, 1989.

Didion, Joan. *The Last Thing He Wanted*. New York: Knopf, 1996.

Dunning, John. *The Bookman's Wake*. New York: Pocket Star Books, 1995.

Faulkner, William. *Sanctuary*. New York: Modern Library, 1931/1958.

Fitzgerald, F. Scott. *The Great Gatsby*. New York: Charles Scribner's Sons, 1925/1953.

Fowles, John. *The Ebony Tower*. Boston: Little, Brown, 1974.

Hammett, Dashiell. *The Maltese Falcon*. New York: Random House, 1972.

Heilbrun, Carolyn. "Discovering the Lost Lives of Women." *New York Times* 24 June 1984: 1, 26-27.

——. "Extended Family." *The Women's Review of Books* 12.1 (Oct. 1994): 15-16.

——. Interview by Diana Cooper-Clark. *Designs of Darkness: Interviews with Detective Novelists*. Bowling Green, OH: Bowling Green State University Popular Press, 1983.

——. *The Last Gift of Time: Life Beyond Sixty*. New York: Dial P, 1997.

——. *Reinventing Womanhood*. New York: W. W. Norton, 1979.

——. *Toward a Recognition of Androgyny*. New York: Knopf, 1973.

——. *Writing a Woman's Life*. New York: Ballantine Books, 1988.

Hillerman, Tony. *The Blessing Way*. New York: HarperCollins, 1970.

——. *Coyote Waits*. New York: HarperCollins, 1990.

——. *Dance Hall of the Dead*. New York: HarperCollins, 1973.

——. *The Dark Wind*. New York: HarperCollins, 1982.

——. *The Fallen Man*. New York: HarperCollins, 1996.

——. *The First Eagle*. New York: HarperCollins, 1998.

——. *The Ghostway*. New York: HarperCollins, 1984.

——. *The Great Taos Bank Robbery and Other Indian Country Affairs*. Albuquerque: U of New Mexico P, 1973.

——. *People of Darkness*. New York: HarperCollins, 1980.

——. *Sacred Clowns*. New York: HarperCollins, 1993.

——. *Skinwalkers*. New York: HarperCollins, 1986.

——. *Talking God*. New York: HarperCollins, 1989.

——. "Taos Restores the Spirit." *The Tony Hillerman Companion*. Ed. Martin Greenberg. New York: HarperCollins, 1994. 395.

——. *A Thief of Time*. New York: HarperCollins, 1988.

James, P. D. *The Children of Men*. New York: Knopf, 1993.

——. *Devices and Desires*. New York: Knopf, 1990.

——. *Innocent Blood*. New York: Warner Books, 1980.

——. Interview by Dina Cooper-Clark. *Interviews*.

——. *Original Sin*. New York: Knopf, 1995.

——. *A Taste for Death*. New York: Knopf, 1986.

Marquez, Gabriel Garcia. *Chronicles of a Death Foretold*. New York: Ballantine Books, 1982.

Morrison, Toni. *Song of Solomon*. New York: Knopf, 1977.

Mosley, Walter. *Always Outnumbered, Always Outgunned.* New York: W. W. Norton, 1998.

——. *Black Betty.* New York: Pocket Books, 1994.

——. *Devil in a Blue Dress.* New York: Pocket Books, 1990.

——. *Gone Fishin'.* Baltimore: Black Classic P, 1997.

——. *A Little Yellow Dog.* New York: W. W. Norton. 1996.

——. *A Red Death.* New York: Pocket Books, 1991.

——. *R L's Dream.* New York: W. W. Norton, 1995.

——. *White Butterfly.* New York: Pocket Books, 1992.

O'Brien, Tim. *In the Lake of the Woods.* Boston: Houghton Mifflin, 1994.

——. "The Magic Show." *Writers on Writing.* Ed. Robert Pack and Jay Parini. Hanover, NH: UP of New England, 1992.

Thurlo, Aimee, and David Thurlo. *Blackening Song.* New York: Forge, 1995.

Secondary Sources

Alewyn, Richard. "The Origin of the Detective Novel." *The Poetics of Murder: Detective Fiction and Literary Theory.* Ed Glenn W. Most and William W. Stowe. San Diego: Harcourt Brace, 1983.

Bakerman, Jane S. "Cutting Both Ways: Race, Prejudice and Motive in Tony Hillerman's Detective Fiction." *MELUS* 11.3 (Fall 1984): 17-25.

Bernstein, Richard. "Well, He's Sure No Angel but Maybe a Philosopher." Review of *Always Outnumbered, Always Outgunned. New York Times* 29 Dec. 1997: 12.

Birkerts, Sven. "The Socratic Method: Walter Mosley's Protagonist, An Ex-Con, Struggles with the Question of Atonement." Review of *Always Outnumbered, Always Outgunned. New York Times* 9 Nov. 1997: 11.

Bonnycastle, Stephen. *In Search of Authority: An Introductory Guide to Literary Theory.* 2nd ed. Canada: Broadview P, 1996.

Bouchard, Larry D. *Tragic Method and Tragic Theology: Evil in Contemporary Drama and Religious Thought.* University Park, PA: Pennsylvania State UP, 1989.

Brady, Margaret K. *"Some Kind of Power": Navajo Children's Skinwalker Narratives.* Salt Lake City: U of Utah P, 1984.

Brooks, Peter. "Freud's Masterplot." *Contemporary Literary Criticism: Literary and Cultural Studies.* Ed. Con Robert Davis and Ronald Schleifer. New York: Longman, 1989.

Bulow, Ernie. *Talking Mysteries.* Albuquerque: U of New Mexico P, 1991.

Campbell, Joseph. *The Masks of God: Occidental Mythology.* New York: Viking P, 1964.

Carpenter, Thomas H., and Robert J. Gula. *Mythology: Greek and Roman.* Wellesley Hills, MA: Independent School P, 1977.

Chisholm, James S. *Navajo Infancy: An Ethological Study of Child Develop-*

ment. New York: Aldine, 1983.

Coale, Samuel C. *Mesmerism and Hawthorne: Mediums of American Romance.* Tuscaloosa: U of Alabama P, 1998.

Descartes, Rene. *Discourse on Method and the Meditations.* Trans. and introduction by F. E. Sutcliffe. London: Penguin, 1968.

Fowles, John. *Wormholes: Essays and Occasional Writings.* New York: Henry Holt, 1998.

Fraser, Antonia. "Kate Fansler among the Foxes." Review of *The Players Come Again. New York Times* 14 Oct. 1990: 36.

Gates, Henry Louis, Jr. *Loose Canons: Notes on the Culture Wars.* New York: Oxford UP, 1992.

___. *The Signifying Monkey: A Theory of African-American Literary Criticism.* New York: Oxford UP, 1988.

Giddins, Gary. "Soupspoon's Blues." Review of R. L.'s *Dream. New York Times* 13 Aug. 1995.

Gill, Sam D., and Irene F. Sullivan, ed. *Dictionary of Native American Mythology.* New York: Oxford UP, 1992.

Greenberg, Martin, ed. *The Tony Hilerman Companion.* New York: Harper-Collins, 1994.

Grossvogel, David I. *Mystery and Its Fictions: From Oedipus to Agatha Christie.* Baltimore: Johns Hopkins UP, 1979.

Hamilton, Edith. *Mythology: Timeless Tales of Gods and Heroes.* New York: New American Library, 1942.

Hutcheon, Linda. *A Poetics of Postmodernism: History, Theory, Fiction.* New York: Routledge, 1988.

Johnson, Barbara. "The Frame of Reference: Poe, Lacan, Derrida." *Contemporary Literary Criticism: Literary and Cultural Studies.* Ed. Con Robert Davis and Ronald Schleifer. New York: Longman, 1989.

Karl, Frederick. *American Fictions: 1940-1980.* New York: Harper and Row, 1983.

Klein, Marcus. *Easterns, Westerns and Private Eyes: American Matters, 1870-1900.* Madison: U of Wisconsin P, 1994.

Klinkenborg, Verlyn. "The Reservation Is His Beat." Review of *Sacred Clowns. New York Times* 17 Oct. 1993: page.

Lehman, David. *The Perfect Murder: A Study in Detection.* New York: Free P, 1989.

Leonard, John. " 'Reflex' and 'Death in a Tenured Position.' " *New York Times* 20 Mar. 1981: 252-54.

Lewis, R. W. B. "It's Not Easy Being Easy." Review of *A Little Yellow Dog. New York Times* 16 June 1996: 18.

Loftin, John D. *Religion and Hopi Life in the Twentieth Century.* Bloomington: Indiana UP, 1991.

Magny, Claude-Edmonde. *The Age of the American Novel: The Film Aesthetic of Fiction between the Two Wars*. New York: Frederick Ungar, 1972.

Marty, Martin E. *The One and The Many: America's Struggle for the Common Good*. Cambridge: Harvard UP, 1997.

Oates, Joyce Carol. "H. P. Lovecraft: The King of Weird." *New York Times* 31 Oct. 1996: 50.

——. "Inside the Locked Room." Review of *A Certain Justice* by P. D. James. *New York Review of Books* 5 Feb. 1998: 19-21.

——. "The Simple Art of Murder." Review of *Stories and Early Novels* and *Later Novels and Other Writings* by Raymond Chandler. *New York Review of Books* 21 Dec. 1995: 32-40.

Pagels, Elaine. *The Origin of Satan*. New York: Random House, 1995.

Poirier, Richard. *The Renewal of Literature: Emersonian Reflections*. New York: Random House, 1987.

Pollitt, Kathy. "Books in Brief: 'Death in a Tenured Position.'" *Mother Jones* 6.7 (Aug. 1981): 65.

Porter, Dennis. "Detection and Ethics: The Case of P. D. James." *The Sleuth and the Scholar: Origins, Evolution, and Current Trends in Detective Fiction*. Ed. Barbara A. Rader and Howard G. Zettler. New York: Greenwood P, 1988.

Purcell, J. M. "The 'Amanda Cross' Case: Sociologizing the U. S. Academic Mystery." *Armchair Detective* 13.1 (Winter 1980): 36-40.

Reddy, Maureen T. *Sisters in Crime: Feminism and the Crime Novel*. New York: Continuum, 1988.

Reynolds, David S. *Beneath the American Renaissance: The Subversive Imagination in the Age of Emerson and Melville*. New York: Knopf, 1988.

Ringle, Ken. "The Robicheaux Recipe: James Lee Burke Cooks Up Cajun Detective Tales Close to Tabasco Country & Right on the Money." *Washington Post* 31 May 1993: D1, D10-11.

Ruddick, Sara. Review of *Reinventing Womanhood*. *Harvard Educational Review* 49.4 (Nov. 1979): 549-53.

Said, Edward W. *Culture and Imperialism*. New York: Knopf, 1993.

——. *Orientalism*. New York: Random House, 1978.

Schwartz, Regina M. *The Curse of Cain: The Violent Legacy of Monotheism*. Chicago: The University of Chicago Press, 1997.

Selden, Raman, and Peter Widdowson. *A Reader's Guide to Contemporary Literary Theory*. 3rd ed. Lexington: UP of Kentucky, 1993.

Soitos, Stephen F. *The Blues Detective: A Study of African American Detective Fiction*. Amherst: U of Massachusetts P, 1996.

Stasio, Marilyn. "Crime." Review of *Cadillac Jukebox*. *New York Times* 18 Aug. 1996: 28.

——. "Crime." Review of *Cimarron Rose*. *New York Times* 10 Aug. 1997: 18.

——. "Crime." Review of *The Fallen Man*. *New York Times* 8 Dec. 1996: 50.

——. "Crime." Review of *The Puzzled Heart*. *New York Times* 25 Jan. 1998: 20.

Strenski, Ellen, and Robley Evans. "Ritual and Murder in Tony Hillerman's Indian Detective Novels." *Western American Literature* 16.3 (Fall 1981): 205-16.

Symons, Julian. *Bloody Murder: From the Detective Story to the Crime Novel*. 3rd ed. New York: Mysterious P, 1992.

Thomas, Brook. *The New Historicism and Other Old-Fashioned Topics*. Princeton: Princeton UP, 1991.

Tocqueville, Alexis de. *Democracy in America, II*. New York: Vintage Books, 1945.

Tuttleton, James. *The Novel of Manners in America*. New York: Norton, 1972.

White, Jack E. "Easy's Early Days." Review of *Gone Fishin'*. *Time* 20 Jan. 1997: 75.

White, Jean M. "Mysteries: 'Death in a Tenured Position.'" Review of *Death in a Tenured Position*. *Washington Post* 15 Mar. 1981: 6.

Williams, Anne. *Art of Darkness: A Poetics of Gothic*. Chicago: U of Chicago P, 1995.

Winks, Robin. *Modus Operandi: An Excursion into Detective Fiction*. Boston: David R. Godine, 1982.

INDEX